TExES

Superintendent (195)

SECRETS

Study Guide
Your Key to Exam Success

TExES Test Review for the
Texas Examinations of Educator Standards

Dear Future Exam Success Story:

Congratulations on your purchase of our study guide. Our goal in writing our study guide was to cover the content on the test, as well as provide insight into typical test taking mistakes and how to overcome them.

Standardized tests are a key component of being successful, which only increases the importance of doing well in the high-pressure high-stakes environment of test day. How well you do on this test will have a significant impact on your future, and we have the research and practical advice to help you execute on test day.

The product you're reading now is designed to exploit weaknesses in the test itself, and help you avoid the most common errors test takers frequently make.

How to use this study guide

We don't want to waste your time. Our study guide is fast-paced and fluff-free. We suggest going through it a number of times, as repetition is an important part of learning new information and concepts.

First, read through the study guide completely to get a feel for the content and organization. Read the general success strategies first, and then proceed to the content sections. Each tip has been carefully selected for its effectiveness.

Second, read through the study guide again, and take notes in the margins and highlight those sections where you may have a particular weakness.

Finally, bring the manual with you on test day and study it before the exam begins.

Your success is our success

We would be delighted to hear about your success. Send us an email and tell us your story. Thanks for your business and we wish you continued success.

Sincerely,

Mometrix Test Preparation Team

Need more help? Check out our flashcards at: http://MometrixFlashcards.com/TExES

TABLE OF CONTENTS

Top 20 Test Taking Tips

1. Carefully follow all the test registration procedures
2. Know the test directions, duration, topics, question types, how many questions
3. Setup a flexible study schedule at least 3-4 weeks before test day
4. Study during the time of day you are most alert, relaxed, and stress free
5. Maximize your learning style; visual learner use visual study aids, auditory learner use auditory study aids
6. Focus on your weakest knowledge base
7. Find a study partner to review with and help clarify questions
8. Practice, practice, practice
9. Get a good night's sleep; don't try to cram the night before the test
10. Eat a well balanced meal
11. Know the exact physical location of the testing site; drive the route to the site prior to test day
12. Bring a set of ear plugs; the testing center could be noisy
13. Wear comfortable, loose fitting, layered clothing to the testing center; prepare for it to be either cold or hot during the test
14. Bring at least 2 current forms of ID to the testing center
15. Arrive to the test early; be prepared to wait and be patient
16. Eliminate the obviously wrong answer choices, then guess the first remaining choice
17. Pace yourself; don't rush, but keep working and move on if you get stuck
18. Maintain a positive attitude even if the test is going poorly
19. Keep your first answer unless you are positive it is wrong
20. Check your work, don't make a careless mistake

Leadership of the Educational Community

Management

Leadership is concerned with the future and with aspects of personality and interpersonal relationships. These concepts involve intangible emotional and philosophical topics. Management is more concerned with the here and now, the mundane duties of daily operations including budgets, staffing, equipment, the nuts and bolts of schools. While principals will not personally do a lot of the jobs required to keep the school running, they delegate and manage the staff who do, and they must be familiar with their jobs. A leader of an organization does not necessarily have to know everything the organization's members do, but a manager does. Principals must be effective as both leaders and managers in their schools.

Administration and staff relationship

Under the leadership of its administrator, an entire school community must work together as a team in order to foster student achievement. Comfortable and confident in his or her role as a leader, an effective administrator knows the importance of a strong relationship with his or her staff. All staff members should feel that they are essential in the success of the school and that their opinions and values matter. By treating his or her staff with fairness, respect, and dignity, an administrator instills in them the desire to perform at a higher level. Any situation in which conflict arises should be dealt with professionally and equitably. Additionally, administrators should interact with their staff not only professionally, but also personally, so long as they do not show partiality to certain employees.

Learning community

One important action an administrator can take to improve the overall success of a school is to create a learning community by encouraging his or her school's staff to work together as a team. A learning community is created when a team of staff members shares the same mission, vision, and values in helping students reach their full potential. When each staff member is knowledgeable about the school's goals, then the team as a whole is stronger, as they are striving to accomplish the same thing. For example, different grade levels within an effective learning community collaborate to reach the school's goals, while individual staff members are motivated to seek continuous improvement in their own teaching methods. Although goals may take a long time to achieve, an administrator must ensure that the learning community never loses sight of what the school's mission is. Another administrative advantage to creating a learning community is that everyone comes together and develops an action plan to solve any problems that might arise.

Value of diversity

For administrators to be effective leaders, they must understand the significance of a diverse group of individuals within their school communities. Individuals who come from different cultures, backgrounds, socioeconomic classes, and educational levels offer a variety of perspectives about a school's issues and situations and are invaluable in decision making, implementation, and problem-solving processes. It can be difficult for someone who has a preferred way of thinking to be openminded enough to view a situation in another way. However, listening to and understanding others' points of views can reinforce to an administrator the fact that only one point view does not allow for subjective, informed decisions. Overall, diversity within a school community can greatly improve the quality and range of a school's programs.

Organization

An organization is a group that sets its own goals, develops ways of pursuing those goals, and controls its own performance. From a sociological perspective, an organization is planned and coordinated by human beings in order to generate a certain product. An organization is an arrangement of certain elements, and these elements are governed by rules in order to complete a task. Each task is completed by individuals through a division of labor. The elements are considered to be the individuals in the organization and how each one communicates with the other. If the elements are coordinated and planned appropriately with everyone's cooperation, then the organization has the ability to solve tasks that are given to them. The benefit of organizations is they offer more enhancements because of the different features of each element, or individual.

Participatory government

Participatory government emphasizes getting everyone involved with the mission and operation of an organization. In regard to education, the concept of participatory government means that every person who has influence on a student's academic achievement, such as administrators, teachers, parents, and students themselves, is involved in the educational process. When everyone is encouraged to participate, all parties feel as if they have a voice and that their opinions matter. For example, participatory government allows parents an active role in helping their children be successful in school. Similarly, students can take ownership in their education. Examples of decisions that can be made together under a participatory government include fundraising, ideas for curriculum development, and school improvement projects. Because participatory government allows everyone to have a part and provides a sense of teamwork, there are fewer barriers between administrators and teachers, as well as teachers and parents.

Participatory management

One of the key elements of participatory management is power. In a school-based management system, decisions are made by team members, including the principal, teachers, and parents, as opposed to a centralized system in which decision-making authority is given primarily to central office administrators. The second element of participatory management is how and what types of information are disseminated. In a centralized system, information originates in the central office and then trickles down to employees. In participatory management, information is exchanged among all involved parties. Two of the most frequents types of information shared in a participatory management system in education include information about ideas and information about performance. The distribution of awards is another element of participatory management because rewards can inspire staff members to be more motivated. The fourth element in participatory management focuses on knowledge and skills.

Plant operations and maintenance

The purpose of plant operations and maintenance is to provide school buildings with services that will ensure a clean, safe, comfortable, and appealing learning environment. Individuals who take part in plant operation and maintenance functions should be qualified and given efficient and effective tools and materials in order to keep a building in the condition it should be. The operations and maintenance division provides its staff with proper training, which includes how to inspect the building for mechanical and structural problems, and helps to maintain an inventory of cleaning supplies. It is important that the staff members in charge of plant operations and maintenance are given sufficient funds for supplies, equipment, and materials necessary for making repairs, cleaning the school, and keeping cleaning equipment in good working condition.

School safety and security

No matter where a school is located, teachers and students alike have the right to be safe and feel secure when they are at school. Students cannot be expected to learn, and teachers cannot be expected to teach, if they fear for their safety. An administrator is responsible for making certain that the district has taken measures not only to protect its teachers and students, but also to make them all feel safe. One way to create a positive, non-threatening school culture is to encourage students and teachers to behave in ways that support a safe and orderly environment by establishing a zero-tolerance policy in regard to violence. Explicitly explained to every student, this kind of policy outlines the consequences of violent behavior.

Preventing school violence

In an effort to make schools safer, many districts have installed metal detectors on their campuses. While metal detectors help prevent weapons from being brought into schools, they do not prevent violence from occurring within the school walls. One way an administrator can address school violence is by implementing not only zero-tolerance policies, but also school violence prevention programs. These types of programs help students develop skills for handling conflict. These skills are built around how students can avoid conflict, how they can respond appropriately once conflict has begun, and how they can remove themselves from conflict situations if other people's behavior makes it impossible to resolve the issue at that time. Another way an administrator can deal with school violence is through mediation. Students can learn valuable life skills when a mediation approach is used. In general, violence prevention training programs are more beneficial to a school campus than criminal enforcement techniques.

If an administrator is seeking resources to help with violence prevention training programs, the Internet can provide useful sources of information that discuss what leads to school violence and what the most effective way of preventing it is. Administrators can also read journals that present the latest research on the early warning signs of violent behavior and how school districts can develop a useful prevention plan. Another resourceful piece of information is the publication *Safeguarding Our Children: An Action Guide*, which provides information on how schools can use a model that stresses prevention, early intervention, and services for children with behavioral and emotional needs. An effective administrator must always stay informed and educated about the latest research and violence prevention methods that can be beneficial to his or her school.

- 4 -

Due process procedures

According to United States law, due process is a principle stating that the government has a duty to respect every one of a person's legal rights; the government cannot pick and choose which rights will be honored and which ones will not. Many states have their own guarantees of due process that are outlined in their state constitutions. When people are involved in procedural due process, they have the right to be notified of any charges or proceedings that will affect them. In a school setting, administrators must ensure that each one of their staff member's rights have been honored before any termination takes place. If a staff member feels that his or her rights have been violated and can prove it, there is probable cause for a lawsuit.

Special education due process hearing

A special education due process hearing takes place when the parties involved present evidence to a qualified hearing officer who acts as both judge and jury. The hearing officer is present to listen to evidence presented by both sides before writing a final decision. There are certain laws that control due process hearings, including the Individuals with Disabilities Education Improvement Act of 2004 and the federal regulations located in 34 Code of Federal Regulations Part 300. It usually takes about five business days from the time a hearing is requested to the time when the hearing officer contacts the parties with a final decision. There is a thirty-day timeframe during which the parties must seek a resolution using mediation or other resolution processes; agreements can be made without the use of a hearing officer. There can be an extension granted if it is agreed upon by the hearing officer.

IEP

An Individualized Education Program (IEP) is an individualized, law-binding document that states what the plan is for a student with disabilities. Administrators must ensure that their staff members are abiding by this document at all times. An IEP is created to give teachers, parents, and other personnel a chance to work as a team to make certain that a student with disabilities is given an equal opportunity to succeed in school. In order to create an effective IEP, teachers, parents, and other school staff must come together and discuss what educational issues the student has been facing both physically and emotionally. The student will then be evaluated, and his or her eligibility for special education services will be decided. If the student is found eligible, then the appropriate services needed for the student will be selected. In an IEP meeting, the findings from the evaluation will be discussed, along with what services and programs are necessary to help the student achieve educational success. The IEP is then written with the agreement of all parties. Finally, the services are provided to the student, and a monitoring process evaluates how well the student is being served.

It is required by law that certain information is included in an IEP. One piece of information required is a determination of the student's level of function and performance. This information is gathered by evaluating assignments and tests and by recording the observations of both parents and teachers. Also required in the IEP are attainable goals that the student can accomplish during a school year. Many times, these goals are not academic; they can pertain to social or physical achievements. It is important that all services a

- 5 -

student requires are written into the IEP document; this includes any modifications that might be made to the student's program. An IEP must also contain information about the extent of a student's participation in a regular classroom and whether he or she will take part in any state or district standardized tests. Other important information in an IEP includes dates and places of services, transition services needed, and methods of measuring progress.

IEP team members

Law requires that specific individuals must have a part in writing a student's Individualized Education Program. If a person is qualified, he or she may fill more than one of the team positions. The goal of an IEP team is to work together to write the IEP within thirty calendar days from the day it was decided that the student is eligible for special education and other services. The key members of an IEP team are the child's parents, because they know their child best and can contribute information about his or her strengths, weaknesses, and health. Other important participants in the writing of an IEP are teachers. At least one regular education teacher must participate in IEP meetings. A special education teacher provides important information about the appropriate ways to educate a student with special needs. Other important members of an IEP team are individuals who can interpret the student's evaluation, a school system representative, and an individual with firsthand knowledge about the student.

FERPA

The Family Educational Rights and Privacy Act (FERPA) is a federal law that helps protect the privacy of students' education records. Any school that receives funds from an applicable program of the U.S. Department of Education must obey this law. FERPA also gives parents the right to examine their child's educational records that are kept by the school. If parents believe that their children's records are incorrect, then they can make a request to change the erroneous content. If the school declines, then the issue will go to a hearing. In most cases, schools must have written consent before any information about a student is released. However, under FERPA, the school can disclose information to school officials who have a legitimate educational interest in a child's situation. FERPA also allows schools to relase records to another school where the student is transferring, to financial aid agencies, or to other officials who have a legal interest in the child because of health and safety issues.

Affirmative action

Affirmative action is a policy or program that attempts to correct the effects of discrimination in the employment or education of targeted demographic groups. By encacting measures to ensure that there is equal opportunity for employment and education regardless of race, gender, age, ethnicity, or disability, affirmative action seeks redress for past discriminations. Many opponents to affirmative action state that it may increase racial tension instead of bringing the parties involved to a peaceful conclusion. Challengers of affirmative action also contend that in the case of college admissions, affirmative action is detrimental to the greater good because it oftentimes allows a minority student who is less qualified to be admitted rather than a student of another ethnicity group who may be better qualified. Because of its potential to both help and harm students, affirmative action is a policy that an administrator must understand. Having up-to-date

- 6 -

knowledge of affirmative action policies and programs will enable an administrator to understand his or her responsibilities when affirmative action applies to students and situations in his or her schools.

Sex discrimination

Sex discrimination can affect employees, parents, and students; therefore, it is important that administrators are familiar with Title IX and are consistently monitoring their schools to ensure that they are following the guidelines of that policy. Title IX applies to all public school districts that receive federal financial assistance. This policy covers academic, extracurricular, and athletic programs. It also pertains to all participants in school programs, including parents, students, and employees. Administrators must also ensure that everyone involved with the school is aware of the consequences of sexual harassment and understands what procedures to follow in the event of a harassment situation. Administrators should make it clear that severe action will be taken against anyone who is guilty of sexual harassment.

FOIA

The Freedom of Information Act (FOIA) was enacted in 1966 and states that any person has the right to request access to information contained in federal agency records. Federal agencies are required to disclose the information when a written request has been received; however, there are nine exemptions that protect certain records from disclosure. If someone wants to make a request, he or she must email, fax, or mail a request to the U.S. Department of Education. While the party requesting the information should receive a response within twenty working days, the actual release of the records could take longer. Most states and local jurisdictions have their own laws about access to state and local records. Administrators must inform their staff about policies regarding the privacy of school records. There should not be any information given out about a student except to the student's parents or legal guardian.

Civil rights

An administrator is responsible for making certing that his or her entire school is aware of civil rights. A person's civil rights are the protections and privileges of personal power that are granted to everyone by law. These rights are written in the United States Constitution and include the right to privacy, the right to a fair investigation, the right to vote, and the right to equal protection. One of the most famous cases regarding civil rights is Brown v. Board of Education (1954), which involved the constitutionality of laws that enforced segregation in the educational system. In order to have an effective school, it is vital that staff members, students, and parents respect and honor everyone's civil rights. Doing so enhances the school's sense of community and, in return, leads to student achievement.

Parental involvement

Besides traditional PTA/PTO organizations, parents can be involved in their children's schools in a number of ways. For example, parents can participate on a one-time-only basis in developing handbooks for student behavior or establishing dress code policies. They may also serve on special task forces, including booster clubs, to oversee school activities that support student clubs and sports teams. Parents can also serve on a variety of committees that foster open communications between the school, as well as on committees that allow parents to mentor new school families by encouraging them to get involved with the school and by helping new students become acclimated with their new schools. Parents may also be asked to serve on governing bodies, such as a district's school board.

Teachers oftentimes fear that parents will interfere with their teaching and prevent them from doing their jobs. Teachers may feel that parents are focused only on their own children and are not interested in the problems and issues affecting the entire school. At times, unfortunately, parents might believe that their own kids are exceptional and have no discipline or academic problems and that many of the other students are bad influences. As for teachers, they are sometimes reluctant to involve parents too extensively in curriculum or classroom issues because of litigation possibilities. Additionally, some teachers may object to parental participation in their classrooms because they feel that while they are held accountable for a child's academic success, parents are not. No teacher can ensure that students attend school, study, complete homework, and make an effort in school, but parents are quick to blame teachers when their children do not demonstrate academic progress.

Parents can offer superintendents additional perspectives on issues and provide a glimpse of the wider community's views on certain matters. Ongoing communication between schools and parents helps a school's staff and administration maintain a customer (i.e., student) focus, keeping them attuned to the needs and opinions of their primary constituents. A school district in which parents are active gets more respect and attention from the wider community. Parental involvement also is positive from a political standpoint because parents are more apt to approve bonds and other school-related issues during elections if they are invested in a school district's policies and activities.

Issues that complicate relationships between schools and parents

The news is filled with daily occurrences of violence and rage from school-aged students. Unfortunately, the result is that schools are viewed by many people as physically dangerous, and parents do not feel that they can entrust their children's safety to the school system. Due to educational theories that seem to come and go overnight, making it appear that teachers do not know what they are doing because they simply adopt and discard educational methods as they are told, conflicts are instigated between parents and staff members. Such policies as zero tolerance garner a great deal of criticism, while school curricular programs are increasingly criticized for being politicized; these kinds of issues cause parents to be cynical and suspicious about what and how their children are being taught. Additionally, widespread social problems, including divorce, drug use, and physical abuse in modern family life, add more stress to the relationship between schools and parents. Many parents are unwilling or unable to interact with their community schools, and the schools do not know how to respond.

Benefits of parental involvement

Giving families the opportunity to volunteer for school committees, programs, activities, and events familiarizes them with their children's academic activities and allows them to learn a great deal about the school and what it is doing for their children. Parents can learn what specific material is being taught, and, if prepared and assisted by the school, they can provide tutoring help at home. When parents get involved in school governance issues, they are more likely to be inclined to support the school district at election times, which can translate into continued funding for the school. Principals and teachers must also use parents as a resource for understanding their students and gaining insight into what educational approaches will work best for different students.

Partnering with community businesses

In many schools, local businesses have provided professionals who tutor students in their subject fields. Local business people can also visit classrooms and talk to students about careers in different fields and what sort of studies are required for each. Businesses also work with Junior Achievement and other similar programs to provide work-study opportunities for high school students. Many high school students need part time jobs, and a number of local businesses are willing to hire and train those students. Business people have an interest in high-performing schools, as they will be hiring those schools' graduates somewhere down the road.

Data analysis required of test takers

The level of data analysis required of test takers is basic data analysis: the ability to read a fairly simple chart. The test will not require any advanced analysis. It is more concerned with determining that the test taker is familiar with the basic format of an AEIS report and knows where to find such information as test scores, student demographics, teacher salaries, operating budget figures, and program information. It is helpful if one has memorized the sections where this information can be found.

Politics inside the campus environment

Every area of academic concern—curriculum, school funding, violence in schools, and test scores—is frequently in the news, and educational issues are hot political topics. Politicians routinely make school funding issues and schools that fall below state and national standards part of their platforms. Although most people commonly report that they are happy with their own school districts, the greater public perception is that the public school system is badly broken and in danger of complete breakdown. Many parents are angry about educational issues they feel are adversely affecting their children. More and more, today's parents view teachers as adversaries who are trying to supplant parental roles by imparting their own values and beliefs in the classroom. Furthermore, parents see administrators as bureaucrats who are more interested in test scores and their own careers than the education of the students in their charge. Principals who are not aware of political issues and social concerns and do not face them head on through open communication with parents and the media risk losing the support of all stakeholders within the school's community.

Reporting academic progress to parents

A principal needs to lead his or her staff members in explaining to parents the factors affecting students' advancement, why their children are placed in particular programs, and why children progress at different rates and in different ways from their peers. Staff members should explain to parents how tests are scored, how classes are ranked, and what students are expected to know to progress from grade to grade. Principals and staff members must be aware of families' different cultures, not only language differences, but also differences in child rearing styles and the role that schools and education are expected to play in their children's lives. The school must not make assumptions about any student's home life based on his or her religion or ethnic background; instead, educators must talk to parents to find out how much they know about the educational system in which their child is being instructed.

Effective public relations

Effective public relations generate good buzz for a school, which enhances the school's reputation and encourages community support of the school. If they see and hear that their local schools are generating positive PR, parents and community members will be more inclined to get involved with the school by donating time and funds, offering services, and participating in activities that benefit the students. When a school has strong public relations ties, the local community is much more likely to support school initiatives at election time because they have evidence that the school is succeeding in its mission.

Legal issues and curriculum content

Education is highly politicized and is frequently involved in litigation these days. School districts across the nation have been sued by parents because of their curriculum content, both what is being taught and what is not being taught. Subjects of law suits have included evolution (some students' religious beliefs support creationism instead of evolution); sex education (some parents do not believe that sex education belongs in the school at all, while others object to the materials being used or the manner in which the subject is presented); social issues such as homosexuality or abortion (again, some parents do not want the subjects discussed at all, and others object to the way they are presented); history (in school districts with a great deal of ethic diversity, there have been controversies centering around contentious historical subjects, including the Texas Revolution, Japanese internment during World War II, and the Vietnam War). More and more often, people have complained about the ways that global warming and other environmental issues are presented in the classroom. In order to avoid litigation, principals and school districts must be very familiar with current laws and policies regarding the content and presentation of curricula in the schools.

Legal issues and student activities

Although students have constitutional rights that schools are obligated to respect, schools have the right to restrict and control what students may say or do. Court systems frequently must decide where the line between the two is drawn, and a principal must be knowledgeable about the laws and cases that apply to his or her school. Students and parents have taken schools and school boards to court over sports. Issues such as who can play, who may be barred from playing, whether girls can play on boys' teams, what effect a student's GPA should have on student athletes' eligibility, and whether a student has been unfairly kept from playing on a team are frequent causes for litigation. In addition, freedom of speech and expression is often a source of controversy, especially in regard to student activities that are held off campus. These types of cases address when a student can be prosecuted for what he has said or written and when a student has a constitutional right to speak or write as he or she wishes. Other potential conflicts related to student activities that arise include dress code violations, behavior and disciplinary matters, and issues of privacy, most often in relation to search-and-seizure procedures and confidentiality of student information. As a result of national media coverage of school controversies, students and parents in today's society are both very knowledgeable about their constitutional rights and eager to defend them.

Documenting communication

Documenting communication with teachers and students is one of the most important aspects of a principal's legal responsibility. Most lawyers will attest to the fact that in the event of a lawsuit, the side with the more complete documentation usually wins. If all communication is documented—communication regarding discipline, personnel issues, access to records, academic progress, athletic eligibility, attendance, etc.—then the principal and the school are in a much stronger position should legal action be brought against them. Even though the state and the school district probably have very detailed policies regarding requirements for record keeping, an effective principal should go beyond policy and document even when he or she is not required to. Keeping records that back up everything he or she says and does will allow a principal to assist the school's legal representatives if he or she is presented with a legal challenge or potential legal challenge. When prinicpals are confident that they have followed the law and can prove that they have done what they are supposed to do, they can concentrate on the success of their schools and students.

Communication with school staff regarding legal matters

Just like principals, teachers and other staff members must be knowledgeable about matters of legal compliance. Principals must ensure that their staff members are aware of federal, state, and local laws and regulations regarding their interactions with students and other employees. Furthermore, staff members should completely understand the legalities pertaining to curriculum content, student rights, due process, free speech, privacy and confidentiality, etc. The school is vulnerable to legal challenges occasioned by staff members' ignorance of or failure to follow applicable laws. To keep them up to date on current legal issues, a principal should hold regular meetings with teachers and staff members, and the school's attorneys should hold similar meetings whenever appropriate. Staff members should be aware of how important legal compliance is in all matters and that a failure to comply with legal standards compromises the school and can lead to their own termination. The principal must also keep staff informed of legal matters involving the school at all times.

School law and litigation

On one hand, schools are much more sensitive today to the needs of all students than in the past, with respect to ethic or socioeconomic background, disabilities, etc.; schools are more inclined to approach education with a view to all aspects of their students' lives, not just that which they learn when they are seated at their desks. Civil and individual rights are better protected and children's emotional needs are better understood. On the other hand, schools and teachers receive less respect and deference than in the past, and most teachers would agree that this has made their jobs more difficult. Parents are less easily satisfied with how schools educate, more suspicious about that which their children are learning, and much quicker to legally challenge subject matter and disciplinary actions. Principals and their staffs must always, at all times, be aware of the possibility of lawsuits as they truly are a constant threat. Therefore every action must be considered and reconsidered in light of its potential for legal conflict. This has made schools more bureaucratic, less flexible and less spontaneous, and a certain amount of creativity has been lost. Teacher-student relations have changed dramatically and teachers report that they are more formal and less intimate with their students for fear of provoking suspicion, or worse. For example, in years past it was common for teachers to hug their students; today this is relatively rare. Conduct and curriculum are highly regulated.

Laws, regulations, and policies

Laws are statutes that are written and passed by elected federal, state, or local legislative bodies. Regulations are rules that have been written by official government agencies that have been granted rule-making authority by elected legislative bodies. Frequently, regulations detail how laws are to be implemented. For example, a law might read that a school must make regular reports of one kind or another to the school board, while the regulations supporting the law will detail what the reports are, when they are due, and to whom copies must be sent. Regulations have the force of law, same as statutes. Policies are usually written by local bodies, such as school districts, school boards, and school administrations. Policies do not have the force of law, but employees of the authoring bodies or people who report to the authoring bodies are required, as a condition of their employment, to follow the policies. Policies cannot contravene existing laws and regulations.

Student use of the Internet

In order to prevent legal action concerning student use of the Internet at school, schools must teach students to use the Internet safely, responsibly, and effectively. Schools must have safety measures in place to protect students from predators and to prevent students from accessing inappropriate or harmful websites; therefore, filtering software is a necessity for school districts. Students must be taught how to avoid accessing obscene or inappropriate sites, along with how different types of computer threats, including URL hijacking, mouse traps, spam, phishing, and spyware, operate. Other issues related to student use of the Internet at school can be adressed by teaching students how to recognize and report predators, how to protect their privacy online and respect the privacy of others, how to comply with copyright laws and avoid plagiarism, and how to observe network security protocols. Classroom instruction can also provide guidelines for students about web etiquette, chatrooms, and libelous or defamatory speech. Many books are available to direct principals and teachers in training students to be responsible users of computers and the Internet. Failure to train and monitor students effectively will leave the school vulnerable to lawsuits.

Partnerships with commercial ventures

Many school districts have allowed businesses to sell and promote their products in schools, including soft drinks, food, computers, and multimedia products. Commercial ventures will also sponsor school activities or fund school projects in return for being allowed to place their products in the school, which, in effect, is advertising in the school. These commercial partnerships can provide much-needed financial resources for the school, but the school must monitor such sponsorships closely. Among the concerns business partnerships present are the effects of commercialism on impressionable children, especially younger children; the danger of exposing kids to food and drink with no nutritional value; forcing children to view advertising that appears in the guise of educational material; violations of student privacy in the context of technology use; and using students as unpaid and unwitting marketing research participants. Parents and other members of the school community should be informed about any commercial sponsorships or partnerships, and the school's legal representatives should review any contracts and arrangements between schools and businesses, all of which must be committed to writing.

Student discipline

A principal and his or her staff should be able to motivate students to demonstrate good conduct without the constant threat of punishment. Many schools have reported success with allowing students to have input in formulating codes of conduct. Such conduct codes stress the importance of respect toward others, academic honesty, and peer-to-peer influence in adhering to the rules of conduct. In some schools, students serve on panels that review charges of code violations. Students are more inclined to police their own behavior when they know that they are expected and trusted to conduct themselves appropriately, especially when they have a role in shaping the rules of their community.

Faith-based organizations

Faith based organizations (FBOs) are often able and enthusiastic participants in the school community, providing much-needed funds and resources for school materials and projects. They also offer volunteers who will counsel, mentor, and tutor students. However, partnerships between FBOs and schools must be closely monitored for compliance with applicable laws, especially constitutional laws regarding the separation of church and state, along with laws pertaining to students' rights and privacy. The programs in which FBOs participate must be secular in nature; they cannot include any proselytizing and must not consist of any explicitly religious activities. The school must be thoroughly objective and neutral when choosing organizations with whom to partner and cannot show any preference to FBOs over secular groups, or vice versa. FBOs must observe the same rules and standards as any other organizations that share school partnerships, and the school must make sure that their programs are safe and appropriate for students. As with any third-party agreements, partnership agreements between FBOs and the school must be in writing and must be reviewed by the school's lawyers.

LAN

Though the upfront costs of installing a local area network (LAN) can be high, it is a sound financial investment in the long run. A LAN will save money on the purchase of software, as the school can purchase one copy of a program and, with the appropriate site licenses and licensing fees to satisfy copyright law, run it off the LAN to computers throughout the campus. Fewer printers are necessary with a LAN because many people can send their print jobs to printers linked to the network, as opposed to every individual computer having its own printer. Administrative staff can share information and paperwork on a network, which saves time and increases efficiency. Once a LAN is installed, the school may be added to a wide area network should the district install one. The one drawback to LAN systems is that when the network is down, all computers associated with the network are down as well. This problem can be mitigated by allowing computers to work in stand-alone mode or by keeping a few computers off the network so that they can always be accessed in stand-alone mode.

Class schedules

A class schedule is one of the most important time management tools a school has. Because the academic day is limited, it is important that the amount of time spent teaching students is maximized, while the amount of time spent on non-academic tasks during the school day is minimized. The National Educational Commission on Time and Learning has recommended an academic day that represents the time students spend on core subjects— language, math, science. The Commission suggests that 5.5 hours a day should be dedicated to these core subjects. Meeting this recommendation is not so difficult in the lower grades, where students usually have the same teacher all day for all subjects. However, the design of the public school for upper grades has always worked more like a factory in which secondary students go through an assembly line for a set number of hours each day, and each subject they must learn is accorded a block of time. In general, all subjects are allocated the same amount of time, regardless of their complexity or nature of study. Schools have begun to experiment with class scheduling options in an effort to move away from the assembly line model and are increasingly trying such alternatives as team teaching, block scheduling, and semesters that are structured more like those found in colleges.

Community familiarity

If the greater community has firsthand familiarity with its local schools, it is much easier to win public support at bond election time. This might be especially important when a school is in need of costly repairs and renovations. Voters are more likely to approve bonds or an increase in taxation if they know what kind of physical plant upgrades the school needs. The community will also be more likely to pitch in and help with maintenance and repairs around the school. Communities frequently organize "clean up the school" or "paint the playground" drives, during which parents and other community members help plant flowers, paint classrooms, install playground equipment, and do other things that do not require professional contractors. Administrators must reach out to the greater community because community members cannot offer their assistance and services if they are not aware of a school's needs.

New technological tools

A large number of schools have buildings that are many years old, and before they can be fitted with twenty-first century technology, their physical facilities must be renovated. Older buildings, for example, do not have telephone lines in each classroom, which might be necessary for Internet access by modem. For Internet that is not accessed through a dial-up conection, the school will need cable, DSL or T1 line access. Most old schools require completely new electrical rewiring before they can accommodate a lot of computers or audiovisual equipment. Before any of this is done, a principal and his staff should make a thorough plan of how they expect to use technology, determining specifically what computers will be used for, where they should be installed, and how many printers and peripheral devices will be required. This will save time and money in the future so that rewiring and further extensive renovations will not be necessary.

Block scheduling

Block scheduling is an alternative to the traditional assembly-line scheduling model. Block scheduling is a generic term covering any of several alternative scheduling models, all of which feature longer class periods so that subjects may be covered in more depth. Many educators feel that six or seven class periods a day is too hectic and stressful for both students and teachers, and the forty-five or fifty minutes of teaching time is too short. In contrast, block scheduling allows for classes to be held less frequently, but for longer periods of time, so that the time spent teaching each class is no less than the time spent under the seven period model. One popular form of block scheduling calls for classes to meet on alternate days, as many college classes do. Another plan, usually referred to as the four-by-four plan, calls for students to take four courses each semester, a plan that is also similar to a college schedule. In a four-by-four plan, the academic day consists of four instructional periods of 90 minutes each; the course is compressed into one semester, as opposed to meeting all year. The total time students spend in the classroom is the same as under the old scheduling model, but with fewer class periods, less time is spent on such non-academic tasks as roll call, turning in assignments, and announcements. There has not been extensive formal research done on block scheduling, but it has been tried in many schools, mostly high schools, and both teachers and students speak favorably of it.

School food service

Childhood obesity is a serious public health problem today, and many experts are focused on the kinds of food children eat in school. Schools now try to ensure that all food prepared in cafeterias is of high nutritional value; most schools have nutritionists or dietitians on staff to consult with cafeteria personnel in menu preparation. A lot of schools no longer allow vending machines with "junk food" and sodas to be on campus in an attempt to limit students' access to unhealthy snacks. Vending machines have always been a source of revenue for schools because schools receive a portion of the money collected by the machines; to compensate for this loss of funds, some schools have contracted with restaurants and other food suppliers for discounted items or revenue-sharing programs. Such cooperative arrangements have been a source of contention with parents and experts who do not think students should be eating fast food. Many schools are trying to limit the amount of nutritionally-poor foods students have access to without incurring added expenses or losing significant amounts of revenue.

Technology leader

One of a superintendent's primary responsibilities as a leader in technology is to provide his or her personnel with appropriate training in technology in order to enhance their efficiency and ability to help students succeed. Many times, however, teachers and administrators are required to attend technology-based workshops but then are not given ample opportunities for hands-on practice of what has been presented, nor do they receive one-on-one feedback during training. It is important for a superintendent to recognize that if a new technology is to be implemented, then district personnel need to be given the appropriate support and supervision during the time of training and implementation. One of the main reasons that programs fail is because staff members receive information about new technology programs in handouts but are provided no help with how to implement those programs. In addition to providing extensive technology training, effective superintendents procure the necessary resources for their schools to keep current with

- 15 -

changes in technology. For example, some superintendents apply for grants that provide laptop computer labs for each classroom. Through such actions, superintendents enable educators throughout the district to help their students become successful.

Culture

A community's culture defines what is important to the community's members. Culture articulates what resources are to be used for, how members are expected to treat one another, what behavior is rewarded and what is punished, and how members deal with the outside world. Culture is, or ideally should be, the glue that unifies and holds a community together. In a district with a strong and healthy culture, there is a general consensus about what is important and what takes priority. Individuals recognize that they are an important component of the culture, that they influence the culture, and that it can influence them. Each school district must understand the cultural components that influence its educational mission.

Disposition of resources

School resources are finite, and in almost all public schools, resource shortage is a constant challenge. Different groups are constantly competing for resources, and superintendents must try to satisfy the needs of each group by allocating the appropriate resources. School staff members look to superintendents to be their advocates to the school board, and to school district and/or state authorities when attempting to obtain needed materials and funds. If staff members feel that superintendents favor certain groups over others, or that there is no commitment to assist all groups in getting what they need to perform their jobs, they may not unite in pursuit of the district vision. Superintendents must decide whether a school district should buy new sports equipment or art supplies, renovate classrooms, buy musical instruments, hire more teachers, or get new books. Making these decisions, and providing convincing explanations for the allocation of resources are important responsbilities for all superintendents. Staff members must understand the decisions and understand why they are the correct choices made with a school's best interests in mind.

Being caught between parents and teachers

Superintendents must not align themselves with one side when dealing with conflicts between teachers and parents. If superintendents side with teachers on all issues, parents will feel that their interests are not valued and they may lose trust in school leaders. Not all teachers are perfect, and parents may have legitimate complaints. On the other hand, if superintendents consistently side with parents, teachers will feel that they lack support from district leaders. Superintendents must ackowledge the efforts and concerns of both teachers and parents. Taking sides in any conflict could lead to the destruction of the campus vision. Superintendents accordingly must learn to validate the different perspectives of parents and teachers in difficult situations.

Communicating negative information

Communication with parents should be forthright and simple, without anger or accusation or condescension, and especially without judgment. Superintendents should not be indirect or unclear when explaining a problem or difficulty with a student's behavior or academic progress. Superintendents should understand that parents who are not fluent in English may be unable to understand certain gestures or phrases. It is important for parents to understand an issue, and the specifics of their children's behaviors. Superintendents need to provide clear information, detailing the exact area in which a student's work is suffering. Examples then must be provided to determine what might be done to correct a problem. Superintendents must express that the school wants to work with the family, and there should be no judgment of the student or the student's family. Communicating negative information should not involve finger pointing or attempts to place blame on someone. Instead superintendents should communicate that there is a real problem that needs to be dealt with in a positive and productive manner.

Conflict with parents

Many parents are focused on the interests of their own children rather than the student body as a whole. Some parents are reluctant to believe that their children have academic or behavioral problems. A parent may say that his or her child never does anything wrong, and think that other children are bad influences. Like teachers, parents may believe that certain school programs are more important than others, and when these programs are not allocated sufficient resources, parents may feel that superintendents are not addressing their children's needs. Curriculum is another area of potential friction for parents and superintendents. Parents today are more concerned with the specific material being taught in the classroom than in decades past, and they are more apt to object if they view any material as too conservative, too liberal, too religiously-oriented or disrespectful of their beliefs. Although they must be open and receptive to parents' concerns, superintendents must keep each school's vision of learning prioritized during any conflict.

Encourage a sense of community

It is important, especially in larger school districts, to instill a sense of community in students. Each school's special events and traditions are important in helping students develop a sense of belonging in the larger community and to lessen some of the anonymity that can occur when attending a large school. Superintendents can play an important part in reaching out to groups that might not feel included in the school, such as students with special needs or students in various alternative school programs. In large school districts, it is very important to avoid student apathy and create diverse academic and extracurricular programs to involve all students. If students feel that they are part of a whole, they are less likely to get lost in the crowd, fall back in progress, or eventually drop out of school. School activities can get students involved and help teachers to get to know their students better as well as students in the school who are not in their classes.

Communicating with stakeholders

As leaders of school districts, it is important for superintendents to be available to students, teachers, and other administrators. The physical presence of superintendents is essential and they should implement well-established practices such as standing at the entrance of schools every morning to welcome students and teachers. Students and parents can stop to chat, and teachers can inform or remind superintendents of ongoing issues and events. Superintendents can see the students who come in, and take note of any problems or concerns that can be shared later with staff members. Both superintendents and teachers can keep each other informed about students' problems, needs, and accomplishments. Frequent student assemblies can serve the same purpose, keeping students informed about campus events and providing an opportunity for students to approach superintendents. Also, each school district can distribute weekly or monthly bulletins to students which might include notes and messages from superintendents.

The three words likely to appear in many test questions are *all*, *collaborate* and *continuously* or synonyms thereof (everyone, cooperate, constantly, etc). The competencies expected of superintendents all share certain traits because they all call for continuous collaboration with all stakeholders of the school community. Superintendents must work with all who have a stake in their school districts, collaborating closely with thosel who work in the school community. Continuous leadership of the school community in the pursuit of the campus vision of learning is important for all superintendents.

Business and parental perception

Today some parents and local communities tend not to see schools as public agencies as much as in the past. Instead, they see the school as producing a product and they think of themselves as the school's customers. These "customers" expect the school to be mindful of their needs and opinions. In this scenario, superintendents are viewed as district CEOs and are held responsible for customer satisfaction. Superintendents and teachers must be responsive to their customers and hold themselves accountable. The school exists for the community, and being friendly to visitors, returning parents' calls promptly, and holding school meetings with parents at convenient times all are essential to creating a positive atmosphere in a school district.

Reaching out to parents

To each out to parents, superintendents can initiate orientation sessions before the school year starts, and invite parents to attend with their children. It is important to ensure that parents feel welcome to visit the school and their children's classrooms. Contacting parents when students do well or exceed expectations is important because often parents are contacted only when there is a problem. Teachers should receive training in how to communicate with parents to encourage active involvement in the school community. Administrative staff and teachers need to take the time to gain knowledge of specific family cultural backgrounds and different customs, values, family structures, and child-rearing practices. If a family needs help beyond academics, the school can offer information regarding community agencies that can provide assistance.

Respond to political and social changes

Political change often is preceded by changes in the socioeconomic conditions or demographics of a school district's community. Superintendents need to be aware of widespread demographic shifts among the student population in advance of any political changes that may follow. Political changes also may be preceded by public dissatisfaction with schools. For instance, the Kansas school board evolution issues, or the role school funding plays in every state election. Some political changes can lead to drastic, and unwelcome, changes in school districts. Budgets for certain programs may be cut, or there may be intrusive government policies. If superintendents are aware of these issues, and respond to them proactively and appropriately, unwelcome changes can be avoided.

Cultural sensitivity

Some cultures view the teacher/parent and school/family roles as separate and distinct spheres that should not overlap. This view means some parents will not realize that they are expected to play active roles in their children's academic efforts. Parents may not realize that they have certain rights, and are expected to ask questions, make suggestions, and contribute to schools. Also, some parents will not expect the level of participation that is asked of them such as providing materials for projects, and transporting students to and from certain school activities. In some cultures, teachers are held in the same regard as doctors or other professionals, and parents might be reluctant to question a teacher, make suggestions, or express concerns about teaching methods. If superintendents are aware of these notions, they can work with educators to plan appropriate approaches to discussions with parents. Remaining sensitive to each culture's customs can help in such discussions and encourage parent participation in school events.

Communicating with non-English speaking parents

The wider school district community, including parents and local business people, may include a lot of people who speak more than one language. School districts should compile databases of these people and the languages they speak. People can be called on to act as translators as needed for parent conferences, report cards, newsletters, and other school information. Translators also could assist students and parents who want to take the GED or pursue other educational opportunities. School staff could help families get in touch with agencies that can provide various services. Families who receive such assistance will feel that they are part of the community, and the translators will become more involved in school districts.

Choosing businesses with which to partner

School districts should choose business partners in fields that fit an appropriate academic profile. Businesses should support subject matter taught in the district's classrooms. Districts must be aware of a company's motives in participating in any partnerships and it must be clear what the company hopes to get in return. Corporate altruism can be a positive thing for schools, but the district must understand what a company is aiming to accomplish. Districts should avoid companies that will attempt to market directly to students. Before choosing any partners, a needs assessment should be conducted throughout the school district to determine exactly what activities and products are needed. The opinions and input of all in the school community should be solicited, especially that of parents, who have a right to know which companies are going to be involved in their children's education. Each company's background and products should be researched thoroughly previous to creating any partnerships. All agreements must be confirmed in writing and approved by a school district's legal consultants.

Public relations

PR is an unavoidable part of superintendents' responsibilities. Every time the school district is in the news, or the community learns of something that's going on at a school, or someone in the community mentions a school to someone else, these are all forms of public relations. The crucial thing for superintendents to do is be knowledgeable about public relations, and take the lead in generating positive PR, creating a "buzz" for their school districts in the community. If superintendents and educators do not take the lead in communicating with the community and the media, public relations for a school may not be positive. Bad news always finds its way to the public whereas good news can be more difficult to publicize. Superintendents need to make a strong commitment to positive publicity through avenues including press releases to local radio and TV stations, and newspapers. School leaders can seek regular spots on radio or local access cable to communicate continuing news about their districts. Also, schools can use marquees to publicize school activities and events for the community to see. Each district must be proactive and train all administrators, educators, and staff members to understand the value of good communication and positive publicity.

Handling media

The way superintendents handle the media is very important because positive media relations are important for school districts. School leaders must be informed and prepared since members of the media can be unkind to those who are misinformed or do not do their homework before dealing with them. Superintendents must get to know members of the media including the names of reporters and producers. Learning about people in the local media involves knowing what areas are covered by different reporters, and how frequently they report different issues. It is important for superintendents to answer questions honestly and simply, without embellishment, without adding pointless details, and without trying to "lead" or manipulate the reporter's coverage. Limited use of educational lingo and jargon also is helpful when communicating with the media, and it is essential not to ask for pre-approval rights on stories. Discretion is important and school staff should remember not to say anything off the record and expect it to stay off the record.

Inviting the wider community into schools

Superintendents can try various approaches to invite the community into a school. They can try a direct approach, sending invitations to community members including business leaders and municipal personnel. Another approach is publicizing back-to-school festivities with student presentations, and awards to community members who have helped schools. Districts can conduct career days, job fairs, or stage all-day curriculum fairs and exhibits. Superintendents can offer use of a district's facilities, such as conference rooms, gymnasiums, or cafeterias to local groups for meetings and assemblies. Also, community members can be invited to volunteer in activities appropriate to their business roles providing career mentoring, tutoring, or being job fair sponsors. Superintendents can identify community leaders and invite them to learn about school activities by sending out press releases and newsletters.

Getting the word out

Most schools today have marquee boards that can be used for more than football game announcements and holiday schedules. These boards can trumpet good test results, awards given to students, teachers or the school, and upcoming events that are open to the public. Superintendents also can communicate with the community by writing press releases for the local media. A district's website is another communication tool, and superintendents could start blogs to connect with parents and students. Students could create posters and multi-media commercials that can be distributed in the neighborhood. Flyers and billboards also can present school information to community members and local businesses.

Advocating for students

Being an advocate for students includes advocating for those students who have the most academic challenges, the most at-risk students. It is not enough to be an advocate for National Merit Scholars and students with good grades. At-risk students need the attention, commitment, and advocacy of dedicated school leaders. Superintendents must help to ensure that all students have equal opportunities in the public school system. Superintendents are proponents of the importance of education in a free society, and the public school system offers the only chance some children will have to get an education. Their roles as advocates make superintendents responsible for giving a voice to all students, especially the most vulnerable and challenged ones.

If superintendents are aware of current issues and concerns in the school community, they are better prepared to lead districts in addressing students' needs. Being aware of the complex ethnic and socioeconomic backgrounds of students is part of the preparation necessary to lead staff in tailoring curriculum and programs to meet each student's needs. If the external community has a high unemployment rate, a high crime rate, or widespread drug problems, students can be affected in various ways. These situations can lead to high dropout rates, lower test scores, or lack of parental involvement. Superintendents can take the lead in combating these problems before they become insurmountable. Too often families who need help from various school and government agencies do not find what they need because all the different agencies operate independently and without awareness of each other. Schools are in a unique position to help coordinate efforts to help these families, by communicating with the various agencies and acting as an advocate and intermediary for the families. Awareness of current political concerns regarding curriculum or disciplinary and budgetary matters in the community enables superintendents to address problems before a district faces potential lawsuits or unfavorable election results.

Grasping current school law

Anyone preparing to become a superintendent must take at least one course in school law, and more would be better. Superintendents must be knowledgeable of current federal, state, and local school law and important cases involving education. Legal reference materials should be available for superintendents and they need to know the school board's legal representatives. In addition to statutes and case law, the state and the school board will have many policies, and superintendents must be familiar with them. Law regulates everything that schools can do, down to the smallest and seemingly most obscure details, and ignorance of law and policy could lead to problems for superintendents and their districts. Student activities, students' rights, teachers' rights, labor laws, constitutional law, due process, free speech, special education, and sexual harassment are all subjects superintendents should research and understand.

Disciplinary actions

Superintendents must be fair and impartial and approach disciplinary actions with an open mind. It is important to resist the urge to side with one person before knowing all details about a matter. When meeting with a student or teacher, a third, impartial person should be present to observe. Superintendents should not talk alone with the student or teacher unless the matter is extremely confidential, and in such cases the superintendents must be keep detailed notes and records of any discussions. Regardless of whether the meeting is private or observed by a third party, superintendents should document all communications thoroughly, and the student or teacher should be asked to sign off on any reports to ensure that everyone agrees on what happened. If superintendents have any questions at all about the legal ramifications of a disciplinary matter, they should talk to the school district's legal representatives before speaking to the student or teacher. It is most important that superintendents are absolutely certain that they follow the appropriate laws and policies, and observe the rights of everyone involved.

Multicultural awareness

Superintendents must take specific steps to communicate with the non-English speaking members of the community, particularly students' families. Parents need to know and understand what their children are learning in school, If parents are aware of the cultural and ethnic makeup of the student body, they will be more inclined to have a positive view of multicultural education including English as a second language, differing perspectives on history, and studies of diverse groups representing students in the district. Some people are apprehensive about people they do not know or understand, so learning about the members of the school's population will promote multicultural awareness. The school community also should know about the school's special education/alternative education studentsl. Schools report that people are more enthusiastic supporters of special education when they know about the school's programs for students with special needs. Knowledge is essential for tolerance and support, and superintendents need to promote awareness of diversity in their districts.

Ethical role model

Superintendents are more than rule enforcers, budget overseers and personnel managers. They also are the leading figures of school districts, and the representatives of schools in the eyes of the community and in the eyes of students. How superintendents are perceived to treat students and teachers sets the tone of the entire school district. If superintendents are hostile or unfriendly, dishonest or unconcerned with others, or partial to certain groups, school districts will be unpleasant places. Some may feel it is inappropriate to compare a school district to a family, but a school is a community of individuals who interact daily in close proximity, and how they interact determines whether a school will be effective in its educational mission. Superintendents who model and promote respect of others, kindness and consideration of students and staff, honesty and fairness, and a constant concern for the needs of all students set a positive example that others will want to follow.

Safety

Safety is one of the most important issues on school campuses today, where violence can be an everyday danger. School safety involves more than hall monitors and superintendents can walk the campus to make sure students are in class. Schools today spend a lot of money on high-tech security devices. Many schools have key-card access systems and metal detectors through which all visitors, students, and staff must pass. Most schools now have their own police officers monitoring campuses, and video surveillance is common. This technology costs money to purchase, install, and maintain, but since horrific school shootings and other incidences of violence seem to be part of the modern educational landscape, such expenses are necessary and demanded by many communities.

Nature of resources

A district's resources include people, money and time. Often there are not enough of these resources. It is imperative that schools have enough teachers and administrative and custodial staff, and all of their salaries are an important part of the budget. Many school districts struggle with being understaffed due to both financial contraints and the critical lack of teachers applying for certification each year. In some districts, competition for good teachers is fierce. Money comes from the state and the district through tax revenues, and schools also must raise money from other sources because taxes are not enough to cover everything in most schools. Superintendents and staff must manage time effectively to accomplish everything that needs to be done. Most of the daily operations of the school district are not performed by superintendents, but by people they manage, and they must be effective managers of time and resources. It is the efficient management of limited money, people, and time that enables superintendents to lead high performing school districts.

Encouraging parental involvement

Many parents need to be told how to get involved with their kids' schools - they do not know what they can or should do and they may not even know that their involvement is welcome and appreciated. Parents who had bad educational experiences themselves – or who did not complete their schooling - may be especially reluctant to involve themselves in their kids' schools. The Superintendent must make explicit outreach efforts, targeting specific people and offering suggestions about what they could do and how they could offer their time. The Superintendent could explain to the parents why their involvement is important to their kids' academic future and how it would help make the school more responsive to kids' needs. If parents realize that their involvement is of real and measurable importance to their kids' success, they are much more likely to be receptive. The school can also provide the parents with materials to help their kids with their school work. School, parent, and student can sign academic contracts for short or long term projects – all three participate in daily or weekly reviews of progress, signing off as things are done according to schedule. Parents and teachers are able to track student's progress and monitor that the work is being done. Parents and teachers are able to track student's progress and monitor that the work is being done.

Most states and the governing bodies overseeing schools now expect and require a high degree of parental involvement. "Site-based decision making" is now the norm in school districts across the country. States and school boards, which often are comprised of parents, view parents as partners in their children's schools. Today's parents are not inclined to leave their children's education completely up to the schools. Parents will not accept being shut out of decision making and other issues. Many schools encounter resistance when trying to get parents inolved in their children's academic endeavors, but there are plenty of parents who feel it is their duty to be involved. If they are not allowed to participate, these parents will make their displeasure known to the school boards and at election times. School choice is a very hot political issue. Parents are much more likely to vote in favor of bonds and other issues important to schools if they know firsthand what the schools are doing and how important certain programs are for their children.

- 23 -

Effective communication with all parents

Report cards and other written information can be made available to parents in their own languages. The school can employ a staff member whose job function is specifically community information, including communication with parents. The PTO or PTA should meet regularly – i.e., more than once or twice a year. Office staff should make an effort to be friendly and open to parents, which includes returning phone calls promptly, maintaining an open door policy (drop-in visits welcome) and offering to give parents campus tours. Parents should be kept informed about what their children are studying at any given time so that they can equip themselves to help with homework and projects. Phone hotlines with prerecorded information can help parents stay current on what is happening in the school and what their kids should be doing regarding home work, outside projects, etc. – especially good for those homes that lack Internet access.

Potential dilemmas

Teachers and other staff might not buy in to the need for PR and proactive communications in the first place. Many teachers are inclined think that the Superintendent, principal, and staff should concentrate on the fundamentals of teaching and that paying too much attention to PR and communications is like pandering to critics. This attitude is short sighted but common. Staff might also be resentful if the Superintendent is seen to be spending too much time on PR and neglecting, in their view, the needs of students and staff. There's also a danger – whether real or perceived – that pushing the school district to the forefront of the community's attention might make it a target for criticism that it would not otherwise have attracted – the "keep your head down and no one will take a shot at it" mindset. This too is shortsighted and not at all beneficial for any school. There is always a danger when communicating with lots of diverse people and groups that you will be expected to be all things to all people, but no one said that being Superintendent was going to be an easy ride.

Application of laws, regulations and policies

In a word: impartially. The Superintendent must have the objectivity and neutrality of a Switzerland or a Solomon, playing no favorites and applying all laws and regulations in a fair and evenhanded manner, regardless of the persons or issues involved. In another word: consistently. Policies, rules and laws must be applied and adhered to in all cases and at all times – applying the rules inconsistently is almost worse than not applying them at all. If small rules are not followed, then larger ones are sure to be broken. If the law is not followed and applied at all times, the school will consistently lose legal challenges. In addition, if the Superintendent is seen to have favorites, is seen to be unfair or inconsistent in his enforcement of laws and policies, he will very quickly lose the loyalty of teachers and the confidence of students and their parents. Ethical and moral leadership is crucial in a Superintendent, and fair, impartial adherence to rules is a crucial dimension of ethical and moral leadership. A Superintendent who cannot be trusted to follow and apply the rules fairly cannot be trusted.

Campus safety

Threats to campus safety do not come only from the outside; unfortunately, there is a lot of student-initiated violence in the public schools today. Today most public schools, especially high schools, feature metal detectors to make sure students cannot bring weapons onto campus. Schools also make periodic searches of lockers, often with police and trained police dogs, to look for drugs and other contraband items. It is very important when conducting these searches that proper attention is paid to due process and to students' rights regarding search and seizure. Superintendents in several schools have faced civil liability and district disciplinary action for overstepping their authority in this regard – by conducting intrusive searches without sufficient cause or without regard to due process and search and seizure laws. "Zero tolerance" policies have also gotten schools in trouble and subjected administrators to unfavorable publicity when children have been suspended for bringing toy water guns or empty pill bottles to schools; these types of cases only cause friction and resentment from students' parents and the community. Schools have also faced dilemmas when they have found students with material that might indicate a propensity or plan for violence – say, an essay in which a student fantasizes about hurting a teacher or his fellow students, or a student's web page that contains threatening statements. Administrative staff must be mindful of students' rights to free expression.

Involving stakeholders in decision making

In order to involve stakeholders in the decision-making process, an administrator must first identify them. Stakeholders in education can be any group involved with education; however, the most notable groups are students, faculty members, teachers, administration, parents, school board members, legislators and community leaders. All these groups have a powerful impact on education. Many stakeholders want to take an active part in education while others choose to take a more passive role. Allowing stakeholders, especially parents, to be a part of the decision-making process can have a positive impact on their child's educational achievements and emotional development. Their ideas and opinions can be extremely helpful and it creates a unity between parents, teachers and administrators. However, there can be drawbacks, for example, if one group of stakeholders takes an active part, they can have too much power. There is a chance that this power could be used to create conflict.

Rational model for decision-making

The rational model for decision-making is viewed as a process that first begins with the administrator admitting they are facing a problem. Then the administrator addresses this issue through a series of steps, which in return comes out with an effective decision. This model focuses on what should be done and requires the administrator to follow certain actions that have already been designed to help achieve the best solution. It is assumed that the administrator is a rational administrator that works in an environment that functions rigidly and in a bureaucratic nature. Obviously, many school administrators do not work in this type of environment. This model does have some advantages; it clearly states the actions an administrator should take in certain situations and forces the administrator to decide which actions are most appropriate. However, this model has also shown that administrators are too quick in making decisions and do not attempt to try and find the true cause of the conflict.

Shared decision-making

Shared decision making, which is also known as participatory or site-based decision making is also built on the idea of choice. This model states that choices are made by the administrator in order to satisfy constraints. The focus of this model is on consensual decision making that is based on the values of the members in the group. The members of the decision making process also have open communication and everyone's status is equal. The whole idea of a participatory decision-making theory centers on the idea of the way administrators make decisions versus how they should make decisions. Some critics believe this way of making decisions limits the control of the decision maker and they believe administrators are influenced by other's personalities and values more than their own reason or intelligence.

Strategic decision-making

When an administrator uses this model, they are making a decision based on information they have gathered for their own knowledge and evaluating the internal and external environment. The environment is made up of interest groups, negotiation, and informal power. In order for this model to work, the members need to identify what the obstacles are as well as what challenges may impact the decision choice. An administrator will want to use this model if they are interested in making a plan that has room for change, is flexible and has a long term effect. It is important that the individuals involved with this decision have the same philosophy and purpose in common. There will situations when unexpected events occur and an administrator may find themselves making decisions based on these unexpected events despite trying to strictly use the strategic decision making model.

Differentiated decision making model

This decision making model does not follow the traditional way of thinking. The administrator needs to take into consideration a variety of points and each point will affect the decision choice in some way. Certain situational variables can have an impact on how the administrator will make their decision choice. This model recognizes that administrators may need to take a different approach in deciding what is best for the school. A decision can be made regarding the goals of the school itself or just about the whole process. Other factors that administrators should take into consideration are ethical considerations, values, culture and climate. It is important that administrators are prepared that different situations will arise and the need for a decision may be needed immediately. The process will not be the same each time, different situations call for different decision making processes.

Process of decision-making

Making a decision is a process that takes valued information and opinions from others and in return make a choice that you think is best. This whole process follows steps in order to achieve that decision. The first step is defining the situation that needs a decision. This is the time to fully investigate and gain an understanding of what the problem is. The next step is identifying the alternatives that can be used to make a decision. It is important for the administrator to know there can be more than two alternatives. After identifying the alternatives, the next step is to assess them. When the administrator is at this step, they should consider if they have the resources or power to implement a certain alternative and what kind of reception will they receive. When a desirable alternative has been chosen, then it is time to implement it. An administrator may encounter resistance or complete acceptance. After it has been implemented, the administrator should evaluate the decision and see if any other decisions need to be made.

Assessing decision-making effectiveness

Assessing decision-making effectiveness is an important process in order for an administrator to improve as a decision maker. Administrators are extremely busy people and this can be a challenge to complete, therefore, often times this step is overlooked. It can be difficult for an administrator to be objective about their decision, especially since they have invested so much of their time. It might be helpful to involve outsiders who do not have vested interest in the assessment process. There is a chance that the decision's effectiveness could reflect negatively on the administrator. However, if the administrator wants continued improvement for their school, they should occasionally assess the effectiveness of their decision. Many times there will not be enough time to assess every time a decision is made; however, if he or she wants to improve their decision-making skills, a periodic check will be in their best interest.

Analysis and input

A Principal cannot make decisions based on instinct or emotions or gut-feelings; while emotions might well play a part in some decisions, and emotional commitment is necessary to be a good Principal, you cannot make a decision to design a new math curriculum because you feel like maybe it might work. You have to have facts and data before you make decisions, especially decisions that will require funding or impact students' lives, and that covers most decisions. You don't decide to tinker with curriculum until you have data on student grades and test scores; you don't terminate teachers or hire new ones unless you have assessed the teachers' performance or you have determined that the ratio of students to teachers in particular classes is too large; you will not build a new gym until you have had inspections done on the existing one and plans submitted for the new one; etc. And you must have help in gathering and analyzing all the data, help from the staff members and professionals in your school whose job it is to know about the gym's condition, the number of science teachers and size of their classes, which teachers are not performing to standards, in which subjects a lot of students are failing or under performing. These professionals make up your team and their expertise is necessary in analyzing data and making decisions.

Empowerment means responsibility, and some people simply do not want more responsibility. If you are in charge of something, and you have decision-making authority, you also have accountability and responsibility for those decisions. Some people equate responsibility with risk and blame, and they want neither. Some teachers and administrative staff are happy to follow orders and, while they may like to contribute and to offer opinions or suggestions, they do not wish to make decisions or lead others. There's a lot of discussion in the professional literature about how to lead such people; most principals accept that they will have teachers and administrative staff who feel this way, and these people can still be valued employees. It is not necessary for everyone on a staff or a team to be a leader, and it is not necessary for every school staff member to have decision-making responsibilities, especially if such responsibilities were to be carried out resentfully, fearfully or weakly. What's important is for the Principal, as a leader and a manager, to know which employees want and can handle empowerment, and which do not and cannot. This will be an integral part of his team building duties

Collaboration

Because the Principal's role today is less that of a top-down imposer of rules and solutions and more that of a leader among professionals, it is necessary for the Principal to collaborate with the professionals whom he's leading. The school is now the site for most of the decisions made about it, and the decisions are made by the school's administrative staff, teachers, councils and others. The Principal cannot realistically make all the decisions himself, and under the school-based decision making model he is not supposed to. The school's professional staff is to collaborate on decision-making – they collaborate on the gathering and analysis of information; on the design and implementation of programs, classes, budgets and activities; on the testing and assessment of students; and on the actual curriculum and instruction used to educate the school's students. Many – maybe most – of the correct answers on the test will be the answers that involve the most people, i.e., consulting with a large group of people, or seeking input from a lot of people. There should be very few decisions that the Principal makes entirely by himself, and those will likely be routine decisions on small matters. The vast majority of the Principal's duties will be performed in collaboration with other school and district personnel.

It usually involves the types of activities that professionals roll their eyes at and profess to hate, but for which no adequate alternatives have ever been found – meetings, brainstorming, and one on one talking and listening. The only way to encourage collaboration is to communicate, whether it is individually in person or on the phone, in meetings or by memo, and the only way to encourage problem solving is by making the problem and its solution a responsibility of others – and that too requires communication. So if the seventh grade math scores are abysmal, you don't tell the teachers "here's the district's new math curriculum – start teaching it next month." For one thing, the district has probably told you that the school has to design its own new math curriculum. So you gather the teachers, and the appropriate admin staff, and you tell them how bad the math scores are, and you explain that it is everyone's problem - yours, theirs, the whole school's – and that you value their expertise and their knowledge and you want them to give you ideas and suggestions about what can be done to bring up the math scores. So now they own the problem and they want to be part of the solution.

Framing a problem

To frame a problem is simply to put it in context. What does the problem relate to, what and who will it effect, what caused it and what might solve it, and who has responsibility for solving it? For instance, the problem is that 67% of your seventh graders have failed the math portion of the most recent STAAR. Frame it – what math curriculum is currently being taught to seventh graders, and how is it being presented? Who are the teachers, what are their experience levels, what were their most recent assessments? What kind of homework have the students been assigned and have they been doing it? How did seventh graders in other schools in your district do on the math portion? What have other middle schools done to bring up failing STAAR rates? Once you have framed a problem correctly, you can break it down, identify the people who can help you design a solution, and start working on it.

Evaluating change

Once you've made the decision that a change is necessary, and you have designed and implemented the change (whatever it might be), it is necessary to monitor the results and evaluate their effectiveness. You've decided to redesign the seventh grade math curriculum because the majority of your seventh graders failed the math portion of the most recent STAAR test. So you do a wholesale redesign of the curriculum, and your math teachers completely redesign their instruction program, and they start doing team teaching and breaking the math classes down into smaller groups. You have to monitor this as you go along – how are the students doing on their homework assignments, have there been complaints from students and parents about the new format, how are the students' in-school (as opposed to statewide mandated) test scores, etc.? You can't wait until next year's STAAR test to see how if the new program is effective – you must be monitoring and evaluating it from its inception.

Support for change

You first want to enlist the support of the people who will be responsible for helping to make the change – if you're talking about redesigning the seventh grade math curriculum, that would be your seventh grade math teachers. They are probably already aware that the students' math scores are way below where they should be and if they are not aware, you need to show them the data. You will discuss the ramifications of those unsatisfactory scores – on student performance, on the school's ranking, on district funding, on the teachers' assessments. When they see the data, and you have discussed the scope and ramifications of the problem, you invite them to help you come up with a solution. People are more likely to welcome and implement change if they are made a part of it, if they own a piece of the solution. Ask the teachers for ideas on curriculum modification or redesign, on ideas for new ways of presenting math material, on help looking at how other schools have taken steps to raise math scores. Once the teachers are on board, you do the same thing with other school and district personnel who will have roles in implementing any needed changes.

Overcoming obstacles to change

It goes back to ownership, participation, and collaborative decision-making – all important concepts in the competencies and all likely to be covered on the test. Before staff members, teachers, and student families will accept change they must be persuaded that such change is positive and necessary. Whether it is a mild modification in curriculum or a wholesale redesign, new courses, changes to extracurricular programs or a new conduct or dress code, it cannot come as a surprise and it cannot be imposed from the top down. Most schools today operate on the site-based management plan, making much of their own policy and their own decisions, and today's schools are under close scrutiny from students' parents, who expect to play an active part in their children's education. They must know about, approve of and want the changes. And administrative staff who will be responsible for implementing changes or making the decisions that lead to the changes must give their assent and support or they will not be effective leaders and managers.

Leadership vs. management

Leadership necessarily involves people; management does not. You can manage paperwork, budgets, assembly line production, or inanimate objects, but you cannot lead them. A manager knows what needs to be done, but a leader can make others want to help get it done. Managers have knowledge and expertise and experience but they don't inspire passion or commitment in others – that takes a leader. Leaders challenge the convention, the rules, the we've-always-done-it-this-wayism, while the very nature of a management role depends on we've-always-done-it-this-way-ism. A manager has to be someone who's been in the organization for a while, or at least in the field, worked at different levels or in different departments and has the same skills and experiences as the people who (might) report to him. A leader can come in from another company, or another field entirely, and take the organization in the direction it needs to go. A manager must necessarily know the functions of the people he's managing, but a leader does not need to. A manager can implement appropriate management techniques as required by competency 007, but that does not mean that he can encourage and facilitate positive change, or promote collaborative decision-making and problem solving, or develop consensus – that demands leadership.

Transformational leader vs. transactional leader

Transformational leadership involves vision, leading others to share in the creation and support of that vision. Transformational leadership takes a holistic approach to the organization, seeking to lead the organization's members in new directions, or helping them to identify and then attain new goals. The transformational leader can inspire stakeholders to care about, share in and work toward the betterment of the organization even without direct reward to themselves; i.e., teachers and staff work to improve the school's rankings and test scores even if it will not mean an increase in their salaries or individual promotions. Transformational leadership involves a lot of intangible rewards. The transactional leader, on the other hand, leads individuals on an individual basis and uses individual incentives and rewards to get better performance – i.e. a raise for all teachers whose students raise their math scores. Transactional leaders appeal to personal wants and needs, while transformational leaders ask for personal sacrifice – and get it. Many professionals think a transformation leader is needed to really change a school.

School-based management and collaborative decision-making

The school-based management model is probably the predominant one in American public schools right now. This means that Principals and their administrative staffs are responsible for more decisions and more outcomes than they have been in the past – most of the funding, curricular and extracurricular activities, instruction and assessment decisions are now in the hands of school administrators. Principals certainly cannot be expected to make these decisions on their own; the demands of gathering and analyzing the information needed to make each decision are enough for more than one person already. So the Principal must delegate a lot of responsibility to others in the school – both teaching staff and administrators. This means training those staff members in the skills they need to make those decisions, and it necessarily means collaborative decision making as well. Because the responsibility is devolved, and many people are responsible for different pieces of the school's operation, decisions will be made by groups instead of individuals.

Data analysis

Up until a decade or so ago, school districts told Principals what the school was supposed to do, and the school did it. Parents sent their students to the school to which they were zoned. You didn't pull your child out of a school if the school was under performing; in fact, how were you to know if the school was under performing? You probably didn't. But today, thanks to increased attention to and pressure on schools to be more accountable to parents for how well they teach their students, schools now have to gather, coordinate and analyze data from every activity in which the school engages. Parents want to know how many students graduate, how many go to college, what the school's students average on the mandated tests, what kind of advanced courses are offered, how the teachers are ranked, how the school is ranked, how many kids have to be put on a special education track...and the school district and the state want to know as well. Schools today have to be run like businesses, with the parents as shareholders and the school boards and government as regulators. This requires a lot of data.

Lead student

The Superintendent is the lead teacher and must also be the school's lead student - always learning, staying current on education research, theory and practice, reading professional literature, attending conferences, and networking with other Superintendent s to know what other schools have done that worked or didn't work. He processes all that acquired knowledge and distributes it among his staff continuously (remember that most everything the Superintendent does, he does continuously). He learns from his own teachers about curriculum and instruction and he helps them to learn from mistakes as well as successes. The Superintendent is the one who must constantly encourage teachers to continue their learning and help them find opportunities for professional development.

Learning for all students

The Superintendent sees to it that the instructional program reaches all students at all levels of learning. This means a flexible instruction program that is adapted to the needs of the students. Students do not all learn alike or at the same pace, and so different students will be reached by different methods. The instruction program will actually be a collection of instruction strategies, and the Superintendent will make certain that school resources are aligned with available budget resources to make those instruction programs reach the students for whom they were designed. There will be regular assessments to monitor the instructional program and ensure that it continues to meet the needs it was designed to meet and to ensure accountability on the part of the school. The Superintendent and other staff will communicate frequently with students' parents and caregivers so that they know what their children are learning and what is expected of them.

Individual behavior

Administrators should have a background in the study of human behavior in order to understand why individuals are motivated to do the things they do. For an administrator, addressing human behavior includes understanding the basic psychological processes of students, teachers, and members of the community. Not everyone is motivated to do things in the same way, as evidenced by the large number of sociological theories about human motivation that have been studied. Administrators are responsible for knowing how to

- 31 -

reach out to people and motivate them to reach their full potential. It is important for an administrator to understand divergent behaviors as well, as they need to know how to deal with the negative actions that some people are inclined to take.

Because people are different, they will exhibit different behaviors when they are in group situations. While some people work well in groups, others work better independently. An administrator may find it difficult to have everyone's participation in a group, especially if participants were not given a choice about being in the group. It is very important that administrators make sure everyone feels valued and knows that his or her opinion matters. In order to receive everyone's full participation, an administrator may assign roles for group members. That way, each person in the group has a specific job, and it is his or her responsibility to make sure that the job is completed. It may be necessary to change roles every so often, because individuals who like to work in groups may always take an enthusiastic but aggressive role, while others may hold back and eventually have their opinions and actions overlooked. Giving reluctant participants the opportunity to have a more active role in the group's responsibilities will likely encourage more all-around interaction. Whatever methods an administrator uses to address individual roles and behaviors within a group, he or she ensure that all group members feel that their input is essential for the group to be effective.

Group dynamics

When an administrator becomes the leader of a group, he or she needs to be aware of problems that may occur within the group. Many times in group situations, no problems arise, and the goals of the group can be achieved quickly; however, in some cases, group dynamics result in problems that must be addressed before the group can move forward with its objectives. At times, an individual has no interest in participating in a group and will lack the level of commitment other members have. Therefore, communication as to why this group has formed and what its goals are should be a top priority so that reluctant participants might understand why they have been selected to be part of the group. Other problems occur when members of a group have conflicts, both personal and professional. As a result, the group is unable to be productive. From the first time the group meets, an administrator must create and maintain a respectful and constructive group environment. Another problem an administrator might have is keeping a group's attention focused on the task at hand, especially if some of the group members are good friends.

It is best to keep the size of groups to a small number because the more members there are, the less comfortable some group members might be. Oftentimes, larger groups cause members to be less intimate with each other, which results in a decline in the frequency of interaction. Another issue that may come up in a larger group is related to the interests of the members within the group. The more members a group has, the more likely it will be for people to share the same interests, dedication, and sentiments. If this is the case, then an administrator may have the problem of small groups forming within the larger group. Naturally, if people within a group have common interests, then there is a good chance that they will want to work with each other. If group members have too much in common, however, then the thoughts and ideas of the group will be too similar. Therefore, an administrator should balance groups by selecting individuals with both common and diverse backgrounds and interests, though finding the right combination of people can be difficult.

Maintaining school-community relations

Maintaining school-community relations contributes to the overall well-being of a school. This is especially true if the school population is composed of diverse ethnic groups that have a wide range of cultural traditions and values. By fostering school-community relations, administrators can ensure that every group is recognized and that their values are considered necessary for the educational success of their children. If parents feel that their values are important, then they will be more likely to have an active role in their children's education. Another way that administrators can maintain school-community relations is by taking advantage of the many kinds of resources offered by the community, such as parent volunteers, business sponsorship of special events, and donations of classroom supplies. Using community resources encourages everyone to be involved in a school's educational success.

Nonverbal skills

One of the most important skills in life is knowing how to communicate with others. For administrators, this skill directly relates to their leadership capabilities and can affect how people respond to them as leaders of their schools. Because many ways of communicating are nonverbal, administrators communicate with others all time, even if they do not realize they are. One way administrators can communicate nonverbally is the manner in which they dress. To maintain an image of professionalism, an administrator should wear appropriate business attire. Standing in certain ways can also communicate nonverbal messages to listeners. For example, administrators who stand with their arms crossed in front of them give the impression that they are closed off from the people they are talking with, even though that may not be the administrator's intent at all. Communication also involves listening as well as speaking. Effective administrators know that listening involves not only hearing the words people are saying, but also making eye contact, interpreting their nonverbal clues, and taking a serious interest in what they are saying.

Writing and speaking skills

Communicating with others is a vital aspect of anyone's life, and administrators are no exception. In order to communicate effectively with staff, parents, and students, an administrator must have good writing and speaking skills. The content of a written document should be checked for spelling and grammatical errors before it is distributed to colleagues because a document with misspelled words and grammatical mistakes does not appear professional. It is also important to remember that anything sent electronically, especially email, can be misinterpreted because the recipient is unable to read the sender's facial expressions and does not have the advantage of hearing that person's tone of voice. Therefore, an administrator should be aware of proper etiquette concerning electronic communication in order to avoid such faux pas as writing a message in all capital letters, which many people consider to be indicative of yelling. Effective speaking skills are another mode of communication that is extremely important for an administrator. In addition to delivering a message with sincerity, clarity, and confidence, an administrator should speak in a tone that is appropriate for the situation and use correct grammar.

Effective school culture

When an administrator focuses on school culture, he or she helps improve the total development of the children served by the school. This involves the development of social, moral, physical, and psychological skills. When a school's culture is brought together, everyone works together as a team to make sure that every child is receiving a quality education. The same school values are shared with everyone, especially the students. Therefore, students know what is expected of them. These values can be communicated through emblematic actions, such as signs or slogans. They can also be communicated by recognizing student achievement and reinforcing positive behaviors. However, if a student is not meeting his or her expectations and causing trouble, then negative sanctions will be necessary.

Problem solver

As discussed throughout this competency the Superintendent will not be solving problems alone – he will be leading others in finding solutions to problems. The biggest part of the Superintendent 's responsibility is decision making, and in one sense all decisions are solutions to problems, if you view a problem as simply a situation requiring action. It need not be a negative situation, just something that requires that something be done. So, the budget is a problem, facilities maintenance is a problem, hiring and firing is a problem, so is curriculum design and community relations. The Superintendent is responsible for identifying those areas requiring solutions or decisions, and he then seeks input and leads teams in designing those solutions and decisions.

Problem-solving skills

Every administrator should know how to approach problems with staff, students, and parents with fairness and empathy. At all times, administrators must be prepared to confront issues, explore them, and then be able to offer several possible solutions for each situation. When a staff member, student, or parent approaches an administrator with a problem, the administrator should react in an appropriate manner by listening attentively with an open mind and empathizing with that person's concerns. By making staff members, students, and parents feel as if their problems matter both to the administrator and to the success of the school as whole, effective administrators ensure that everyone involved in a problematic situation feels important. After truly listening and understanding the concerns that a staff member, parent, or student has, then an administrator should gather more information about the issue from other people, as well as from any additional available resources, such as other school administrators or school district policies. The last step an administrator should take in solving a problem is to set goals and establish problem-solving steps in order to resolve the issue.

Message content

While much of an administrator's daily communication is conducted in a casual manner, he or she will find times when a more formal approach to communicating is appropriate. When such a situation arises, it is important that an administrator construct his or her words in a careful and thoughtful way. Before delivering a message, an administrator should determine who the audience is, what the purpose of the message is, and whether the message is going to be shared via an oral or written form of communication. It is also important for an

- 34 -

administrator to remember that his or her every word has the likelihood of being be heavily scrutinized. When constructing their messages, administrators need to make sure that their ideas are clear and that the words they choose express their desired goals. Before distributing a message, administrators should consider how other people will respond. For example, if his or her goal is to persuade, then an administrator should acknowledge other people's opinions and realize that facts alone will not change someone's opinion.

Cross-cultural communication

An administrator should always take into account the various communication styles of staff, parents, and students. Everyone has learned how to communicate differently depending on who taught them, where they were raised, and what culture they come from. Being successful in communicating with someone from a different culture requires effort. Because different cultures have their own communication practices, administrators should be educated about some of those practices. For instance, some cultures discourage eye contact. Other situations call for administrators to be aware of the physical distance between themselves and the people they are communicating with to avoid insulting someone by invading his or her personal space or by appearing to be standoffish. Another important factor for administrators to consider is their speed of speech; when English is not someone's first language, he or she might have difficulty comprehending what is being said if it is being spoken too quickly. Perhaps the most important thing to remember about communication is that listening is just as important as speaking.

Feedback

Even though an administrator may clearly communicate a message that is grammatically correct and appropriate in tone, his or her intended message may not have been completely successful in its delivery. An administrator's message is effective only if it is understood by its audience and acted upon in the ways the administrator had intended. An administrator must be open-minded about the feedback he or she gets from the people who received the message. Without feedback, administrators would never know the true impact of their messages and might not realize that someone's input cannot only clarify their original message, but also improve their future communications. Administrators should encourage honest feedback and be able to accept it gracefully in the event of negative responses. Staff members should feel that their opinions matter and not live in fear that their jobs may be in jeopardy if they do express dissenting opinions.

Public speaking

Effective public speaking skills are crucial to all administrators because they are responsible for speaking at many public events, PTA meetings, student assemblies, and school board meetings. When speaking to a large group, an administrator must speak loudly and clearly and use larger gestures than he or she would in a smaller setting. If everyone present cannot hear the administrator's message, then he or she will quickly lose the crowd's attention. It is also important that the information the administrator gives is up to date. Good speaking skills include using an outline or notes in order to stay on track. However, if a speaker uses notes, he or she should consider them to be a guide and never read the words verbatim. Furthermore, an effective public speaker avoids saying "um" and "ah" when pausing to consult notes or to answer questions. One way to improve people's public speaking skills is to videotape them giving a speech a few days beforehand so that they can make any corrections in their speech and movements before addressing other people.

Effective listening

Effective administrators must have strong speaking and writing skills; in addition, they must know how to interpret and listen effectively to both verbal and nonverbal forms of communication. If an administrator does not know how to listen, he or she can misunderstand what is being communicated, which creates the possibility of problems arising. Listening entails more than hearing the words being spoken; it involves showing a legitimate interest in what is being said and genuine empathy for the speaker. Many people are not good listeners because listening is a skill that takes practice and may even involve a change in the listener's attitude. To be an effective listener, a person must be willing to learn from others and hear what another person has to say without interrupting. If administrators are unsure of their listening skills, they can find many resourceful books about how to be a successful listener.

Community of leaders

Successful administrators understand the importance of building a community of leaders that is comprised of staff members, parents, and students. When people feel as if they are apart of a group, then they more readily take responsibility for learning, commit to school goals, and understand why those goals are important. When teachers, parents, and students are told what to do, they oftentimes simply go along with the status quo and never assume leadership of anything related to the school. The result is that everyone accepts a passive, ineffectual role in the educational process. Effective administrators know that empowering others to have an active part in supporting the school's mission can have a powerful impact on student achievement. In addition, administrators recognize the importance of providing the necessary resources and support that will allow others to become leaders in the school community.

Promoting parental involvement

Parents are often hesitant to get involved with school functions or speak up about issues affecting a school district because they often feel that their opinions do not matter to school officials. In some cases, parents may have previously had a negative experience with administrators or teachers. Because of this, an administrator should attempt to make those parents feel valued and important, both to the school and to the success of their children. An effective administrator knows the significance of parental involvement and realizes that he or she must invite, recruit, and motivate all parents to participate in school functions and to offer input when decisions concerning their children are being made by the school district. If an administrator's efforts to involve parents produce no results, he or she may choose to offer parents incentives or rewards in order to encourage parents to take that first step toward involvement. Administrators can reassure parents that being involved in their children's school district does not mean that they have to speak in public or chair a committee. Parental involvement can include such acts as volunteering to chaperone a field trip, speaking to high school students about career choices, and donating time to work at fundraisers.

Negative reactions to authority

When administrators are faced with negative responses to their authority, their first reaction may be to become defensive or upset. However, the appropriate way to handle such situations is to investigate and examine the reasons why others are responding in a negative way. Although feelings of hurt and anger—and possibly betrayal—are normal, effective administrators have the ability to put those feelings behind them and move on to problem-solving. Having one's authority challenged can be turned into a positive situation when an administrator understands the concerns people have and is willing to address those concerns from the perspective that he or she can learn from them. The key to diagnosing the reasons for people's negative reactions is having a non-confrontational discussion with the parties involved. Every effort should be made to avoid putting anyone on the defensive.

Exercising authority successfully

There are numerous reasons why people question and challenge authority. However, if an administrator follows certain guidelines, then administrative authority can become less of an issue on campus. Administrators are obviously going to have to make some very difficult decisions and issue controversial directives to others. One thing an administrator should consider is how and in what style he or she will present the directive. Regardless of how professionally the directive is given, a person will resist it if he or she does not feel that it is in their best interest; issuing an order to someone who is not motivated will most likely result in failure. An administrator should also consider the strengths and weaknesses of his or her audience before giving a directive. To increase the likelihood of successful results, administrators should also explain the rationale behind the directive. Finally, they should acknowledge that not everyone may understand the value of what they have been told.

Positive response

When an administrator is an effective communicator, he or she creates a more positive, encouraging environment throughout the school. If administrators open a meeting by stating their true feelings or reactions to the situation at hand, then they can establish a secure environment from the onset because staff members will be at ease when they perceive that they are meeting in a safe atmosphere in which they can freely speak their minds. Because an administrator can control the attitude of the group he or she is addressing, chances are that the group will be more positive if the administrator enters into the meeting with a positive attitude about a situation. It is crucial that an administrator talk to the staff in a non-threatening manner; nothing will cause a person to become defensive faster than feeling that they are being personally attacked. An administrator must also learn how to become open to and accepting of others' personalities, opinions, approaches to issues, and methods of communicating.

Choice of staff members

After an administrator has developed a clear vision and has established goals for his or her school, he or she must staff the school with individuals who share that same vision. With the power to hire, promote, and demote staff members, an administrator must remember that every time he or she fills a position, whoever is hired for that position has the potential to change the school's culture. While it would be impossible to find someone who shares the exact same vision as the person who vacated that position, an administrator should strongly emphasize the school's values and goals during the hiring process. Because a school culture can take years to develop, a newly-hired staff member must understand what the school seeks to accomplish and be committed to doing whatever he or she can to contribute to the school's purpose.

Leadership appointments

An administrator can shape a school's organizational culture by making leadership appointments within the organization. Leadership appointments include positions such as a committee chairperson or a department head. Before making campus leadership decisions, an administrator must carefully consider what person best reflects and will most effectively promote the mission, goals, and ideals of not only the individual school, but also the school district. Because the person an administrator selects serves as an example for other staff members, appointing people to leadership positions allows an administrator to emphasize the qualities he or she looks for in a leader. However, because an administrator's choice can appear to be mostly subjective, he or she must be prepared for challenges and resentment from others who are upset when they are not chosen. Such responses oftentimes lead to a negative impact on the entire school environment.

Informal leaders

Administrators have definite influence in shaping school culture by appointing leadership positions; however, schools also have informal leaders who have not been selcted by administrators. Informal leaders are those individuals whom other staff members look up to and seek guidance from. Most often, informal leaders are the people who have the greatest interaction with other staff members, and their opinions and values are respected by the majority of their colleagues. Occasionally, a school's informal leaders will be the same people who are its formal leaders. If an administrator wants to shape the organizational culture of his or school, then he or she needs to identify the informal leaders of the school and develop a relationship with them. In many instances, a school's informal leaders are already in place before an administrator takes a position at the school. If administrators want their goals to be achieved, they must secure a commitment from the school's informal leaders.

Conflict between formal and informal leaders

Conflict between formal and informal leaders is always a possibility. There are many opportunities for disagreement about a variety of topics, and any type of conflict can make it harder for an administrator to build a unified organizational culture. Of utmost importance for an administrator is listening impartially to all parties involved in order to understand the main reason for the conflict. Both formal and informal leaders should be given the opportunity to voice their opinions and feel that their viewpoints are important and are being considered by the administrator. An administrator can use his or her influence to persuade one of the dissenting parties into a direction that is more suitable to the school's overall organizational culture; however, this may not work every time. Although no single correct way to handle conflict between formal and informal leaders exists because of the number of possible sources of conflict, an administrator with strong conflict resolution skills can usually guide a difficult situation to a peaceable solution.

Being attentive to others

Administrators can be effective communicators by being attentive to others. This does not mean that an administrator must show up at all school functions, PTA meetings, concerts, and other functions; rather, being attentive means being helpful and supportive. Oftentimes, administrators are so busy that while they are engaged in conversation with a teacher, parent, or student, they are simultaneously trying to complete other things, which prevents them from fully listening and being completely involved in the conversation. This lack of attention can give other people the impression that they are not important or that they are a nuisance to the administrator. Effective administrators are aware of the value of using their eyes, body, and face to reassure listeners that they are giving them their undivided attention. Doing so makes a clear statement to the other person that the administrator is listening attentively to what he or she has to say. When holding a meeting, administrators must be free from distractions, including cell phones, pagers, or palm pilots.

Asking questions

For an administrator to gather information about issues, he or she must ask precise questions in order to investigate the matter fully. However, an administrator does not want to ask an excessive number of questions because the other person in the conversation may feel as if he or she is being interrogated. An administrator should ask questions in a way that will extend the conversation so that he or she can gather the kind of information that is more difficult to obtain in other ways. Open-ended questions are most acceptable when they are asked during brief conversations, in a public environment, or if there are times when asking questions could result in a threatening or dangerous situation.

Community volunteers

Effective administrators know that in order to build a successful school culture, they must encourage community volunteers to participate in the school's success. Asking community members to volunteer their time will help them realize that they can have a major impact on student learning. If a school has a strong volunteer program, then parents and community members will be actively involved in their children's education and feel that their skills are useful and important. This bond can help break down the barriers between teachers and parents. Community volunteers also have a major impact on teachers. If volunteers are actively engaged in meeting students' needs, then their involvement can provide teachers with more time to plan other activities in the lesson plan. As a result, teachers' scheduling can become more flexible.

Self-nurture

Administrators have an extremely difficult job; they must motivate, coach, lead, attend meetings, and maintain the mission and goals of their schools. While all of these job duties can be highly rewarding, they can also be emotionally draining. Being overwhelmed by the demands of an administrative position can lead to burnout among many administrators, a condition that negatively impacts the rest of the school. In order for administrators to perform their responsibilities effectively, they must take care of their own needs along with those of their staff and students. It is important for administrators to find a healthy balance between their work and personal lives. Sleep, relaxation, fitness, and a nutritionally-balanced diet enables an administrator to be a healthy, well-adjusted person. When administrators have found ways to balance their responsibilities, they become healthier and happier individuals, as well as great role models for staff members, students, and parents.

Empowering teachers

When administrators empower teachers, they allow them to have a voice in decision-making processes. As a result, teachers feel valued, which motivates them to improve their performance. As leaders of a school, administrators facilitate the school's goals by encouraging teachers to create and share their ideas for not only their classrooms, but also the entire school. The more power teachers have, the more responsibility they assume in helping their school achieve success. Administrators should make it clear that each teacher is solely responsible for carrying out his or her duties and performing them to the best of their ability. However, administrators themselves are responsible for providing each teacher with the necessary training and education that will enable them to acquire appropriate decision-making skills. In order to make teacher empowerment successful, the school board members have to be in support of it as well.

Communication barriers

Every message an administrator sends out will be interpreted in different ways from the people who receive it. Sometimes, a message will not be successfully communicated due to factors that are not in the administrator's control. At times, an administrator will send out a message that they believe is extremely important, but the recipients of the message may not have the same level of interest or sense of immediacy as the administrator. Another barrier to communication results when the person hearing the message lacks the background knowledge needed to understand the content of the message. Certain buzzwords or phrases require a listener to have some extent of familiarity with them in order to fully comprehend the message. Furthermore, understanding the group of people who will be receiving his or her message can help an administrator know how the message should be written to avoid any potential misunderstanding.

Social barriers

Social barriers that may detract from the meaning of a message include a person's age, gender, and position in the school hierarchy. Because pedagogy is influenced by trends in education, new teachers who have been educated under newer methodologies might interpret information differently from more experienced teachers. Also, older teachers who are accustomed to how things have been done for years might be more resistant to a message detailing changes in the management of the school. Because men and women have their own ways of communicating with others, the meaning of messages both given and received by each gender can vary. Males are often misinterpreted as arrogant or harsh, whereas females are sometimes wrongly stereotyped as weak and lacking in leadership ability. People's positions within a school's hierarchy can also detract from the meaning of a message. Staff members who teach different subjects or grade levels may not interpret a message in the same way. Similarly, a superintendent is more likely to interpret another administrator's message on a different level than teachers will because their responsibilities differ so vastly. Administrators should be wary of communicating in ways that may be inappropriate for their audience. Despite an administrator's best efforts to present clear messages, however, every recipient will develop his or her own interpretation of what the administrator is attempting to say.

Enhancing school culture

Before administrators can enrich their school's culture, they must first have a good understanding of what the school's organizational culture is. After this has been determined, then the administrator can move on to enhancing school culture. If the school culture is not an effective one, it will be a challenge for the administrator to change it. The administrator must envision the future of the school and identify what goals will lead to the improvement of the school. An administrator must also make it a priority to meet the needs of the teachers and students. Enhancing the school culture will more likely be achieved if the administrator views a problem as an opportunity to find solutions rather than yet another burden to deal with. A school's culture will also be enhanced if teachers are encouraged to be creative in their classrooms, are given opportunities to share their ideas, and are made to feel that they are a vital part of the improvement of the school. The most important factor that will enhance school culture is for everyone to stay focused on student achievement.

Subcultures and countercultures

It is well known that effective administrators know how to shape and lead an effective school culture. Administrators can easily get the impression that their schools operate under one culture. This, however, is highly unlikely because every school culture is comprised of a wide range of personalities and opinions. A school can have multiple organizations that make up a culture, subculture, and even countercultures, with each group seeking to define what the school stands for based on the interests of its own members. The most common examples of subcultures and countercultures can be found in secondary schools, where there are several departments and subjects areas. Many of the departments are themselves a subculture; furthermore, subcultures are likely to exist within the department as well. Such structures can be an extremely difficult challenge for an administrator who is trying to understand and gather information about the school's culture and trying to set goals and expectations accordingly.

Building character

One of the many responsibilities an administrator has is building the character of the students he or she serves. What happens at home cannot be controlled, but what happens at school can. Administrators should always set high expectations for good student behavior. However, if administrators expect students to behave and act in accordance with certain standards, then they themselves must provide students with examples of good behavior in the school environment. For instance, students should see staff members using kind words and showing positive attitudes. Changing students' attitudes can have a major impact on their work habits and levels of achievement, both present and future. Character building in school provides students the opportunity to develop such character traits as responsibility, kindness, compassion, trustworthiness, and integrity, qualities that can apply to the rest of their lives.

Norms

Norms can be described as unwritten rules that state what others believe should and should not be done; norms are important in society because they represent the values and beliefs that help regulate and control people's behavior. Effective administrators understand that a group cannot be forced to believe in certain norms. Every person who works at a school already has strong beliefs and values of his or own. If an administrator wants an effective organizational culture, then it is important for him or her to hire staff members who have similar norms and values that the administrator feels are essential for a school to be effective. If staff members feel that they are in an environment where they share values and beliefs with their colleagues, then their work performance will be greater, and they will have more job satisfaction. If a school's norms change, it is often a result of personnel changes.

Expectations

The expectations of an organization are developed based on the norms of the school. While it is impossible for administrators to live up to every expectation staff members might have, they should always be aware of what their staff members expect from them in order to fully understand and enrich their school's culture. It is also important that the merit of these expectations be evaluated before an administrator devotes too much time to meeting them, because some expectations may be too unrealistic or might contradict the school's goals and mission. If expectations are too high, then conflict within an organization can result. On the other hand, if expectations are too low, then people may not reach their full potential. Ultimately, this will have a negative effect on students and their academic potential.

Symbolism

It is important for an entire school community to understand the expectations and sanctions that have been established by the school. Values and expectations can be communicated symbolically in the form of slogans, group rituals, or awards banquets. If students are expected to act in a certain way, then staff members and administrators should be expected to exemplify that same behavior. The focus of symbolic activity is not what is said, but what actions are taken to reflect a desired behavior. For instance, if students are expected to read, then they should see teachers reading. Administrators should also apply communicating through symbolism to staff members. If administrators expect something from their staff members, then they should take the lead by demonstrating the behavior as well.

Emphasizing academic effort and achievement

If administrators want their schools to be effective, then they must place emphasize academic effort and achievement. There should still be an emphasis on student behavior and character building; however, successful schools also stress effort and achievement as highest priorities. Ways of communicating expectations for academic effort and achievement to the community include developing a clear mission statement and preceise educational goals that can be included on all communication sent by the school. Another effective way of communicating that effort and achievement are of top priority is through the staff member's attitudes. Staff members in effective schools understand that they all must adopt the attitude that their students are capable of high achievement. If students have someone who truly believes in them, then they will believe in themselves. Teachers should also adopt the attitude for themselves so that they can help each student in their classes reach his or her full potential.

Path-goal theory

The path-goal theory describes the type of leadership in which administrators and other school leaders encourage and support their team members in achieving existing goals by providing a path they can follow. Leaders can make the path easier by eliminating any factors that may cause the followers to be unsuccessful and by offering awards as they follow the path. Removing any roadblocks will help team members feel capable of achieving their goals, and providing rewards will help encourage them. The disadvantage with the path-goal theory is that it assumes there is only one way of achieving goals and that the leader is the only one who can create a correct path. It does not allow for others to develop their own ideas and creative ways of achieving goals.

Transformational leadership

Transformational leadership is a type of leadership that is exercised through individuals instead of over them. This type of leadership requires group decision making, teacher empowerment, and a thorough knowledge of the value of change and its processes. An individual who can demonstrate transformational leadership knows how to create a team-like atmosphere and is always focused on school improvement. An individual with transformational leadership qualities knows the importance of implementing the team approach and also realizes that doing so can be difficult because a reassignment of roles will be necessary. When everyone is working as a team, each person contributes and feels a sense of ownership within the school community. As a result of a unified school community under transformational leadership, teachers will want to perform at a higher level, and student achievement will be greater.

Communication at every level

An effective administrator knows the significance of encouraging communication at every level throughout the school organization. In some cases, there is communication from principal to staff but not from staff to principal. It is crucial for administrators to encourage staff members to communicate with them and to convey the attitude that staff members' opinions are important to the success of the school. In order for staff members to communicate effectively with their principals, they must feel that their ideas, opinions, and feelings are valuable to the school. There will be a decrease in communication if staff members believe that what they say is not important, which can result in a campus-wide lack of trust and respect. In order to gain the confidence of staff members, a principal should work to develop strategies that build both organizational and personal trust.

Expanding information sources

If administrators want to hear truly informative feedback about their messages and job performance, then they must expand their sources of information. Many times, their sources are limited because there is a misconception that an administrator is receptive only to positive communication. Staff and other members of the school community may feel that their opinions and ideas will cause them trouble; therefore, they do not express their opinions honestly. This is especially true for those individuals who have views contrary to the majority. This could lead to a situation in which an administrator receives feedback and evaluations solely from groups of people who view things in the same or similar way as the administrator. It is vital that administrators receive feedback from a variety of sources in order to do their jobs effectively and to serve everyone's best interest.

Expectations

The behavior of an administrator can be influenced by different factors, including what expectations others have for a person in an administrative role and how an administrator's personal needs influence the success of a school. There will less conflict if the administrator's personal needs and the expectations of others are similar in nature. While it is not a necessity for an administrator to conform to others' expectations, it is important for him or her to understand them. There will be several different groups, including teachers, parents, students, school board members, and community leaders, that will expect an administrator to act in a particular way in certain situations. It would be impossible for an administrator to understand why all of these groups have the expectations they do; therefore, the administrator should focus more time on developing relationships that could have a positive impact on his or her effectiveness as an administrator.

The main factor in determining the direction of a group and its expectations depends on the situation and the group's decision-making process, which is why it is important for an administrator to understand the group's expectations for someone who is in an administrative role. A situation may occur when a group is accepting of an administrator's making a decision without consulting them; however, the opposite may be true in another situation. It is important that an administrator carefully evaluate the situation and then base his or her decision-making process on what he or she understands about the group's expectations. Conflict is likely to arise if the situation is handled in an opposing manner from what the group expects.

Clarity

Role expectations are generally not written down in a manual or expressed directly to an administrator, and many times the administrator may be completely oblivious to the role expectations of different groups. Another problem that can arise is that administrators may have different understandings of terminology in the field of education. If role expectations are clearly communicated, or written down, it would help lessen the possibility of administrative role uncertainty. Another potential source of conflict is the fact that many administrators have inaccurate perceptions of what others' expectations of them are. The possibility of role conflict can occur if expectations of the group and administrator are not the same or if the administrator perceives them to be different. Other sources of conflict when role expectations are not clear include situations in which an administrator believes that the expectations are the same within a group, when in reality they are different. In addition, an administrator might not realize how strong a group's belief in role expectations is.

Role expectations

A group's expectations may be so intense that its members believe there is only one way an administrator should conduct himself or herself in certain situations. An effective administrator must investigate and attempt to understand fully why a group is so adamant about certain issues. Furthermore, an administrator must be able to determine whether a group believes that there is only one way he or she should act or if the group would be receptive to the possibility that an administrator can act appropriately in ways other than what the group may deem most effective. If an administrator has the freedom to act however he or she feels is appropriate in any given situation, then he or she will naturally feel much less pressure. An administrator's response to a group's role expectations would typically be completely different if he or she felt obligated to act in whatever manner a group expects. If administrators choose to ignore others' expectations during an intense situation, there is a chance that the group will complain, and the administrator's status will suffer.

Intra-role conflict

If conflict arises because administrators are uncertain about which roles they should play in certain situations, it is referred to as intra-role conflict. Such confusion can create a difficult situation because the administrator may lose confidence in his or her ability as a leader and become unsure about what is best for the school. Although an administrator might be uncertain about what role to choose in a particular situation, he or she must be certain of the correct action that should be taken in order to prevent or bring an end to conflict.

Extra-role conflict

If conflict is experienced by an administrator because of external factors and is not the result of his or her own inner doubts, it is referred to as extra-role conflict. Extra-role conflict occurs when certain groups challenge the role the administrator has chosen by imposing their own expectations on him or her. For example, an administrator might require that teachers follow certain procedures regardless of their years of experience; however, some veteran teachers might refuse to follow those procedures and continue what they did in the past. Administrators should be certain of the role they must play and be confident in their decisions, even if some teachers completely disagree with them. Although administrators may be aware of staff members' disagreement, they should consider other options without second-guessing themselves about which role is best for them. Extra-role conflicts can create extremely difficult situations for an administrator, and it is important that he or she handles them promptly and in a professional manner.

Other types of role conflicts

It is the responsibility of an administrator to work with a variety of individuals and groups who have different views, ideas, and backgrounds. With so much diversity and so many opportunities for interaction, there is a strong likelihood that conflicts will arise concerning what roles are appropriate for an administrator to play. At times, an administrator's personality is incompatible with the roles that are expected of him or her; someone's personality cannot be changed. There could also be an incompatibility between what the administrator expects of himself or herself and what the group expects. Additionally, there can be differences between the expressed expectations of two or more groups in regard to the administrator's role in the same situation. In some cases, individuals within the same group will not agree on what their expectations are. In this type of situation, it will be nearly impossible to avoid having role conflict; however, effective administrators will be equipped with the knowledge and managerial skills to handle it professionally.

While administrators can take several steps in order to prevent role conflict, it is important for them to realize that their own personalities, attitudes, and behaviors could be the cause of some of the problems they encounter. Administrators need to be aware of the fact that the way they treat people, make decisions, and use their authority can cause conflict. Administrators should decide if conflict occurs because of unavoidable circumstances, or if conflict could have been prevented if he or she had taken a different approach to the situation. For an administrator to be truly effective, then he or she must consider the possibility that some conflicts may be the result of their own actions and not automatically assume that other people or factors are the cause of conflict.

Consequences of role conflict

Role conflict results in a variety of consequences. If, for instance, administrators repeatedly find themselves in situations of conflict, they can become very frustrated and overwhelmed by the stress and tension that result from pressure situations. Constant conflict can impair their effective decision-making skills. By far, the worst consequence of role conflict for an administrator is being dismissed from his or her position. In regard to an individual whose group is always at conflict with an administrator, repeated conflict can cause that group member to have a negative attitude about other staff members, especially his or her administrator. A person's recurrent negative feelings can develop into hostility toward the administrator, as well as create a deep lack of interest in the school and its goals. This would have a definite negative impact on the students who are in that teacher's class. Conflict can have both major or minor effects; the determining factor about how major the impact will be is based on how well the conflict is handled.

Preventing role conflict

If an administrator wants to prevent or reduce the likelihood of conflict, then it is essential that clear job descriptions are developed for every position within an organization. When individuals understand what is expected of them and what their responsibilities include, they are less likely to fail to meet the expectations of both their colleagues and established evaluation criteria. In many situations, individuals who do not know their responsibilities may assume roles that belong to other people, which can result in their being viewed as overstepping the boundaries of their positions. It is best if an administrator reviews job descriptions and makes certain that they are clear and cannot be misinterpreted. It is also helpful for an administrator to review a job description with both the person who occupies that position and someone who has expectations for the person in that position. Periodically reviewing a job description with the staff member who holds that position also aids in gaining that person's full commitment to his or her role in the school.

Reducing role conflict

It is crucial that an administrator select appropriate personnel in order to reduce the potential for role conflict on a campus. When people interview for a position, they must be told what will be expected of them and what type of person it ideally takes to fill that particular position. Once this has been communicated, then the hiring committee can be confident that the individuals they are considering for a job have been properly informed about the school's policy concerning personnel. An administrator can receive insightful information during the selection process, especially from staff members who hold certain expectations about that position. For example, teachers can provide invaluable input about what they expect from the school's library media specialist. Once a person has been hired, his or her responsibilities and expectations should be clearly expressed again and should then be reviewed periodically so that role conflict can be minimized.

Social conflict

Social conflict occurs when groups within the school community are at odds with one another. Poor communication is often the leading cause of social conflict. Because teachers can develop negative attitudes and be unwilling to strive to achieve their school's goals if they do not feel encouraged or appreciated, it is important for administrators to give feedback and express their gratitude for all the work that their teachers do. If a school has an organizational structure that allows an administrator to make all the decisions without considering his or her staff's opinions, then there will be an increase in social conflict. Schools that empower teachers and depend on group decision-making processes will occasionally experience conflict; still, these conflicts are usually more minor than those that occur in schools controlled primarily by an administrator. Other factors, such as personalities and different values, can be the cause of social conflict; however, these things cannot be changed in people, only managed appropriately. Social conflict can also be the result of a lack of resources for staff members and the programs they want to promots; therefore, it is the administrator's responsibility to ensure that available resources are distributed fairly.

Situational leadership

Situational leadership is based more on the situation at hand and not on the people involved. Different situations call for different styles of leadership. This theory states that an administrator should base his or her style of leadership on the situation he or she is facing at that moment in time. In some cases, an individual may be chosen to lead in one situation and not chosen for another situation. Many times, school boards may be looking for a person who can handle introducing change and at the same time be looking for someone who can be a mediator during conflict. This can cause a problem because as circumstances change, the administrator who was chosen for one leadership position may not be needed when the situation does not occur anymore. An administrator who is successful at situational leadership must have the capability to adapt and be flexible.

Concept of empowerment

Leadership does not involve just one person; it involves empowering others to contribute to making decisions and working together to achieve the school's goals. Administrators can empower their staff members by allowing them to make decisions and express their opinions freely. When staff members feel as though they have voice and they are important to the success of the school, there will be an increase in their desire to achieve the school's goals. One way an administrator can empower his or her staff is by rewarding them for their successes. An administrator can also empower his or her staff by using words of encouragement and letting them know how much they are appreciated. It is also imperative that administrators generate excitement for teaching and express their pride in the teachers. Empowerment can also be observed in the behaviors of administrators and how they interact with their own superiors.

Appropriate communication channels

If an administrator wants to have an effective message, then he or she must select an appropriate channel of communication for delivering that message. Communication channels should be based on the content of the message. An administrator needs to consider what he or she is intending to say and decide whether the content of the message would be better understood if it were presented in one form rather than another. The administrator should also identify his or her audience: students, parents, teachers, or other members of the community. Administrators also need to consider the size of their audience, as well as the objective of the message. It is also crucial for administrators to be honest with themselves and recognize what their strengths and weaknesses are as communicators; certain communication channels may be more effective than others depending on an administrator's strengths.

Social networking sites

Many educators feel that students should not be allowed to access social networking sites while they are at school. These are not secure sites, and anyone can read and post on them. Because online identities are almost impossible to verify, pedophiles and predators can masquerade as students, and identity thieves can access personal information that computer users may not even be aware they have revealed. As a result, myspace.com and other social networking sites are the cause of a great deal of concern among parents, educators, and law enforcement officers. Nevertheless, the use of the Internet cannot be prohibited in schools because it provides students with useful tools for expressing their creativity, accessing information for assignments, and communicating with teachers and other students. In an effort to address legal and safety issues associated with accessing online social networking sites at school, teachers can offer instruction about online safety and explain the consequences of posting personal views and information on these sites while at school. Some teachers believe that forbidding access to popular sites without offering online alternatives does not teach students about online safety. Schools can set up internal bulletin boards, and teachers can show students how to create blogs that are accessible only to other students or people specified by the student. When used correctly, blogs and online communities can be very effective ways for students to communicate with each other and with their teachers.

Technology in the classroom

Technology can be used in the classroom in a number of ways. Younger students use creative software such as Kid Pix for drawing and making slide shows. Older students can use digital photography and drafting programs for the same purpose. Font programs can teach kids to write in cursive, while word processing programs allow students to compose papers more easily. Students of all ages can use educational software programs that teach spelling, grammar, and math skills. The Internet frequently replaces costly textbooks for teaching art, history, and science. Most newspapers are available online and can be used for social studies and current events; it is not necessary for students to save papers and clip articles from them anymore. There are a large number of resources aimed at teachers, with ideas for lesson plans and assignments incorporating technology in the classroom. It is important that staff members receive frequent training so that they are aware of all the instructional possibilities for computers and the Internet.

Positive environment

In order for a school to be a productive learning environment, a superintendent must help campus administrators create and maintain a positive learning environment. One way this can be achieved is by building a school culture, which means fostering relationships among a team of parents, teachers, and students. Major elements of of this culture are district-level and site-based planning committees that are composed of staff members, parents, and representatives from the community. These committees collaborate with superintendents and school administrators in planning, budgeting, goal setting, and decision making. Because these teams know what the core values of the school are, they are motivated to uphold these values. Such values include clear expectations for students, holding students accountable for following school rules, and recognizing students for academic achievement. Everyone is familiar with these values because the superintendent communicates them effectively. A superintendent who wants to build a successful school culture also knows the importance of repeating, explaining, and discussing these values with everyone involved. Superintendents also know that once these values have been communicated to the team members, the members will continue to build this culture based on the strengths and values of the school.

Group meetings

Group meetings are a common occurrence in the educational field. In most cases, superintendents will lead the group and be in charge of planning and conducting district meetings. Sometimes someone else will be responsible for carrying out those functions, but superintendents ultimately are responsible to make sure the functions are carried out in an effective and productive way. In general, superintendents believe their meetings are meaningful and productive. However, some staff members view meetings as a waste of time. Teachers often feel meetings do not provide resourceful information and the planning of them is unsatisfactory. Superintendents must ensure that the information provided at meetings is valuable. In addition, each meeting must have a clear purpose, and not be a time merely to distribute or collect paperwork.

Values and ideals

Superintendents need to stay true to each school district's values and ideals. Without a vision and focus, creating policies to move schools in positive directions will be much more difficult. Establishing a clear mission about where a school should be going will help the instructional focus of teachers, and help influence student learning. Superintendents play the biggest role in developing school district goals, yet they should not decide these alone. Outlining each school's goals should be a group effort. Superintendents need to get teachers, students, and parents involved. Without cooperative efforts and a clear focus, the organizational culture will be harder to change in positive ways. Superintendents are extremely busy and can easily get caught up in the everyday duties of managing a school district. However, it is important for superintendents to stay focused on each school's mission and not lose sight of it.

Data gathering and positive change

Data drives today's school curricula, programs, reports, and testing. The combination of school-based decision making, a multitude of mandated assessments, and parents' increased expectations of accountability of school leaders make data analysis a vital part of school leadership duties. Data informs superintendents and principals regarding how well, or how poorly, students are performing, and what the student population really looks like, via demographic data. Data also helps determine how well teachers are doing their jobs, how well-funded school programs are, and if funds need to be reallocated. Superintendents can use the data they have gathered and analyzed to paint a complete and accurate picture of each school district's performance. With this information, superintendents can convince staff, both at the school and at the district levels, of the need for changes to a school's mission and program. Data also can be an accountability tool used to determine how well schools are following the visions they have created and which areas may need revision.

Actual data that schools collect

If it can be measured and given a number, then it is data and it is probably required by law that it be tracked. Even if it is not required, it most likely is useful to document various types of data. Students' data includes the following: demographics (age, race, number of students per grade) and test scores. Teacher data includes areas of specialization, assessment reports, and certifications. Student and teacher data are necessary when planning new curriculum, removing or modifying existing curriculum, planning for needed equipment, or designing new instructional programs. Assessment data can help educators to identify areas of testing where students are performing adequately or better, and in which areas they need improvement, which will require curriculum and instructional changes. Budget data identifies where money is spent, and how it can be reallocated to focus on supporting the curriculum and instruction necessary to help students perform better. Data regarding the community including demographics and socioeconomic data help educators design specific curriculum and instructional programs, offering specialized programs to support each school's unique group of students.

Assessing staff abilities

Administrators should assess staff abilities to find their strengths and to find ways to keep encouraging those strengths. An effective administrator is a mentor and has the ability to encourage their staff and make them believe in themselves. An assessment can also give an administrator an opportunity to determine what the staff's needs are. Some teachers may need more material because there is a shortage. Others may need more support and encouragement. After assessment is not a time to pick on the weak, it is a time to bring up the ones who need help by offering guidance. In order to have an effective school year, the entire school needs to come together and work as a team. Making sure the staff's needs are met will help ensure that the student's needs are met and in return, there will be student achievement.

School-based community

A school-based community involves everyone in the decision-making process, including teachers, parents, and students. By working together, all three groups have essential roles in promoting a school-based community that focuses on continuing to improve the school. In addition to having a positive effect on student behavior and academic performance, this type of community encourages parents to take an active part in their children's education. When the team members are able to work together and make decisions, it creates a feeling of ownership and responsibility. Aware of the school's mission and goals, everyone is dedicated to helping the school achieve them. Although it may be difficult at times for everyone to agree on certain issues, conflict may be reduced if individuals can agree on issues by using "no fault" problem solving, collaborating with others, and making decisions by consensus. Such methods are more successful than voting because voting encourages people to take sides instead of working together as a school-based community.

Arbitration

When conflict cannot be resolved using mediation, it may be necessary to use arbitration. This process involves the parties at conflict explaining their point of view to an unbiased third party, known as an arbitrator. Each party must agree to accept the third party's decision, and they must commit to carrying out that decision before they even discuss the issue with the arbitrator. The best way to choose the person to be the arbitrator is to evaluate the type of conflict causing the problem, as well as the circumstances surrounding it. Using an outside party for arbitration is not common in the school setting; it is more common to use a superior within the organization. The growing trend of arbitration is a reflection of the fact that traditional means of conflict resolution are failing to achieve results.

Community's vision of learning

A school community consists of more than parents, grandparents, and other caregivers; a school community's stakeholders include anyone who lives in the community served by the school, even if they do not have children who attend that school. Basically, the stakeholders in a school community are everyone whose life is touched even tangentially by the school. It is comprised of the staff at area daycares who care for the students after school, the local businesses that will one day employ people who were educated at the school, and the local municipal leaders who have governmental oversight of the school. All are vital to the achievement of the school's vision; a school cannot operate in a vacuum. Because students, who are the very reason the school exists, live in the surrounding community, the school needs the support and resources of that community. Members of the community have ideas to offer, as well as talents and resources to donate; furthermore, they can share in the governance and operation of the school. Because of the value community members offer their local schools; superintendents must lead the school community in soliciting, attracting, and keeping the involvement of the greater community.

Importance of stakeholders

Any realistic and achievable vision that is to be carried through from development to implementation must be the result of consultation, cooperation, and collaboration with the entire school community, not just the district and campus professional staff. Because the school cannot exist and thrive on its own as a self-contained world, it must have the support and participation of all who live in the community. Members of the community will not participate in the school's vision if they have not participated in its proposal and preparation; people are seldom willing to shepherd a project they have not helped create. All community stakeholders must feel that they have part ownership in the school; in fact, a school is one of the places where people learn to become community members.

After goals are reached

When positive results have been achieved, expectations exceeded, or goals reached, the most important thing to follow is praise. Because any success will be the result of extensive planning and effort, people need to know that their work is recognized and celebrated. From proposal through preparation to implementation, a school's vision of learning requires a great deal of work from many people. Just as individuals are much less likely to contribute to a vision in which they do not feel they have some ownership, so are they much less likely to give their best to a vision when they do not feel that their talents and work will be acknowledged. Recognition is as important to some people as remuneration; teachers cannot be expected to be content only with getting a paycheck, nor can students be expected to be content only with making good grades. All people, adults as well as children, need recognition and praise when they have succeeded in reaching or surpassing their goals. People strive even harder when they know that their efforts are part of a larger effort and that they will be recognized and appreciated for their contributions.

Sources of data

Most everything a school does, and everyone it serves, can be identified, quantified, and measured by some statistical approach. For instance, the equation of teachers combined with students under an educational program supplemented by funding results in test scores, grades, and a wealth of other statistical data. If schools can measure the output, then they can more accurately determine the right kinds of input. If a school knows how many students it serves, along with their ages, ethnic backgrounds, levels of English proficiency, test scores, grades, economic class, and risk factors, then the principal can more readily determine the resources that he or she needs in order to put the campus vision into place. A principal must be able to know what data he or she needs, how to gather that data, how to understand the data, and how to use the data to project the needs of the campus. When these things have been done, a principal can answer such questions as the following: How many teachers does the campus need for each subject? How much funding does the school need for different areas? What programs are not performing? What programs should be added to make the school more successful?

Culture and community

Culture is the personality of a community, which is comprised of people with diverse personalities from different cultures. When a principal is leading the proposal and preparation of a campus vision of learning, he or she must know and understand the culture of the community, because he or she ideally needs all community members to contribute to the proposal. A principal must also know who makes up the community, what values are represented, what fears and dreams are shared, what traditions and rituals are observed, and what problems are most discussed; all these of these factors are a reflection of the community's culture. As a person's experiences over time alter his or her personality, community cultures may also undergo transformation as the members of the community change. Effective principals must be attuned to such changes.

Superintendents should be the guiding forces in campus culture, leading by example and inspiration, but never by harsh command or fiat. Superintendents can enable teachers and staff to create a culture wherein students are challenged to learn and to grow intellectually and where staff members also thrive intellectually and professionally. A school district is not a self-contained and isolated world. Schools coexist within wider communities, and superintendents must invite and encourage all members of the outside community including parents, caregivers, local businesses, and municipal governments to be part of the school community and to participate in its vision of learning.

Successful working relationships

Superintendents are responsible for setting the tone of the campus working environment, and they must be sensitive to the needs and talents of a large and diverse group of professionals. Superintendents must take steps to foster a culture of respect and openness to new ideas and innovative learning techniques. A campus professional community includes teachers, counselors, and administrative staff. This diverse group resembles an orchestra comprised of many different instruments producing many different sounds. Such instruments do not always produce the same notes at the same time, but when playing together, they produce harmony. Superintendents must be the conductors of their symphonies, ensuring that all the players know their parts, respect the parts of others, and that they all enjoy playing music together. Times of discord and tunelessness will be unavoidable, and during such times superintendents' leadership skills are indispensable.

Innovative thinking and risk taking

If superintendents have taken steps to foster environments where a school district's staff members collaborate effectively and all members function harmoniously, then they will be open to new suggestions and ideas. Superintendents who are receptive encourage their school communities to be the same way. It isn't always easy to come up with new ideas, but it is reasonable to look back and reflect on what has not worked in the past. It is imperative to analyze past mistakes and figure out what went wrong. Superintendents can determine the flaws and missing components of past ideas. Two very common phrases, "brainstorming" and "thinking outside the box," describe precisely what is needed to spur creative thinking and risk taking. Superintendents need to encourage campus staff members to think big, to think creatively, and to express their ideas without fearing rejection or embarrassment. Trial and error is essential to this ongoing process.

Realizing the vision

All members of the community must be involved in the proposal and preparation of a school's vision of learning. Superintendents must foster a healthy working environment for each school's staff, leading the efforts to maintain cordial relationships and professional cooperation. All members of the school community must feel that their needs are being addressed and that they are important participants in the school's mission. Superintendents will continuously collect and analyze data produced from the school's activities and use the data to make adjustments and modifications in programs and processes as needed. They will encourage staff members and others in the community to offer ideas and solutions to solve problems or build upon successes. Superintendents will acknowledge all successes, both large and small, that the school community produces.

Protecting the vision

School communities, led by superintendents, must continuously monitor a school's progress. Protecting the community's vision of learning involves careful consideration of the following questions: Are students meeting and exceeding expectations? Have improvements been made in the areas that have been targeted? Are test scores and other data reflecting positive growth? Analysis of these questions requires superintendents to look at various sources of information available to keep a constant watch on all of a school's activities. This process allows for adjustments to be made to programs that are not performing well or processes that are not yielding their intended results. Adjustments and revisions are important because no plan or process proceeds exactly as it was intended. If superintendents set up systems for rigorous monitoring of all school functions, then modifications may be made promptly when needed. Such modifications protect each school district's vision of learning so students can stay on track and improvements at each school can be made accordingly.

This is how we've always done things around here

If superintendents make suggestions for new ideas and programs, it is not encouraging to hear "This is how we've always done things around here." If a district needs improvement in any particular area, it is because past programs or policies didn't work, or didn't work as well as was expected, or they no longer work as they once did.   "We've always done it this way" can be an excuse and superintendents can explain to the school community that if something isn't working, change is necessary. It is important to use past mistakes as learning opportunities, but past mistakes should not be repeated. Just because something has never been done, does not mean it won't work, and when people become afraid to try new approaches it means that they have lost their excitement and passion for their job. This danger arises in any job, but it is an ever-present danger in a campus community, which requires so much emotional and intellectual energy of its staff. An openness to new approaches, new ideas, and new programs is not only the primary way to ensure that a campus community does not stagnate, it is also a great preventative for burnout.

Modifying implementation plans

When superintendents lead a school district staff in collecting and analyzing all the sources of data derived from students and the rest of the school community, they can get an accurate picture of campus progress. This constantly changing picture will inform superintendents, on an everyday and annual basis. They will be able to see whether or not a school district is on track with its vision and if there is a good pace to progress. In this way, superintendents will know as early as possible when changes need to be made in plans, processes, or personnel, and what those changes should be. All the data, when analyzed together, serves as a compass directing the school community so it knows where the district vision is, and where it is headed.

Leading preparation

Superintendents must communicate with a school's professional staff to articulate their commitment to creating a healthy work environment. To lead in the preparation of a district's vision of learning, superintendents also must get to know the community's members and understand the culture of the community in order to comprehend the expectations of a school district. Understanding the school district's current status requires that superintendents find answers to the following inquiries: Does the district have a lot of at-risk students? What is the number of native English speakers? Are there programs for gifted and talented students? Finding answers to these questions helps superintendents prepare each district's vision , and lead staff and the community in assessing the needs of each school's unique student population.

Appropriate responses to diverse needs

Groups in the school community may differ in socioeconomic class, religion, or nationality. Accordingly, when one group feels it has been excluded from participation in the district vision, superintendents have to find ways to reach that group. Trying something new is always a risk, and always necessitates new ways of thinking. Communicating with diverse groups can be risky because people can get offended and feelings may get hurt. Superintendents must be knowledgeable and sensitive to each group's culture. Superintendents might be afraid of offending someone, but this fear should not prevent them from reaching out to different groups. It is important to identify where there may be a lack of community support, especially when there is a lack of parental involvement. Issues with parental involvement permeate many failing schools, and superintendents must support innovative thinking to find ways to get parents more involved in campus culture. Reaching out to parents and the various members of a school community challenges superintendents and their staff members to think creatively and take risks when implementing new ideas.

Superintendents cannot know who the members of a community are until they have gathered and analyzed the necessary data. Of course, such data does not reveal everything about a community, but it is an essential component of the larger whole. Superintendents must know the racial, religious, and socioeconomic makeup of the student population. Different programs must be designed for at-risk students as well as National Merit Scholars. Language learners with varying degrees of English language proficiency will need appropriate support and scaffolding. Also, newly arrived immigrants may face different problems than those born and raised in the community. Superintendents must know and appreciate the distinct needs of all of these unique groups of students. Various sources of data, when analyzed and understood, help superintendents identify members of the student population, and this knowledge is vital to leading a district's educational mission.

Inclusion

Because the cooperation and participation of all community members is vital to each school district's success, superintendents must strive to reach those who have declined to get involved or those who feel that their participation has not been welcomed. Often these people may be minorities in the community. Some people may feel that they are outsiders in the school district's community and perhaps in the past they have been treated as such. Superintendents must make changes by reaching out to all who have felt left out of the community. Such efforts could be as simple as inviting people to participate in school events and meetings. Participation can promote connections to the campus vision and people will work harder when they feel connected and take ownership of shared goals and ideas.

Administrative Leadership

The competencies of Administrative Leadership require that superintendents know how to **APPLY** principles of effective leadership and management in relation to campus budgeting, personnel, resource utilization, financial management, and technology use. Also, superintendents must know how to **APPLY** principles of leadership and management to the campus physical plant and support systems to ensure safe and effective learning environments in their school districts.

Instructional Community Leadership

The Superintendent knows how to **FACILITATE** the design and implementation of curricula and strategic plans that enhance teaching and learning; ensure alignment of curriculum, instruction, resources, and assessment; and promote the use of varied assessments to measure student performance.

The Superintendent knows how to **ADVOCATE**, nurture and sustain an instructional program and a campus culture that are conducive to student learning and staff professional growth.

The Superintendent knows how to **IMPLEMENT** a staff evaluation and development system to improve the performance of all staff members, select and implement appropriate models for supervision and staff development, and apply the legal requirements for personnel management

The Superintendent knows how to **APPLY** organization, decision-making, and problem-solving skills to ensure an effective learning environment.

School Community Leadership

The Superintendent knows how to **SHAPE** campus culture by facilitating the development, articulation, implementation, and stewardship of a vision of learning that is shared and supported by the school community

The Superintendent knows how to **COMMUNICATE** and collaborate with all members of the school community, respond to diverse interests and needs, and mobilize resources to promote student success.

The Superintendent knows how to **ACT** with integrity, fairness, and in an ethical and legal manner.

Summary of the Superintendent's role

It can be distilled into four steps: **PROPOSE** it, **PROMOTE** it, **PREPARE** it and then **PROTECT** it. The Superintendent must lead the effort to develop (propose) the vision for his/her school community. Then he/she must be able to articulate (promote) it to other members of the community so that they can participate in it. Next, he/she must lead the community to actually implement (prepare) the learning vision that they have proposed. Finally, once the vision has been pictured, and proposed, and prepared, the superintendent helps to steward (protect) it – guiding the community as they all work together in the educational mission they have envisioned.

Instructional Leadership

School's pupil personnel service

Administrators must maintain the organizational and operational elements of their school's programs and services. One of these services is the pupil personnel service. It includes school counselors, school social workers, school psychologists, and other qualified professional personnel involved in providing assessment, diagnosis, counseling, educational, therapeutic, and other necessary services. These staff members work together in order to assist with any student who may have a learning disability or any other issue that may hinder his or her learning capabilities. The goal of pupil personnel service is to work together to ensure that every student is given the opportunity to reach his or her full academic potential.

Gifted programs

Most all schools have a gifted and talented program, and one of the duties of an administrator is to oversee the organizational and operational features of the program. Administrators need to ensure that the policies written for a school's gifted and talented program are followed appropriately. If a student is performing at a higher level or has the potential to perform at a higher level, then that student should be selected to participate in an ongoing screening procedure. The screening and selection committee should collect and assess data about the student's performance from multiple sources. It is important that all students from different populations and backgrounds have been considered for the program. A committee that has been well trained in the area of gifted and talented education will make the final selection. Administrators must also be knowledgeable of the proper appeals process regarding district decisions if parents challenge why their child was not chosen to be in the school's gifted and talented program.

Special education services

In order for a student to receive special education services, he or she must first be evaluated. If the diagnostician who interprets the evaluation information determines that special education services are needed, then the student will have access to them. A team of individuals creates an action plan that outlines what services the student needs in order to meet his or her educational goals. This action plan is called an Individualized Education Program. Because this plan is a law-binding document, it is imperative that an administrator ensure that all staff members are following this plan and that the student is receiving the services enabling him or her to achieve the goals that have been established in the Individualized Education Program. A student may require more than one service in order to benefit from special education; these services can include speech therapy, counseling, physical therapy, audiology services, and alternative transportation to and from school.

Provisions for students with disabilities

The Individuals with Disabilities Education Act (IDEA) was created to ensure that children with special needs are provided a free appropriate public education that includes the services necessary in order to meet their educational needs. It is the responsibility of the state and other public agencies to ensure that schools are giving children with special needs the education and services they are entitled to at no cost to the parents. Additionally, schools must provide parents or guardians with a student's Individualized Education Program (IEP). The IEP is a document that states what the student needs in order to be successful in school. If a parent or guardian has a disagreement with the IEP, then he or she can ask for a due process hearing. A neutral hearing officer will make an independent decision with the goal of resolving the issue.

Other services

One of an administrator's many duties is overseeing a number of campus operational functions, which includes monitoring student activities. It is important for students to have opportunities to participate in programs that relate to their interests because students who are involved in activities they enjoy will more likely have confidence in themselves and have a higher sense of self-esteem. Common programs that captivate the interests of students include student council, choir, cheerleading, band, athletics, and theater, among others. Administrators must also handle ancillary services, a responsibility that can consume a great deal of his or her time. After considering the rules and regulations for services and materials that are outsourced, many school districts have begun outsourcing ancillary services and have discovered that doing so allows administrators to focus more of their time on educational responsibilities.

Establishing staff development priorities

An effective administrator realizes that teachers do not know how to learn, implement, and accomplish everything on their own. While administrators should provide staff-development training for each teacher, they must keep in mind the fact that not every teacher needs help in every area. Establishing staff development priorities should be based on the staff's needs, both individually and as a group. Staff development needs to be arranged to improve teachers' skills in a particular area. This is extremely important, especially if a school is implementing a new program, and teachers should not be expected to know how to use new teaching methods without the proper training. In many instances, teachers view staff development as something they have to attend in order to fulfill their professional development requirements instead of an opportunity for enrichment; staff development should offer teachers engaging, practical ways to improve their teaching skills. Administrators should set priorities according to what kinds of staff development are important for the success of the school.

Changing a person's behavior

If an administrator uses referent influence as a way to change a person's behavior, this means that others are able to identify with the administrator as a person and react positively to him or her. Certain characteristics that others can identify with include a strong character, an outspoken personality, and a compelling leadership style. These kinds of characteristics enable an administrator to gain the cooperation of other administrators, teachers, parents, and students even though those people may question the decisions made by the administrator. Referent influence typically refers to qualities that people perceive as favorable ones; however, the same character traits might not have a positive impact on everyone. While some groups respond positively to certain traits, others may view them as a sign of weak leadership. Another potentially problematic issue with referent influence is that superintendents are already in a position of leadership, and their authority has already been established; therefore, they might not be aware that they are lacking any character traits that could make them more appealing to other members of the school community.

Using rewards to influence the behavior of personnel means that administrators have certain rewards that they can give individuals who obey and carry through with decisions the administration has made. One issue with this type of influence is that an administrator may not receive enough funding from the school board and other bureaucratic agencies to have enough rewards to distribute equally to the people who comply with his or her policies. If an individual or group receives rewards that are not offered to others, this is likely to be considered preferential treatment, which is not viewed favorably in the field of education. Although these problems may occur, administrators themselves can develop other kinds of awards. For example, an administrator can offer staff members a free period or an additional lunch break, as well as support a new activity a teacher wants to implement.

Positive reinforcement

An important—yet often overlooked or underestimated—type of reward that an administrator can offer is positive reinforcement. This kind of reward is practically limitless and can be given out in the form of written or verbal communication. Taking time out of the day to tell a teacher or other staff member that he or she is doing a great job can have a major impact on that person's attitude, quality of work, and level of output. Any administrator can give positive reinforcement, but an effective one knows that reinforcement must be clearly related to a certain task that the staff member is doing. If compliments are given out randomly, then they can seem meaningless and will not be of much value; as a result, the behavior an administrator seeks may not occur. Another problem associated with positive reinforcement rewards is that administrators who want to avoid appearing insincere by being too generous with praise might not offer enough positive reinforcement. Successful administrators can find a balance between showing an appropriate amount of appreciation and not showing enough.

Staff development activities

In order for a school to achieve success, an administrator should involve each teacher in the planning and implementation of staff development activities. In addition to enriching teachers' skills, staff development activities are tools that enable teachers to help each other throughout the school year. One of the primary responsibilities an administrator has in implementing staff development is to help teachers assess their needs and ensure that they have the necessary tools and support to carry out their duties. Staff development activities can provide exciting, progressive ideas to enhance student achievement; however, if teachers do not have the necessary materials to perform these lessons, then their goals will be difficult to achieve. Administrators should also provide each teacher with classroom management and teaching models of these activities, which will make it easier for a teacher to implement the new lessons instead of simply hearing about them during a single staff development session.

Indicators of achievement

To have an effective school, an administrator must have clear goals and objectives for curriculum, instruction, and learning outcomes. In addition, these goals and objectives should be well-known and understood by everyone who is involved in the educational process. Even if a school's goals and objectives are clearly stated and widely known, an administrator must confirm that they are being achieved. One indicator of achievement is ongoing student assessment. Once data has been collected from student evaluations, an administrator can carefully examine the data to determine if students remain weak in the same areas or if they have shown improvement. Another indicator of achievement focuses on the opinions and attitudes of staff members. An open line of communication is crucial to any administrator who seeks a high level of achievement in his or her school. Because they are the ones actually following curriculum guidelines, staff members can most objectively and effectively judge whether a curriculuar plan is working or if there is still room for improvement.

Evaluation

Evaluations are established to determine teacher competence and to foster professional growth and development. Evaluations provide teachers with useful feedback concerning classroom needs, ideas about new teaching techniques, and advice on how to improve the learning environment in the classroom. Administrators can perform informal evaluations by conducting a "walk through" observation, during which an administrator observes a teacher for a few minutes; the administrator may or may not take notes at that time. During formal evaluations, an administrator will observe a teacher for a longer period of time, taking detailed notes and assessing classroom activities, lesson plans, teaching methods, and classroom records. Additionally, administrators evaluate how involved the students are in the lesson. All of this information is recorded and compared with certain domain requirements that the teacher is expected to fulfill. A post-observation meeting will follow, allowing the administrator to deliver feedback about the teacher's strengths and weaknesses in the classroom and to discuss strategies for making improvements.

Even the most experienced teachers may be concerned that evaluations are not productive and do not show the full extent of a teacher's capabilities. Many teachers are concerned about the fact that they have little, if any, input in the evaluative process because state laws and school boards establish the criteria by which teachers are evaluated. Another concern is the length of time an evaluator spends in the classroom. An evaluator will visit a classroom for about 45 minutes, and that short amount of time is the only exposure that an evaluator will have to that classroom and teacher during the entire school year. Most teachers believe that an evaluator cannot gather enough quality information to make an accurate assessment of their teaching methods and classroom success. Teachers are also concerned that evaluators might not be properly trained or may have little experience teaching in a classroom themselves. A lack of familiarity with the grade level or subject being observed is also a source of concern. Also, some teachers feel that the results of evaluations neither promote teacher development nor resut in the development of effective programs for professional development.

After a teacher evaluation has been conducted, the administrator and the teacher have a post-evaluation meeting. At this meeting, the administrator will present the positive and negative findings of the evaluation and discuss them with the teacher. During this time, it is important for administrators to remember that they are leaders and that leaders encourage members of their team and not bring them down. The positive findings should be highlighted first, followed by constructive criticism to address the negative. Post-evaluation meetings provide both the administrator and the teacher with the opportunity to set goals for any improvements that need to be made. If any changes are to be implemented, then the administrator should offer such resources as books, mentor teachers, or research findings that can help the teacher make improvements. Without exception, evaluations should be used as a tool to discover any changes that need to be made in order to enhance student achievement.

Formative evaluation

An administrator should be aware of problems associated with the implementation of a new program before these problems grow into a major crisis. Conducted during a program, a formative evaluation serves to represent assessments of a program's strengths and weaknesses before a conclusion can be drawn about the success of the program. In the early stages of a new program, this type of evaluation is a useful tool for an administrator because unanticipated problems are most likely to occur at the onset of a program. In order to prevent the problems from escalating into a crisis, an administrator will usually take immediate action. The most important aspect of a formative evaluation is that it provides an administrator with adequate information about the progress of and responses to a newly-implemented program. As information is gathered into a formative evaluation, no decision concerning the discontinuation of a program should be made at that time. The implementation process should be given enough time to improve itself before that decision is made.

Summative evaluation

A summative evaluation provides valuable information concerning whether a new program is meeting a school's objectives. This type of evaluation requires the collection of data, along with subjective interpretations of the data. The kinds of summative evaluations that administrators may use include comparisons of student behavior, achievement, and attitudes before and after the implementation of a new program. It would also be informative to collect data on the teachers' and parents' attitudes before and after the implementation process. In order to collect this data, an administrator must consider exactly what is to be evaluated, what information is needed to complete the evaluation, and what method is the most appropriate use. No one method of collecting data is the correct one; administrators have a variety of options for summative evaluations, including questionnaires, interviews, and content analysis. If an administrator chooses not to assess a new program that has been introduced on his or her campus, then other stakeholders in the school may make their own assessments using their own methods and opinions.

Portfolio

A portfolio is an assessment tool that consists of a collection of work produced by a teacher that expresses his or her talents, knowledge, and skills in teaching. Some items that can be included in a portfolio include the teacher's background, what subjects he or she teaches, any state exams that have been taken, and the teacher's personal statement about what it means to teach. In addition to being used as a means of assessment for administrators, portfolios can provide teachers themselves with feedback concerning ways they can improve their teaching. If an administrator wants teachers to implement a portfolio program, it is important for him or her to understand that portfolios take time to create; a busy teacher will not be able to produce a quality portfolio in a day or two. It is also important that both teachers and administrators support the use of portfolios because the program will fail if nobody is willing to put forth the effort to create a useful portfolio.

Technology

Many of today's teachers continue to use the constructivist method of teaching, meaning that a teacher shares his or her knowledge of a subject with the expectation that students will be able to remember everything they have been presented and then be able to demonstrate what they know on a standardized test. Unfortunately, this teaching method does not take advantage of one of today's most effective teaching tools: technology. An effective administrator should encourage staff members to find ways of using technology as a tool to enhance the constructivist way of teaching. Technology should not be used as a substitute for teaching, but as a way to improve students' learning by enriching a teacher's way of teaching. Incorporating technology into their curriculum can sometimes be difficult for teachers, especially the ones who are accustomed to the constructivist method of teaching. Teachers should, however, avoid relying excessively on technology to the exclusion of other teaching methods because they run the risk of sacrificing personal relationships with their students.

In order for students to be successful, teachers must create a classroom environment that engages them in the learning process. One way to accomplish this is to offer a variety of activities, including those that use technology as a tool for teaching. When an administrator observes a teacher, he or she should look for ways that the teacher interacts with students using computers or other technology in the classroom. A teacher who incorporates technology into his or her lessons provides students with the opportunity to work together and share their knowledge with one another. Because a class is made up of both students who are very familiar with computers and those who have little experience with technology, administrators and teachers alike recognize that such collaborative educational opportunities improve student performance for all student populations.

When deciding what kinds of technological equipment their schools will use, administrators serve as major decision makers. In addition to consulting with other education professionals, including the school district's superintendent, to select equipment that is necessary to build a technologically-advanced school, administrators will sometimes arrange usage agreements with local businesses or other educational institutions. Administrators must be wholly committed to keeping their campuses supplied with current technologies. Administrators must also make sure that their staff members receive adequate training in using the equipment; a teacher cannot be expected to implement technology in the classroom if he or she does not know how to use it. Administrators should show full support of newly-implemented technology. At times, they may have to market new technology or technology-based programs to their staff in order to encourage them to be supportive of the changes. If an administrator clearly states how new technology can benefit the staff as well as the students, then staff members will be more likely to use the technology in their classrooms.

Curriculum design

After there has been a decision on what the curriculum goals are it is time to make a decision on the curriculum. The administrator and staff basically have two choices to make; one is to keep the current curriculum and renew it or begin a new curriculum. It is best to renew a curriculum if there are minor adjustments that need to be made in order to improve student achievement. When choosing this option, the administrator and staff need to take a look at the curriculum and determine where improvements need to be made. The only improvements that may need to be made could be adding a new course or just implementing new activities. It is best to begin a new curriculum if the decision has been made to change of the focus of the learning experience and redesigning the school's educational goals.

Holistic curriculum development

The holistic approach to curriculum development focuses on the student's way of thinking in regard to how it is affected by his or her surrounding environment. For years, research in the field of education has shown the importance of a student's culture and environment in the acquisition of knowledge. When educators use a holistic approach in regard to students, curriculum planning is based on the developmental needs and interests of the children served by the school. Rather than following one certain program, teachers observe and take notes about what interests students and then share this information with other team members in order to develop appropriate learning activities. If students share a common interest, then that may be developed into a thematic unit that enables students to pursue this particular interest. Such student-directed projects can incorporate many skills, including writing, reading, singing, painting, and mathematics, in both large and small-group settings.

Integrating curriculum

There are ways to integrate curriculum and still maintain separate subjects. One way is correlation, which means the school can have two subjects that use a curriculum in a way that they support each one of the two subjects. For example, if students are reading literature from a certain era, then in social studies students are studying events that occurred in that same era. Another way to integrate is using skills across the curriculum. All the skills involving reading, writing, social studies, science and math are reinforced throughout the curriculum. There is also the unified curriculum, which means the curriculum of a particular subject and its divisions are focused more on the overall objectives and not divided. The last way is informal integration, which means the teacher can simultaneously bring in content from one curriculum while emphasizing another.

Effective instruction

There have been times when the principles of effective instruction have been described as art and not something taught to teachers in college. A teacher must possess certain qualities about themselves in order for their instruction to be effective. One quality is the teacher must show an honest interest and enthusiasm for the subject they are teaching. If the teacher is not interested the students won't be either. In the classroom they must also show respect and interest in each student. The students should be allowed time to ask questions and discuss with others about the subject matter. The objectives should be clear and the students should know what is expected of them. Any class activities, homework or projects should reflect what has been discussed in class and graded appropriately and fairly. The tests and papers should accurately measure what has been accomplished through the course objectives.

Instructional objectives

Instructional objectives are very specific and describe what the student is expected to do. Therefore, it is important that when deciding what the objectives are going to be, teachers and administrators know exactly what they expect from their students. Instructional objectives are also determined by what the outcome will be. They will state what the student should be able to accomplish after the teacher has finished his or her instruction. It is important to make sure the objectives are used to ensure that learning is clearly focused on a goal and that both students and teacher are on the same track. When determining instructional objectives, it is also important to ensure they line up with the lesson plan. It does not make sense for a teacher to teach a lesson on a certain topic, but the objectives do not follow the same topic.

Learning activities

When choosing learning activities that reflect the instructional objectives, it is important to remember that these activities should encourage students to have meaningful interaction between other students and the instructor. Activities can include anything from writing papers, doing projects, group discussion and hands on activities. It may be difficult for the teacher to decide which activity is best; therefore after deciding the instructional objectives, a teacher should keep them near by and use them as a source for deciding which activity to use. There are different levels of objectives and the instructor will want to choose the activity or activities based on that particular level. It is important to remember that whatever activity is chosen, it must support the student in learning the instructional objectives. It must also align with what the lesson is about.

Assessments of student achievement

One way to determine instructional strategies and priorities is to examine the assessments of student achievement. Student assessments give administrators and instructors a chance to see on what level the students are achieving or struggling. If students are struggling in a certain area then it is time to decide if a certain teaching method needs to be changed or adjusted in some way. Priorities also need to be set in regards to deciding what teaching methods need to be changed and which ones work best with what student. If the assessments show students are achieving in certain areas, then administrators will know certain methods are successful. Priorities should be set on how to decide continuing with this achievement. The instructors should be asked if they need any additional materials to continue on this road to success.

Instructional method

Many factors need to be considered before a teacher chooses a particular instructional method. Many excellent teachers have acquired the ability to use and transition from one method to the other. One factor to consider is the age of the students. Some methods may work better with younger children than with older and vice versa. Teachers should also consider the developmental level of their students. Another factor to consider is the number of students and the space available. Certain methods just work better with a smaller group while others work best with larger groups. There can be times when the number of students is appropriate; however, the space may not be available. One of the most important considerations is to pick a method that will best reflect the instructional objectives. There is not a "best" method for teaching, it is just important to consider all factors and pick the one that fits best at that time.

Direct teaching method

When a teacher chooses the direct teaching method he or she must have complete knowledge of the subject and content taught. He or she should have good oral communication skills. All the content used for teaching needs to be organized in advance. The learning objectives and goals are very specific and the students are told exactly why the learning material is important. Using this method makes it easier for the teacher to measure student achievement. The direct teaching method is also widely accepted and it is good for teaching specific facts and basic skills. However, there are some disadvantages. This method does not allow for the teacher to express his or her creativity. Material needs to be followed in a precise order. This method is not particularly helpful with higher-order thinking skills.

Team teaching method

The team teaching method has been used at many grade levels in many different schools. Different schools may use this method in different ways; there is no correct way to use team teaching. This method involves the students switching classes and having different teachers throughout the day. Team teaching can be divided by subjects, where the student has a different teacher for each subject. It can also be divided by just two teachers, in this situation one teacher may take math and science and the other will take language arts and social studies. If this method is chosen it is important that the teachers have good communication between each other. The teachers should make sure the goals are the same. Team teaching fails when there is no communication and a lack of respect and honesty exists.

Group instruction

Group instruction involves all the students hearing the learning material at the same time. The teacher gives instruction, directions and explanations to everyone at once. This method is useful if it used at small increments during the day. The disadvantage to this method is that there are students who benefit better with more individualized attention. They could get lost in the instruction. Group instruction can also be given in small groups, called small group instruction. This method allows the students to get more individualized attention from the teacher. It is also an opportunity for the teacher to examine how well each student is learning the material. It is important that while the teacher is involved with small groups the other students are actively engaging in other activities. If they are not they could cause a distraction to other students who are receiving small group instruction.

Contract method

The contract method involves writing a contract between the student and teacher that outlines what the student is to learn, what the grade will be and how it will be learned. The teacher and student sign it and it is agreed that the student is responsible for achieving the goals that were stated in the contract. This method allows for the student self-directing. The student feels more empowered and takes ownership in their learning. They feel like they have the ability to teach themselves and still depend on the teacher for a backup. The contract method can also be used for behavioral changes as well. This method is not used in many schools. It should also only be used with students who are of the appropriate age and who are going to take it seriously. This is a big responsibility to put on a student, and the students selected should be chosen wisely.

Individualized instruction

Individualized instruction involves the teacher carefully examining a student and deciding which instructional method is best to use with that student. Every student is different and his or her learning style is different. If a student is struggling and needs more one on one attention, then it is the responsibility of the teacher to make sure that student gets what they need. Finding the right instructional method may take a few times to get it right, it may be helpful to get the parents involved and ask them which way they think the student will learn best. Individualized instruction caters to that particular student and it is needed for student achievement. This method makes sure that student is getting their educational needs met in order for that student to achieve success.

Interdisciplinary approach

The interdisciplinary approach is used to encourage learning across the curriculum. Lessons are set up to make thematic units in all learning subjects. Each subject will be connected to this thematic unit. The teacher is making links between each subject. When this method is used the student is able to learn without fragments during day and at the same time have a stimulating learning experience. The teacher chooses a topic or theme and then brainstorms activities to do in each subject area that revolve around this topic. Questions are then thought of in order to serve as the scope and sequence. The teacher can determine a grade by evaluating standards of performance levels or by using rubrics that evaluate the students completed work assignments.

Instructional resources and research data

When an administrator is deciding what the curriculum needs are, he or she has several resources they can turn to. One of the best resources is the personnel. The teachers and teacher aides are vital to this decision. They are the ones teaching the curriculum and they are experts at knowing what additional needs there are. They will know if there needs to be more activities or if there should be an integration of another curriculum. There could also be a need of more materials. Many times there is a material shortage and not enough for each teacher to give to the students. The finances are another useful resource to use. Administrators need to be extremely careful and use the finances wisely when it comes to curriculum. Advisory groups, community agencies, and institutions can also be extremely resourceful when deciding the needs. These can give their opinion on what they think will best for the students.

Theory of behaviorism

The theory of behaviorism states that if a new behavior pattern is repeated so many times it will become automatic. This theory is associated with the Russian physiologist, Pavlov. He performed an experiment on a dog. The dog would salivate when it saw food, so Pavlov would ring the bell seconds before he showed the dog his food; therefore, he trained the dog to salivate after hearing the ringing of the bell. Another famous psychologist associated with this theory is an American, John B. Watson. He performed an experiment on a young boy named Albert. Albert was initially not afraid of a white rat, but when the rat was shown to Albert along with a loud noise, he soon became afraid of the rat. Skinner is also associated with behaviorism except he studied operant behavior. According to his studies the learner behaves a certain way according to the environment.

Theory of cognitivism

This theory states that learning involves using certain information that has been stored in the brain. One of the most famous psychologists associated with this theory is Jean Piaget. A key concept of the cognitive theory is schema, existing internal knowledge that has been stored in the brain and compared to new knowledge. There is also the three-stage information processing model, which means information is inputted through a sensory register, then is made into short-term memory and last is made into long-term memory and used for storage and retrieval. Other key concepts are a meaningful effect, which means information that has meaning is easier to remember and learn. Serial position effects mean that a person can remember items on a list if they start from the beginning or end. Some other effects that are associated with this theory are; practice, transfer, interference, organization, levels of processing, state dependent, mnemonic, schema, and advance organizers.

Theory of constructivism

The theory of constructivism states that a person develops their own knowledge based on their past experiences. This theory states that each learner is unique because every learner comes from a different background and experiences. Social constructivism encourages the unique traits in each individual learner. The learner should become involved in the learning process; therefore, the responsibility of learning does not solely rest on the instructor. The learner will take an active role rather than be passive. This theory also states that the learning environment should be set up in order to challenge the learner to their full potential. The instructor's role is not to just give the information and answers according to a curriculum, but rather to encourage the learner the find conclusions and answers on their own. The goal for the instructor is to help the learners become effective thinkers and challenge themselves.

Behavioral views of motivation

There many behavioral learning theorists that have created techniques of behavior modification based on the idea that students are motivated to complete an assignment because they have been promised a reward. This reward can be praise, a grade, a ticket that can be traded in for something else, or it can be a privilege of selecting an activity of their choice. There are also operant conditioning interpretations that explain why some students like a certain subject while others have a strong dislike for it. For example, math, some students love it and others hate it. The students have love math, may have been brought up to love it. Their past experiences may have shaped them this way because they have all been positive. On the other hand, the students who hate math may have had negative experiences.

Cognitive views of motivation

Cognitive theorists believe people are motivated because their behavior is influenced by the way some think about themselves and the environment around them. This view of motivation is heavily influenced by Jean Piaget who developed the principles of equilibration, assimilation, accommodation and schema formation. He stated that children naturally want equilibration, which means a sense of organization and balance in their world. The cognitive theorists also believe that motivation comes from one's expectations for successfully completing a task. John Atkinson proposed motivation could also come from a person's desire for achievement. Some are high-need achievers and will seek out more challenging tasks, while others are low-need and will avoid challenging tasks. Those who avoid them do so because they have a fear of failure and that alone outweighs the expectation of success. William Glasser stated that for someone to be motivated to achieve success they must first experience success in some part of their lives.

Humanistic view of motivation

The humanistic view of motivation is heavily influenced by Abraham Maslow, most famous for Maslow's five-level hierarchy of needs. He proposed that everyone has five levels of needs and each level needs to be fulfilled first before moving on the next level. The bottom level is physiological needs, needs people need to survive, food, water, air and shelter. If this level is satisfied then people will be motivated to meet the needs of the next level, which is safety. After this level comes belongingness and love and after this level is esteem. These first four levels motivate people to act only when they are unmet to a certain point. The highest and last level is self-actualization, which is also called a growth need. Self-actualization is often referred to as a need for self-fulfillment. People come to this level because they have desire to fulfill their potential and capabilities.

State functions concerning curriculum

The development of curriculum at the state level involves creating guidelines concerning the development and implementation of curricula and ways of assessing student achievement. The state also creates the tests and other performance measures that are required for each academic subject. They should take a limited approach and focus assessment on language arts, social studies, science and math. There has been a movement toward assessments to test the student's ability to complete projects and open-ended problem solving rather than the tradition pencil and paper methods. It is also the responsibility of the state to provide the needed material and resources to local school districts. Often times the most desired resources are monetary support and technical assistance. The state must also decide the graduation requirements in terms of credits and competencies. These functions are general and allow the district more ownership in deciding what their needs and strengths are.

- 68 -

District functions concerning curriculum

Each district can implement any program of study they feel is necessary for their schools, however, it would be to the district's advantage if the program is consistent for each grade level and uniform for each academic subject. If the district ensures a consistent and uniform program of study this would help guarantee equity that all students across the district are getting an equal education. Another advantage is it makes it easier for a student to transfer within the district. A parent will not have to worry that their child is not on the same level with other students simply because they changed schools. The school district should create a mastery core curriculum that will explain the subjects that all schools will offer. A mastery core will also explain the goals and objectives of each subject. However, there is still the freedom and flexibility for each school to development their curriculum using the mastery core for guidance.

School functions concerning curriculum

After the school has received the curriculum's goals and objectives from the state and district, it is time for the school to make choices. The school's decisions will be made under the leadership of the principal and teacher leaders. The school will also collect the appropriate input from parents and then build a curriculum that is guided by the mastery core. The school should identify their goals and needs and then supplement any classes they feel are necessary to add in order to meet the student's needs. As a team, there will be a decision about the schedule, curriculum integration, and how to align and implement the curriculum. If this process is to be successful, it is important that the principal has strong leadership skills and is well informed and active in the development process.

Classroom functions concerning curriculum

After the state, district and school have performed their functions concerning curriculum, now it is time for the classroom teachers to enhance the curriculum using their personal style. The teachers can carry out the curriculum either as an individual or as a member of team or department. This is an opportunity for the teachers to develop yearly calendars and from there develop specific units of study based on the calendar. When making a yearly calendar this allows for the teachers to plan activities ahead of time, for example field trips or guest speakers. This is a time when a teacher can enrich the curriculum by using their own unique style of teaching that meets the needs of the students. Teachers know the students best and know when there is an area that needs to be taught in a certain way in order to gain student achievement.

Evaluating data from tests

Effective administrators know that in order to keep the school progressing, there needs to be a monitoring system of tests, feedback and evaluating student performance. The data collected from standardized tests and state assessments is important but they do not give a complete picture of the student's progression. These tests are resourceful to the teacher in order to plan for daily instruction. The more relevant feedback comes from monthly curriculum-based assessments. These help keep teachers and administrators focused on specific goals that are more short-term and easily measurable. Without collecting the data from these sources, teachers and administrators will have a more difficult knowing if the instruction and curriculum is meeting the needs of the students. They are left to guess about their success. However, if a school does collect all the important data, it needs to be organized in an orderly fashion.

Cooperative learning method

Cooperative learning models are becoming more popular in the school systems. This type of learning model states that students are more likely to gain achievement if they are working as a member in a small group. Many schools are accepting this learning style because it is also the same model that many corporations use. Groups are formed and each group is responsible for a certain goal. However, each student in a group is also responsible for some part. Everyone must prove they have participated and learned something. Therefore, it is extremely important that the teacher is certain that every student knows what the concepts and goals are. After the teacher has given each task, then they come together to work on solving that task together.

Author's Chair method

The Author's Chair is a strategy that allows students to share with other students the writing work they have created on their own. This is the final step in the writing process. A special time is created for the student to read aloud their final product with the audience and then receive feedback from their classmates. The feedback is beneficial for the writer and audience because both of these parties can improve their writing. It is important that the teacher stresses that comments from both the author and audience are respectful and accepting. This process is used to help students realize their ideas are worthy of sharing and to develop their sense of authorship. It also enhances the student's listening and attention span skill, for the ones who are a part of the listening audience.

Drill and practice

Drill and practice is a very familiar instructional strategy to many teachers. This method uses repetitive practices of specific skills in order for students to retain the information. It is often used for the memorization of spelling words and math problems. In order for drill and practice to be effective, it must be used with appropriate strategies to develop certain competencies. Many times teachers use this method for beginning learners or for certain students who may be experiencing learning problems. This method should be used only if the teacher is absolutely certain that it is the most appropriate form of instruction to use. There are software packages that can be purchased for the use of drill and practice. It is important to use the ones that provide feedback to students as to why they got an answer correct or incorrect.

Guided reading and thinking

The guided reading and thinking strategy is a way for the teacher to guide a student's comprehension of a reading selection by asking the students questions. The focus of this instructional form is to use context to predict meaning. The purpose is to help students develop story sense and to help students learn the purposes for reading. Comprehension is acquired by helping students use their past experiences and knowledge of language. One way teachers can use this method is by having the students predict what the story is going to be about by just looking at the cover and reading the title. Then, their guesses can be listed in a story grid or outline. While reading, teachers should stop and ask the students questions about the story and compare what is happening compared to their predictions. Assessments and evaluations can be made by assessing the student's abilities to comprehend certain types of texts.

Scaffolding

The instructional technique, scaffolding, is a process where the teacher models how to perform a certain learning strategy and then the responsibility gradually shifts to the students. Scaffolding is intended to be temporary because some of the work is being done for the students who are not ready to complete the task by themselves. Teachers can perform this strategy by modeling the task and thinking out loud in either direct of indirect instruction. A teacher can adapt this instructional technique by pairing students up according to development level or by engaging students with cooperative learning. Students can help other students in the cooperative learning style; however, teacher assistance is still needed. A teacher can assess the students by using anecdotal notes, student self-assessment or by using graphic organizers. These types of organizers are scaffolding tools that visually represent ideas.

Importance of sound testing methods

You cannot know if students are learning what the curriculum is designed to teach unless you test the students regularly; by testing the students, you will be testing the curriculum and the instructional program. If student scores are less than satisfactory, and show no improvement over time, then either the curriculum or the instructional program needs to be redesigned. But you won't know this unless you test, and in order to get accurate results you must use sound testing methods. Such methods have been tried and proven to work; they have been used in other schools and other districts; they have been approved, or mandated, by states and school boards; and they are appropriate to the areas being tested.

Changing curriculum program

As the school's population and the wider community changes, the needs of its students will change. Changes in the political and economic climate and in society will affect the school's curriculum as well; for instance, think of how much time is spent on subjects covering technology and information today – it's necessary because technology and information now make up such a large portion of our economy. Twenty and thirty years ago, that wasn't the case – then, traditional industries and manufacturing were a large part of the economy and the subjects included in school curricula reflected that. Science is more important than ever in our economy, as is the global nature of that economy, and schools are trying to address that with an increased emphasis on science subjects and foreign languages. In another twenty or thirty years there will almost certainly be different forces at work in the economy. Schools must teach what is relevant to their students and as that changes over time, so too will any given curricula.

Adding technology to curriculum

Advances in technology have a big influence on the economy, and if it affects the economy it should be addressed in the schools. The last twenty years have seen an exponential increase in technological advances, especially in the computer and telecommunications fields, and these advances have had a profound impact on education. Today, the schools that do not have adequate information infrastructures – enough late model computers for their students, fast and reliable Internet access, video technology – put their students at a grave disadvantage academically, socially and economically. Without these technologies students will have trouble getting into college or finding jobs, and they will be cut off from information that others their age have access to. Not only are these technologies enormously effective in teaching and in helping students to learn, but also the technology itself should be addressed in the classroom, as it is so large a part of our economy.

Curriculum and testing assessment

School and district staff cannot know what kind of curricula the students need, what type of instruction will be most effective, until they know exactly what are the strengths and weaknesses of the school's existing curriculum. It is a given that there will be areas needing improvement – you must identify those areas and identify exactly what form the improvements must take. Hopefully there will be areas in which the school's existing curriculum is strong – these areas should be protected and, if appropriate, emulated in other areas. The needs assessment must address: targets – what is to be accomplished for the whole school (specific grades, specific academic subjects); specific methodology, tools and techniques for instruction; hard deadlines and general timelines by which to measure progress toward the targets; tests and measures that will be used to constantly track progress, or lack of it, in each specific target area.

Student demographic trends

As the wider school community population changes, the social and cultural expectations of the school's families will change and the curriculum will have to evolve to reflect that. Although some aspects of the core curriculum will remain the same across the state and nationally – math, the sciences, and English must be taught – social studies and history curriculum will reflect the experiences and values of the student population. A school whose student population is predominantly Asian and white will not concentrate on the same holidays, social studies events, momentous historical events, etc. as a school with a predominantly African-American and Latino population. Teachers want to engage students with material that speaks to their experiences, their cultural expectations and their daily lives, and so curriculum must be designed to be meaningful to that school's population.

Occupational/economic trends

The curriculum, even in the lower grades, must reflect current economic reality. Thus today's curriculum doesn't concentrate on manufacturing and other traditional industries, as did the curriculum of thirty years ago; today's curriculum emphasizes science, information technology and international factors affecting global business. Science and technology represent the largest portion of our economy at present, and school curriculum must address this in order to prepare students for college and the world beyond. And because information technology has allowed people all over the world to be more intimately aware of other countries and other peoples, and to be aware of events occurring thousands of miles away as they unfold, the curriculum must address the societal and political effects of this information age.

Aligning curricular and extracurricular programs

However much attention sports, arts and other extracurricular activity may seem to garner, the basic mission of the school – all schools – remains the academic curriculum, and all extracurricular activity is supposed to enhance and support it. When extracurricular activities detract from the curriculum – draining students' and teachers' time and efforts, and school and community resources – trouble ensues. The community does not want to hear that the school district must raise taxes to cover a shortfall in books or equipment budgets when millions were just spent on a state of the art athletics facility. Parents do not want to see their children's time so taken up with drama club, track team, booster club or community service that they don't have time for homework or time with their family. The focus of the school, and of the teachers and students, must be on the coursework. Everything is – or should be – secondary to that.

Problems with student assessment strategies

Assessment is testing, and testing takes up a lot of students' and teachers' time. It's been estimated that the time spent assessing student performance may take up to 30% of a teacher's professional time – grading homework, making and grading tests, communicating with parents about grades and academic progress. In addition, because of the numerous state mandated tests that occur from third to twelfth grade, many teachers feel that they spend all their time "teaching the tests" instead of teaching actual curriculum material. In addition to the time taken by tests, the very design and implementation of testing strategies is tricky. You must be certain that you have found a reliable method of testing what you actually intend to test, that you are actually measuring what you have planned to measure. The assessments must be uniform across the school district and must be conducted over a period of time before any meaningful data can be gathered and interpreted.

Professional staff development and curriculum planning

The fact that curricula change constantly over time means that teachers must be lifelong learners; they are students too. As the curriculum changes, teachers must keep abreast of changes in their subject areas and in current pedagogical theory and methodology. If a teacher does nothing but teach, day in and day out, with no time given to professional development – conferences, training, continuing education – then she will stagnate. Her expertise will become obsolete and she will no longer be an effective educator. Although the Principal is not a teacher, he is the curriculum and instructional leader of the school and in that role he is the teachers' teacher – he must see to it that teaching staff have regular opportunities for rewarding and meaningful professional development so that they can constantly grow and learn to meet the changing academic needs of their students.

Curriculum development as a contentious issue

Nothing elicits such strong reactions and opinions from all school stakeholders as does the curriculum; it is probably the most highly litigated aspect of school law, even more so than discipline matters. Most parents take very seriously their role as their children's primary teachers of cultural and religious values and belief, and they do not want to see their children exposed to material that, in the parents' view, undermine or contradict those values and beliefs. Subjects such as sex education, controversial historical events, and scientific subjects like evolution are among the subjects that have attracted opposition from

- 73 -

parents. But in a public education system, the values and beliefs of all students must be balanced with the educational needs of all students, and the schools are responsible for teaching students what the social and economic realities of the community require. The Principal plays a key role in trying to achieve the balance, trying to communicate to parents that the school respects the values and beliefs of all its stakeholders while at the same time ensuring that the school curriculum addresses the academic needs of all students.

School control

In addition to controlling what students are taught, the school can have some control over how students learn, and can help students learn. Research has shown that some areas within the school's control include: use of time (number of days per school year and number of hours spent in school each day); rate at which material is covered; size of classes; composition of classes (age based, ability grouping, etc.); what students do while in class; how teachers assign the work; and how students manage the time it takes to perform assigned projects. The school can help students learn at their maximum capacity by making sure that classroom time is used wisely, that teacher-student ratios are appropriate, that students are placed in groups that will help them learn, that teachers assign appropriate types and amounts of homework, that students are taught useful time management skills, etc. Students have to be taught how to learn and this is part of the school's educational mission.

Relationship between curriculum, instruction, resources and assessment

The curriculum (subjects) must be taught via an effective program of instruction (pedagogy); the proper resources (books and other materials) are necessary to impart the curriculum and implement the instruction; and appropriate methods of assessment must be devised to test the students and ensure that they are learning what the curriculum is meant to teach. This is what is meant by the repeated use of the term "alignment". All four factors – curriculum, instruction, resources and assessment – must be aligned, balanced, fit together to accomplish the fundamental purpose of the school, which is the education of its students.

Curriculum program review

Some of the questions to be asked when planning or redesigning a curriculum will be: what do the students need to learn and when should they learn it – i.e., at what grade levels? Have the students been learning what they need to know? In what areas are test scores weak or strong? What can staff do to help students learn what it's been decided they need to know? What kind of training do the teachers need to help the students learn? Does the curriculum address state and school board mandated requirements?

Curriculum alignment

The curriculum is the bedrock upon which every other aspect of the school and its mission rests – the curriculum is the material that the students must learn, and that is the reason the school exists in the first place. The school serves many important social functions for the community but it exists to educate students. The curriculum can make the difference between a failing school and a good one, between a majority of graduates winding up unemployed or the majority of them going on to college and employment. The best teachers in the world cannot be effective educators if they do not have an effective curriculum to teach. Alignment of curriculum simply means that the curriculum is appropriate for the students to whom it is taught; that it covers what students are expected to learn; that it is taught by effective pedagogical methods; that it is supported by appropriate and necessary resources; and that it can be quantitatively assessed by means of student testing.

Environment

The Principal must lead the effort to make the school an open, welcoming environment where staff and students feel comfortable accepting intellectual challenges. The school, through its instructional program, should make students and staff *want* to learn, *want* to grow and expand. New ideas are sought and welcomed, and there is no but-we've-always-done-it-this-wayism. An environment of physical and emotional safety, high expectations for staff and student, flexible instruction targeted to meet individual students' needs and abilities, necessary technical and physical resources, frequent assessment and accountability and respect for student diversity is an environment in which staff and students are free to excel.

The main elements are resources and materials; staffing and scheduling; and student safety. Inattention to, or lack of, any of these elements lessens the school's ability to educate students. The school must have adequate resources and materials for instruction, including books and media and physical equipment as well as a safe and well-maintained physical campus. Classes must be scheduled to allow all students to get where they need to go with a minimum of trouble and confusion. Classes should be well composed for the students – i.e., by age, or by grade level or by academic ability, etc. The teacher to student ratio is very important, as is adequate administrative staffing so that the school operates smoothly. And safety - physical and emotional, in the classroom and on the campus in general - is of paramount importance. School safety is a big concern today with violent incidents occurring with alarming regularity, and with violence on a lesser scale happening in classrooms every day. The Principal who does not devote time and resources to improving and maintaining school safety will find himself with a failing school.

Formative and summative assessments

A formative assessment is done before designing and implementing programs or strategies. It's a needs assessment; it involves collecting all pertinent information to form a complete and accurate picture of a district, a campus, a program, and a class. It's necessary to do a formative assessment before making changes or embarking on new projects because without it you can't know what kind of strategy you need, whom you'll be targeting, what problem or issue you're trying to address, etc. The formative assessment gives you the map you need to get to where you're going. Once you get there, you do a summative assessment, which is a complete and accurate picture of the district, campus, program or class as it looks after the strategy has been implemented and monitored for a while. The summative assessment allows you to see how well or how poorly your project has turned out.

Student social and emotional development

Students don't learn in a vacuum. Schools cannot be – or should not be - cold institutional places of dry pedagogical instruction. Students spend a minimum of 6 hours a day, five days a week in school – that's a significant portion of their waking hours and as a result, school is where students get the majority of their social interaction and resulting social and cultural development. Kids will develop socially in school whether the school actively seeks to enable or enhance that development or not; the point is that by actively seeking to enable and enhance students' social development, that development is much more likely to be positive, functional and healthy. Inattention to students' social and emotional needs will result in a dysfunctional environment where learning is impossible, safety is threatened and negative behavior will flourish.

Non-classroom activities

Educators have long recognized that students learn better when their education is not limited to rote learning or to nothing but the lecture and homework class structure; indeed, one of the recognized strengths of the American educational system, even with its currently tarnished reputation, is that the system is *not* centered on rote learning. Students learn better, and more willingly, when their minds and personalities are actively engaged, when they are allowed input and initiative in their lessons and projects, and when they are socially engaged. Curriculum-oriented clubs like the French or Science Club; arts-centered activities like band or drama; intellectual pursuits like chess club or speech and debate; even sports – such extracurricular activities, when properly balanced in proportion to the curriculum and not allowed to interfere with students' actual academic efforts, help to enhance a student's overall school experience.

Improving the instruction program

Education is one of the most heavily researched and reported professional fields in the world. Every time something new is tried in the classroom or the school, it is studied, measured and reported. Principals and teachers must participate in such research and remain current on the literature that reports it. They must attend conferences and take advantage of other opportunities to learn about current classroom and curriculum program research. Being aware of what has and has not worked in other schools and districts will help staff plan for their own school. Schools that take innovative approaches to classroom management, student discipline, the choice of curriculum material, and methods of instruction are emulated if these approaches are successful. In this way curriculum and instruction programs evolve and improve over time and across school districts, and this is how educational theories and methods fall out of favor as new and hopefully better ones replace them.

Teachers can plan lessons around eliciting student ideas and encouraging student initiative. These ideas and initiatives should be recognized and rewarded. Students can suggest their own projects and assignments, to be approved by teachers. Students can then grade each others' resulting work, in addition to the teachers' official assessments, and students can get school-wide recognition for their efforts. The school could start an ongoing "Recognition Board" of some type that continually features student work of exceptional merit. The school could also set up Student of the Month or Student of the Quarter programs with specific criteria for recognition. Schools have also reported success with peer to peer tutoring – older students tutoring younger ones in particular curriculum areas, or students with advanced skills in certain subjects offering tutoring to students whose skills need work.

It is not always the case that the school lacks resources to accomplish its mission; what often happens is that too many resources are pointed towards one or two areas, leaving other areas without, or resources are going to programs no longer needed. When a thorough formative assessment is conducted the school can get an accurate picture of its current needs – what is working well, what is working poorly, in which subjects students are excelling and in which subjects they need help. Once the picture is in focus, the school can reallocate resources to meet its current needs – new equipment in the science labs, new books for mathematics, less money spent on history materials because more have become available online, etc. When resources are properly aligned to needs, instruction will improve.

Assessment and the instruction program

Students will perform better, and they will be more willing participants in their own education, if they know from the outset what they are expected to accomplish. By incorporating assessment into the instruction program students have a clear understanding of what they are supposed to learn and how they will be expected to demonstrate their learning. They will also have an opportunity to make the connections among what they are being taught, how they are expected to apply that knowledge, why the teachers are presenting that knowledge in the way they are, and how that knowledge will be tested. If the assessment is planned to be more than answering questions on a test, but rather demonstrating knowledge of a specific subject through particular projects, then students will not plan to just regurgitate whatever they hear in class, but to actively participate in learning and to anticipate how to apply what they're learning.

The best outcomes are the ones that can be assessed and quantified: raised student test scores; decreased special education referrals; decreased alternative education referrals; decreased absenteeism; decreased disciplinary incidents; increased parent involvement; increased graduation rates; increased teacher retention. All these measurable outcomes should appear if improvements and adjustments to the instruction program have been designed and implemented properly. If such adjusts do not result in measurable improvements in these and other necessary areas, programs need to be modified or replaced.

Responsiveness to student diversity

Diversity does not refer only to race, gender or ethnicity. It also refers to culture – the language, background and values of the family; social factors – the stability or dysfunction of the family; and the innate differences of temperament and ability from student to student. These differences must be taken into account when planning the instructional programs. The programs must display sensitivity to different cultural attitudes while at the same time maintaining academic standards to which all students are held. In this regard, the school really does have to be all things to all people.

Creating conditions conducive to learning

School safety is of paramount concern to school personnel and parents today as public schools in recent years have seen undreamed of levels of violence from students and from people outside the school preying on students. The public schools are perceived by many people, rightly or wrongly, to be physically dangerous places to which parents are loathe to send their kids if they have other choices – and parents are insisting on other choices. And besides the issue of unusual violence, such as school shootings or hostage incidents, public schools have seen a steep rise in the level of classroom violence and generally bullying among students and violence toward teachers. School district have begun hiring their own police forces and training teachers and administrative staff in anticipating and handling potential violence in the schools. Programs teach school personnel to recognize and respond to bullying incidents. More parents are willing to sue schools they feel are not adequately protecting their children's safety. Students do not learn when they do not feel physically safe, and curriculum, instruction and resources do not matter if students' basic physical safety cannot be protected. The Principal must devote time and resources to improving and maintaining campus security.

Social and cultural development

Extracurricular activities must be designed to support and enhance regular academic work. The activities of sports, clubs, artistic endeavors and charitable and community work must be based on what students are learning in their classes and must not take up so much time that students cannot do the work required from those classes. Many schools restrict athletic eligibility to students maintaining a set minimum GPA, or require members of curriculum-based clubs to do extra credit work in those specific classes, or do not allow musical or dramatic rehearsals and performances to take place during regular school hours. In this way schools ensure that extracurricular activities do not compete with classroom instruction, but instead enhance it. The extracurricular activities are important to students because activity outside the classroom allows them to meet and socialize with others sharing their interests and to develop talents and interests that will serve them well in college and beyond. A curriculum of nothing but pedagogical instruction leads to a stagnant instructional program and bored students, and bored students do not learn.

Instructional flexibility

Different students learn differently – that's a truism. *How* they learn differently is important and may be based on any of many factors: age, emotional maturity, native talent, personality traits (shy, outgoing, deliberate and careful or excitable and busy). Other factors outside the student's own personality and demographics might also affect how he or she learns – cultural expectations, the family's style of child rearing and discipline, the parents' attitudes toward school and study and their involvement or lack of it in their children's daily lives. Decades ago, when public schools were relatively homogenous, educators did not take all these variable factors into consideration when planning curricula and instruction programs; today it is necessary to do so. Today educators – teachers as well as administrative staff - are trained to tailor their teaching to the needs and abilities of their students and to design curricula and instruction that will reach different groups of students. So while all schools will teach the material that they are mandated by government and school boards to teach, and all schools will test their students according to state and federal mandates, how they teach that curricula will vary between schools and within schools.

Rethinking school organization structures

When teachers and administrative personnel are exposed to other methods of instruction, through research and conferences and professional literature, it inspires them to think of new ideas for teaching. Innovation inspires innovation, and seeing what other schools have accomplished by taking risks and thinking creatively inspires teachers to do the same. Educational theories coming from academe filter down to public school staff who are encouraged to adopt and adapt the methods they read about. And by reading current research and attending continuing education classes, teachers can see what has *not* worked for other schools and so avoid making the same decisions.

Telecommunications

Technology must be integrated into the entire school – classrooms, curriculum, instructional programs (i.e., the teaching tools), and information infrastructure. Technology is both taught in the classroom and used to teach in the classroom and out of it, and when integrated into the information infrastructure it enhances and supports the campus' communication with its stakeholders and the wider community – the campus website, communications with parents and other schools, with the district and state, etc. This is where the participation of the community is important, as schools partner with local businesses, other organizations and other schools to form networks and assist with the financial and physical requirements of technology integration.

District curriculum-based assessments

After the curriculum guide has been created and all the necessary resource materials have been purchased, the district's testing office will develop a testing program. These tests will not duplicate or replace any of the state required tests; these will only be used as a supplement. A Superintendent can use their leadership to ensure these tests do not take up too much time for Superintendents, teachers, and students. Many times districts will develop too many tests and it takes away time from the teacher to teach the students. Superintendents should also ensure that these tests do not require an excessive amount of monetary funds to develop, administer and score. The goal of these exams should be to provide educators and parents with information about student achievement and the results need to come in a form that everyone can understand. Superintendent's who want to have an influence on the district testing program should focus on these concerns.

Articulating the importance of education

The public school system is the only chance many students will ever have to obtain an education, and an educated citizenry is the basis of a functioning democratic society. Therefore the public school Superintendent's role as curriculum and instructional leader is his most important. The curriculum which the school follows will determine what, and how well, students will learn; if the curriculum does not include the material students need to equip themselves for life after graduation – college and/or employment – then the public school system has failed its students. No matter how devoted the school's Superintendent and staff may be, no matter how talented its teachers, if the curriculum does not match the students' needs than they will not receive the education necessary for them to succeed as adults. As the curriculum and instructional leader of the school, the Superintendent is responsible, at least in part, for his students' success or failure later in life.

Curriculum revision

Curriculum redesign takes a long time to plan and implement, and it takes a long time to see any results. If it is not approached as a long term project, then when results are not achieved quickly teachers and staff may get discouraged. Any curriculum redesign projects must have realistic deadlines and timetables built into them. Before designing the new curriculum, a review of the existing curriculum – a needs assessment - should be conducted – what will be retained, what will be modified, what will be discarded. The input of a school's stakeholders must be solicited when conducting the curriculum redesign and any proposed accompanying instructional program. Curriculum design is usually undertaken by a committee, either at the school or the district level. It is not a one person job, and the Superintendent will have a large say in the people who will serve on the committee. The Superintendent might be the curriculum committee coordinator, or she may choose another person. In any case the Superintendent will have to be deeply involved with the committee's work and will almost certainly be a member of the committee.

Active participation with curriculum development

Just as student families will be more involved in the school if they feel that they have ownership of the school's mission and activities, so teachers will be more passionate about teaching a curriculum program that they have hand a hand in designing. Teachers are professionals, specialists and experts in their fields, and they expect to have more responsibility than simply imparting a curriculum that's been mandated from on high. Some districts allow teachers more discretion and autonomy in designing curriculum, and instructional methods, than others, but even districts that take a more top-down approach to curriculum development will be receptive to teachers' ideas if the Superintendent takes the lead in soliciting, collecting and passing on those ideas. Teachers will be more excited about and more committed to teaching curriculum that they have helped to develop. The Superintendent can help them do this by establishing communications between staff and district in the curriculum review process.

Beliefs about the fundamental purposes of a school and how people learn (value judgments) affect ideas about curriculum. A school's teaching staff are all experts in their particular fields and they will have definite ideas about what subjects are most important to the core curriculum; about how students in particular grades are most effectively taught; how much homework and what types of projects should be assigned; and a host of other issues. Some teachers have informal and highly interactive teaching styles, with lots of back and forth between teacher and student and lots of student-driven projects; other teachers have a more traditional approach; the two groups may view each others' teaching styles with suspicion and/or derision. Another aspect of curriculum development involves the amount of time and effort that can be required of teachers; many school districts have collective bargaining agreements with teachers' unions that limit the amount of time and type of activities that can be required of teachers outside of school hours. So how much time the teachers can devote to curriculum planning, and the types of activity outside the classroom required by the curriculum and asked of teachers, may limit what the Superintendent's options.

Selecting instructional materials

Texts, software, and other media resources should be selected only after the mastery curriculum has been developed. Often districts make the mistake of purchasing textbooks and then developing a curriculum based on the materials that were purchased. Textbooks should be used to enrich the curriculum, not as the sole basis for creating it. Administrators have a powerful voice and influence in the district's selection process and should use their influence to ensure that their schools are getting the appropriate materials necessary to improve student achievement. One way of choosing appropriate texts is to read through the books and mark the page numbers that correspond to certain learning objectives. Administrators then can choose texts that are the closest fit to the curriculum objectives and discuss their findings with their selection committees.

Design and implementation

Design and implementation involve a great deal of preparation and practice. These words describe the essence of the duties of school staff and principals. Everything principals do, or help others to do, involves the design of programs, activities, courses, and tests. After they are designed, such programs and assessments must be implemented, or put into practice. The word facilitate helps describe principals' primary goals to help, aid, lead, and support the design (plan, proposal) and implementation (preparation, construction, building) of the school's curriculum. This process may seem intangible and challenging until principals see their schools filled with students who are learning effectively.

Alignment

Allocating resources effectively and equitably for instructional needs is one way to discuss alignment. It is imperative to align resources to match instructional needs, and to determine what needs to be done versus what educators want to be done. It is important to consider if the best choices involve implementing new instructional programs or making adjustments to existing ones. Also, school staff must collaborate to determine what physical resources, printed and electronic media, lab equipment, AV equipment, etc. will be required and how much will they will cost. Teachers' needs are an important component of alignment, and it is important to assess when and if teachers need new or added training, books, or conferences. Careful alignment is vital for budget purposes (and "resources" almost always means, or at least includes, budget). In order to be aligned, everything must be outlined in a budget, and everything must be spent accordingly. If budgetary needs are not prioritized, a school's needs and resources will not be aligned or allocated properly.

Time management

Time management in the classroom is an essential part of effective teaching, and time management is one of the most important skills teachers can help their students acquire. Time spent in the classroom on administrative and other non-teaching details such as attendance, activity preparation, assignment details, and lunch money collection needs to be minimized. Lessons need to be planned to engage students and keep their attention for the duration of the class. Students need to be taught how to approach projects in a timely manner and they must learn how much time should be spent on assignments, what should be done first or last, and how to prioritize and organize different tasks. Effective use of time can raise a student's overall grade point average, and teachers must be model these important time management skills.

Recognizing one's mistakes

Sometimes a program, policy, decision, or project will not work as it was intended. It is possible that a program was a mistake to begin with, or maybe it has not been monitored or adapted properly since its inception. Regardless of how it happened, once a mistake is discovered or it is apparent that something is not working, it is important to take action, and to take responsibility. The mistake needs to be corrected, or taken apart to evaluate the situation. It may be necessary to start over and that might be the best option. To keep going with something that clearly is inffective, just because a lot of time and effort went into it, is counterproductive and ultimately harmful to a school. It hurts the ego to admit that an error or mistake was made, and it is frustrating to see hard work go for naught. It is tiresome to think about all the new work that will now be required, but professionals need to accept responsibility and get to work. Good leaders acknowledge their mistakes and then take the necessary steps to correct them.

Instructional method conflict

How students are taught can be as controversial as what they are taught. Teachers are frequently the subject of vehement opposition, including legal opposition, when parents decide that their teaching methods are offensive, emotionally distressing or physically dangerous. Teaching methods that have occasioned controversy, for example, include teachers who attempt to teach classes about discrimination by dividing classes and showing marked preference to certain groups of students over others for a period of time; teachers teaching about repressive or violent governments by having actors burst into classrooms dressed as soldiers or terrorists; students being shown graphic material depicting sexual or violent content; and students being asked to perform tasks that might be considered too dangerous for their age group. Teachers should not be designing their instructional methods in isolation – the Superintendent is the instructional leader of the school as well as the curriculum leader and should be aware of, and have an active role in, how teachers decide to present the material they teach.

Responsibilities once an instructional program has been designed

Once school staff members have designed (planned) and implemented (prepared) curriculum and instruction programs, the hard work is far from over. Once a program is up and running and achieving positive, measurable results, the inclination may be to relax and want to move on to the next project, but this just is not possible. Curriculum/instructional programs will not succeed unless they are monitored, revised, and rigorously maintained. Superintendents and principals need to measure, assess, and make adjustments in accordance with each instructional program. It's not enough to meet initial goals because goals change. Schools are like living organisms that grow and evolve in reaction to changing conditions.

Performance weaknesses in teachers

It is ethically wrong and generally, illegal to wait until the end of the school year to tell a teacher that his or her performance has been substandard. It also is a disservice to the students and the school. Teachers with performance weaknesses need to be talked to, coached, and assisted as soon as problems become apparent. In some cases, this may mean not waiting until the scheduled formal assessment to address a teacher's job performance issues. In many states, employment laws require that an employer have documented evidence of poor job performance or other termination-deserving behavior before an employee is terminated. Even if it is not required by law, such issues could arise in the event of a related lawsuit. It therefore makes legal and financial sense to conduct regular, written evaluations. Formative assessments should be done at the outset of a teacher's employment, so that his or her strengths and weaknesses can be known immediately. This process allows teachers to receive training in the necessary areas. Summative assessment comes later, and regularly, as teachers are evaluated on an ongoing basis, and they continually are encouraged and aided in professional development.

Continuously, continuing, and continual

Most everything you do as Superintendent will be done over and over. You will not design, implement, assess and modify your curricular or extracurricular programs one time. Your students, your school board, the state's educational requirements, prevailing educational theory, political and economic conditions – all will change over time, and the school must change as well. "Sound, research-based practice" will change over time. What was considered educationally sound over 30 years ago is no longer practiced, so expect the "design, implement, assess, modify" paradigm to last throughout your career. This is true of all the duties, all the processes, and all the responsibilities listed and expounded on throughout the exam.

Creating an instructional program

The superintendent leads the campus' professional staff in creating an instructional program that teaches students what they are expected to know at their respective grade levels and prepares them to handle material presented at subsequent grade levels. This is accomplished by using the appropriate resources and pedagogical methods and by testing students frequently and at regular intervals to see if they are learning what they are expected to know and how well or how poorly.

Facilitating

Facilitating is the Superintendent's primary responsibility. Making things happen – proposing, planning, budgeting, discussing, researching, consulting, leading, managing – it is all facilitating. She does not teach the classes, but she helps the teachers get the training and materials they need to teach and she helps them in designing the curriculum and instruction. She does not write and mail the checks for payroll and operations, but she plans the budget that pays for everything. She does not clean the school, paint the buildings, or mow the lawn, but she has to make sure that it all gets done. She is the one parents will call if they have questions or problems, even though she is usually not going to be the subject of the question or problem. She is the one who communicates to the district on behalf of the teachers and vice versa. Although the school district requires many people to make it operate efficiently, it needs one person to make it all happen – and that is the Superintendent.

Advocate, nurture, and sustain

The Superintendent must advocate (promote), nurture (protect) and sustain (persist with) a teaching program – which includes the curriculum and the methods by which the curriculum is presented – that is geared toward each students' needs and abilities and challenges each student to reach his or her maximum academic potential. The curriculum and instruction program will also allow teachers to grow professionally, giving them opportunities to learn about current educational research and theory and allowing them to try innovative programs in their own classrooms. By promoting the curriculum and instruction program the Superintendent encourages students and staff to commit to it and contribute their own efforts to it; by protecting it he ensures that the program receives needed resources and attention; by persisting with the program he ensures that it is monitored regularly, adjusted or modified as necessary and, most importantly, regularly assessed through agreed upon methods to confirm that it is filling the academic needs for which it was designed. Lastly, all this is made possible by the Superintendent's leadership in fostering a campus culture of learning, respect, high expectations, open communications, and involvement of all district stakeholders.

Achieving the campus vision

The Superintendent is the ethical leader (001), cultural leader (002), the communications leader (003), the vision leader (004), the curriculum leader (005) and the instructional leader (006) of the school. In all of those roles, he is the figure that all school stakeholders look to for the ethos, the environment, the character of the school. He sets the tone for working relationships and working conditions on campus. If he works to create an atmosphere of collegial trust and cooperation, of intellectual exploration and risk taking, of open communications among and between staff and students, of ethical and legal conduct, of high expectations of staff and students, and of a genuine love of and commitment to education, the campus vision will be achieved.

No project is ever fully completed

The school is a dynamic, ever growing, ever changing organism. The students change, the teachers change, the administration changes – new people come and go and the people who stay change as well, as they grow intellectually and enhance their skills and expand their experience. It is for this reason that staff evaluation and staff professional enrichment is never over; it is never a one-off. A teacher is hired; trained; evaluated; trained some more; evaluated again; trained some more, and so on. Constant evaluation and constant professional growth should be the norm because the alternative is stagnation. No matter how well you have done it, you can do better. No matter how much you have accomplished, you can do more.

Design, implement, evaluate, revise

"Design, implement, evaluate, revise" can also be explained: propose, prepare, appraise, perfect. In this context, we are talking about designing a professional development, a recruiting plan, or an evaluation plan. All plans relate to staffing issues – hiring, training, retaining, educating, evaluating and sometimes terminating staff. Once a plan for one of these staffing tasks has been proposed, it must prepared and put into effect. Once the plan has been used for a predetermined amount of time, it needs to be evaluated – has it done what it was designed to do, and how well? Have new teachers been adequately trained? Are staff members taking advantage of relevant professional development opportunities? Have staff members been evaluated using the chosen assessment tool and do all agree that the evaluations were fair and accurate? Once the plans have been used and evaluated, they will need to be modified, tinkered with and tuned up, in order to make them better. The design/implement/evaluate/revise paradigm is present in almost everything the Superintendent and the school do.

Successful teachers, schools, and Superintendents

If you wanted to be completely mercenary and pragmatic about it, a teacher's successful professional development is in a Superintendent's own best interest, and here's how. The school exists to educate pupils and to do that it needs teachers. Successful teachers – those who inspire and get excellent results from their students – become successful in part because they continually learn and grow and add to their expertise, and to do that they need professional enrichment. Schools whose students continually excel and show excellent scores on the all-important mandated tests are exemplary schools, and their Superintendents are recognized as exemplary Superintendents. So, successful teachers=excelling students=exemplary schools=exemplary (recognized, praised, well-compensated) Superintendent. Of course, it is in everyone's interest – most importantly the students and the community – for the school to be exemplary.

Changing expectations and views

Some time ago, the Superintendent was seen as the boss, or the head teacher, or the general of the school. The district told the Superintendent what needed to be done; the Superintendent designed the rules, told people what they were, and disciplined those who did not follow them. Most schools had a very top-down style of authority and leadership – this was common and widely accepted. Today's Superintendent, however, is expected to be more CEO and less general, more leader and less dictator. A Superintendent has to have skills more commonly associated with business leaders – data analysis and financial skills; leadership and management skills; team building, consensus building, and personnel management skills. The Superintendent has to be seen as a good communicator, a good people person, a trustworthy leader and a dedicated educator all at once. And he has to be comfortable with transparency and accountability; he has to let the district, the school staff and the students' parents and the wider community know what's going on in the school (both the good stuff and the bad stuff), and he has to take responsibility for making needed improvements and designing solutions to problems. He also has to expect and accept input from everyone in the school community.

Educational standard

Standards are learning goals. Standards are found on lists of educational competencies (concepts and contexts) that each student should attain by certain benchmarks (primarily grade level). Standards are not curriculum. Standards do not instruct schools or teachers on how to teach their students. Day-to-day teaching decisions are left to the local school officials, while standards provide big picture guidance about what students should learn in order to be ready to successfully meet future learning opportunities. Modern standards typically focus on higher order thinking skills and suggest that students go beyond knowing "who" or "what" and towards "how" and "why." Modern standards coincide well with student-centered learning pedagogies (e.g., problem-based, project-based, discovery-based) that offer student opportunities for deeper thinking and greater creativity.

Standards-based curriculum vs. traditional curriculum

Modern standards (such as the Common Core) are centered on the development of higher-order thinking skills. A traditional classroom typically features students sitting in rows and columns of desks led by a teacher who disseminates required knowledge. Because one-size-fits-all teacher-centered instruction (with passive student participation) is not as effective with helping students develop higher-order thinking skills, standards-based classrooms tend to feature more student-centered pedagogies (e.g., collaborative problem solving, student discovery projects) with students actively participating in the learning process while teachers coach individual students. Higher-order thinking skills are developed as students verbalize their understanding with their learning partners. A standards-based classroom features more activities and fewer lectures. A standards-based classroom is focused on student learning rather than on covering a set list of topics. Standards-based classrooms rely upon the professionalism and training of teachers to adjust their instruction regularly to accommodate for the diversity of student and classroom learning characteristics.

Importance of formative assessment to standards-based student-centered learning

Summative assessments are the traditional fare of the classroom; they are closed form tests (or quizzes) on which students work individually and for which students receive some numerical score. These assessments provide a numerical measure of a student's progress towards some learning goal(s) but fall short of providing the teacher with feedback that might guide future classroom activities. Alternatively formative assessments (e.g., teacher observations, student reflections, group problems) are non-numerical open form appraisals of student progress. Though they do not provide quantitative data to represent student progress, they provide qualitative (sentence-based) feedback to guide classroom instruction. There is no one way to teach towards higher-order thinking skills, and student engagement with classroom materials is a key to success. As such, formative assessments are vitally important. They provide the guidance a teacher will need to tailor his or her classroom activities to a given class's unique characteristics. Formative assessment empowers a teacher to individualize curriculum towards students as they attempt to develop higher-order thinking skills. Without an established program of formative assessment, it is highly unlikely that any classroom will successfully empower students to develop the thinking skills called for by the standards.

Support needed to implement a standards-based curriculum

The success of any implementation of a standards-based curriculum is dependent upon classroom teachers, who will require the support of educational leaders. Transitioning teachers and students from a traditional teacher-centered classroom to the student-centered classroom capable of fostering the development of higher-order thinking skills requires a stable pedagogical foundation developed through professional collaboration, fruitful discourse, and patient progress. No teacher or class will be successful in a transition directly from lecture-based instruction into high-ordered thinking. Rather, students and teachers must be gradually acclimated to new ways of classroom interaction. As an educational leader, you can facilitate a professional environment in which teachers can comfortably grow as educators. Teachers are generally receptive to a non-threatening collaborative process in which pedagogical goals are clearly communicated, specific strategies for student engagement are developed, and teachers have an opportunity to have their concerns addressed. As teachers gain experience with student-centered learning they will become more comfortable with the greater depth of learning required by the standards and will begin to better align their classrooms with the standards.

Reassuring concerned parents

Parents can become frustrated when they are unable to help their child with homework. In particular, their frustration may stem from a misunderstanding of modern classroom techniques for learning standard materials. They may say something like, "Why don't you just teach it the way I learned it?" As an educational leader you can both support your teachers and relieve parental frustrations, if such a question is ever brought to you. Regardless of the situation, always remain positive; any negativity will only fuel parental frustration. Encourage parents to speak with the teacher. Perhaps there is some misunderstanding of the intent of an assignment. You can encourage the parents to allow the student to do his or her own homework and ask questions of his or her teacher the next day. After all it is expected that the student will do the work, not a parent. Finally you might suggest the parent talk to family friends or relatives who may be more familiar with the material. Stress to the parent that education (for student, teacher, and parent) is not intended to be an individual endeavor. All parties should be encouraged to seek assistance when necessary.

Administrative Leadership

State initiatives

The state has a crucial and legitimate role in the development of the curriculum frameworks and an administrator can be proactive and get involved with the foundation documents while they are being developed. An effective administrator should use their influence at the state level in order to achieve what they think is best for their school. In order to achieve this, administrators need to stay informed about new ideas that the state may be developing. Knowing in advance what the situation is, is better than trying to react to what is already happening. The state professional association is a great source of information. It is also important the administrator knows how the legislative process operates formally and informally. In addition, if an administrator wants to have a voice in what they believe in, then they need to be knowledgeable of the latest facts and research information. The best source is going to be professional journals.

State level operational procedures

One of the most important operational functions of the state is to set minimum standards for all elementary and secondary schools. In addition, the state is responsible for the funding of schools, which is primarily done through real property taxes. State governments are also responsible for creating laws that ensure the proper operation of public schools; these laws vary from state to state. When state educational agencies are involved with curriculum development, they develop guidelines for the development and implementation of curriculum plans, along with the objectives students are required meet in each academic subject. The state also creates standardized tests and other performance measures in order to assess student achievement. Furthermore, it is the responsibility of the state to provide necessary materials and resources to local school districts so that students have the opportunity to accomplish the learning goals set forth by state educational agencies. Another operational function of the state is establishing statewide graduation requirements in terms of credits and competencies.

District level operational procedures

Operational procedures at the district level consist mainly of developing policies in regard to curriculum, funding, and teaching. Guidelines for such policies are developed through locally-elected school board members who are responsible for ensuring that state laws and regulations that govern the operation of schools are followed exactly. When a district must make decisions about its curriculum content, it can implement any program of study it feel is necessary for the success of its schools; however, it is advantageous for a district to implement programs that are consistent for each grade level, as well as uniform for each academic subject. The school district should create master guidelines concerning core curriculum content that will explain the subjects that all schools within the district will offer, including the goals and objectives of the subjects or courses offered by each school.

School level operational procedures

Each campus must enact and regulate the operational procedures that have been established for it by the school district. However, schools are also responsible for designing and implementing their own operational procedures. It is important that these procedures are expressed clearly to staff members, parents, and students. When a school is making curriculum decisions, it must first receive curriculum goals and objectives from state educational agencies, as well as from the school district itself. The school will also seek appropriate input from parents and then build a curriculum that is guided by the all of the information and guidelines they have gathered. Schools should identify their goals and needs and then add any classes they feel are necessary in order to meet the students' needs while fulfilling their obligation to state and district organizations. As a team, school representatives will make decisions about scheduling, curriculum integration, and aligning and implementing the curriculum.

State educational agency contributions

State educational agencies have considerable power in contributing to the success of school-based management by providing different kinds of support to schools. Districts should be encouraged by state educational organizations to use school-based management as a tool to increase student performance, as well as enhance overall school conditions. Superintendents and the central office staff should be well educated about state guidelines related to school-based management, such as the fact that individual schools will need a great amount of authority and flexibility in order to make this type of management system effective in the improvement of the district's schools. In order for a school to properly implement the school-based management process, staff members need proper training and research-based information. States can provide these valuable resources and offer on-site assistance to help schools with the process. If state educational agencies can offer these services and a school's implementation process is successful, then those agencies can be confident that they are meeting the federal government's highly-regulated accountability requirements.

School district contributions

Schools will not be successful in a school-based management system if they do not have the support of the school district. School districts can help with school-based management success if they clearly express to all stakeholders what it means to have a school-based management and why it is desirable to use this type of organizational structure in the individual schools. Stakeholders should also be informed when a school-based management process will take place and how long it will take to fully implement it. Districts can also help by assessing a school's needs and providing the resources in order for the school-based management system to be successful on that campus. Districts should allow its schools the complete authority they need and encourage them to have an on-site council that includes at least one representative from each of the following groups: campus staff members, the business community, school administrators, and parents. This site-based council should be responsible for decision making and carrying out improvement plans.

To some degree, a school district will typically specify to its schools how a school-based management system should function; however, the campus principal will have a strong influence over the site-based operation as well. A principal can make the implementation process more successful if he or she thoroughly explains to the staff and parents why the school is making a change over to this type of management, along with emphasizing that the change is being made in order to help improve student achievement. Principals need to highly educate themselves about site-based management systems so that they are able to answer all questions that teachers and parents may have. Principals should also emphasize that site-based management systems provide a way to make important campus-wide decisions as a group, and all members will have a voice. A disadvantage to school-based management is that the complete implementation process can take up to five years.

Role of federal government

The primary role of the federal government in regard to education is to carry out the legal responsibility of protecting the right of every citizen to acquire free public education and to have an equal opportunity for learning. The federal government must also strive to improve the quality of education by funding research, providing aid to students, and understanding effective teaching methods so that they can disseminate information related to methodology for educators. The federal government solely funds and administers schools that are established for dependents of military and civilian personnel who are serving overseas. Although funding for these schools is received from the government, the schools are operated by local school boards. In regard to postsecondary institutions, the federal government does not exercise any control over the establishment of colleges and universities or the standards they maintain, with the exception of some academic programs that prepare a person for a career officer in the military.

Role of state government

Each state has its own laws to govern the operation of public schools. These laws establish and regulate the policies and requirements for the proper operation of public schools. In most states, a state board of education enforces these laws under the leadership of a chief state school officer, who works alongside professional educators. The laws that govern membership into the state board of education and the selection of its leaders vary from state to state. The primary responsibilities of the chief state school officer include distributing funds to local education authorities, overseeing the certification of teachers, providing training programs for teachers in order to improve standards, administering state laws, and providing certain advisory services to superintendents and school boards. State governments also play a role in deciding the length of the school day and year, establishing graduation requirements, and regulating school transportation, health services, and fire protection. They must also ensure that private schools follow the proper approval processes for licensure or accreditation.

Role of local authorities

With the exception of Hawaii, states are divided into local administrative districts, and each district has the responsibility of regulating the public schools encompassed by its district. The board of education, which usually has about five to seven members, governs the local district and operates the public school system via the district staff and the superintendent. The school board and superintendent have the responsibility of preparing the school budget, hiring personnel, maintaining school buildings, ensuring that students have appropriate transportation to and from school, and providing funds for school equipment and supplies. In addition to conforming to state law, local educational authorities are also responsible for carrying out regulations that govern the operations of schools. There are some limitations on the actions of school boards, which are regulated by state legislatures or state education agencies.

Role of national associations

Most national associations are non-profit membership organizations that represent their members' interests before the government. Other responsibilities of an association include assisting its members with certain services and helping regulate standards that are within their areas of interest and jurisdiction. Although national associations are non-governmental organizations, they can have a powerful influence in national policymaking and are sometimes consulted by the federal and state governments according to the association's area of expertise. Many teachers' unions can provide teachers with services, such as legal council, and give teachers a voice when they believe reform is needed. If, for example, a teacher feels that there are factors hindering his or ability to teach and the district has not made an effort to improve the situation, then the teacher can go to his or her professional union, which can use its influence to put pressure on individuals to fix the situation.

Zero-based budgeting

Zero-based budgeting is an approach to budgeting that is based on the idea that all activities will be examined before they are included in a school's budget, regardless of whether they were part of the budget the year before. When using a zero-based budgeting process, it is important that administrators remember what the mission and goals are of the school before beginning to make the budget. An administrator will have to examine each program and activity that was in the budget the previous year and determine if those programs and activities proved to be essential for students to achieve success. In doing so, an administrator may have to rank the importance and necessity of each program. Once the administrator has determined which programs will remain or be added to the budget, then a decision needs to be made about how to allocate resources to each one.

Site-based budgeting

Site-based budgeting moves authority and resources away from centralized administrative power and places financial responsibility on the district's individual schools. When districts choose to use a site-based budgeting approach, a campus has the authority to determine its own staffing levels within district guidelines, as well as choose its own vendors and service providers. Each campus also has the freedom to make purchases without filing special paperwork or asking for permission from the school board or from central administration. When schools use site-based budgeting, the decision-making process is left in the hands of the campus administrator, teachers, and, at times, community leaders. This type of approach allows more flexibility within the school and can build a culture of trust among administrators, staff, parents, and students. This approach can also increase student achievement because the school can make important decisions regarding its students because staff members have firsthand knowledge of the needs of their students.

Distribution of financial resources

Because most of a school's financial resources come from the district, the district can determine what resources the school will receive. In addition to having the power to distribute financial resources to a certain individual, group, or program, an administrator can also acquire financial resources from a variety of sources, such as government or private grants. An administrator can work with staff members, parents, and possibly students to develop ways to earn money for the school. Possibilities could be donations, bake sales, carnivals, or other fundraisers. It is the responsibility of the administrator to make the final decision about how these funds will be distributed. Financial resources can be distributed for use in a number of ways; they can be used to improve school buildings or fund special projects that teachers might want to undertake. However, an administrator must ensure the funds are distributed equally so that no favoritism is shown.

Centralized budget

In a centralized budgeting system, a school district pays bills, collects revenues, distributes resources to the schools as needed, and ensures that all individuals are given an equal portion of revenues. A district's overall risks are low with a centralized budget; however, so are the rewards for individual campuses. Because a school is not allowed to control its own income, a campus is dependent on the economic situations of other campuses at any given time. This type of budgetary system does not allow for individuals to be creative and does not enhance an individual's entrepreneurial spirit. Although districts that use a centralized budget attempt to distribute the revenue equally so that conflict is not caused between the district's schools, it does not eliminate the possibility of conflict within the budgeting department as to how much funding each school will get.

Decentralized budget

In a decentralized budgeting system, each school pays for its own expenses and retains most of the revenue it generates, giving the inidvidual school more financial responsibility and accountability. This allows for more freedom to be creative with ways to generate revenue and how the funds will be used. This type of budgeting process can have high risk, as there is no additional financial support from the district if a school's money runs out. However, a school's potential for growth is much higher with a decentralized budget than with a centralized budget. For instance, there is no limit on how much money one school can earn; this, in return, can motivate staff members, teachers, parents, and students to generate additional funds for the school through fundraisers and donations. Administrators must ensure that the strategic planning for spending funds aligns with the school's mission and goals.

Collaborative budgeting process

While a principal is ultimately responsible for setting and overseeing his or her budget, much of the budget will be allocated to programs and processes run by other people, such as those staff members to whom the principal has delegated budgetary responsibility. For instance, a vice principal might be in charge of the budget for the school's custodial staff, while the campus librarian has his or her own budget for purchasing books and other materials for the school's media center. Similarly, teachers know what they need in order to teach their classes and will most often depend on departmental funding for those things. A principal must consult with all staff members so that he or she has a comprehensive picture of all the school's financial needs and obligations. It is also important that the budgeting process is open to examination and that staff members know what goes into the budget; treating the budget like classified information will generate mistrust among the staff, and morale will suffer. A principal is also responsible for communicating with the district about staffing budgets, and the district will have guidelines and formulas it expects the principal to follow when preparing the budget. The more information a principal has from knowledgeable sources, the better he or she is able to prepare a workable budget.

School-based decision making is the model for most public schools today, but when it comes to budget processes, most schools still must follow very detailed policy and procedural guidelines set by school districts. Districts often have standard formulas for administrative salaries, the number of teachers a school should have, how much money a school receives for special education, how frequently a school is allowed to make physical plant upgrades, etc. A principal and his staff members may have some flexibility in certain line items and may be able to request more money or staff when needed. In general, however, the district will have in place set guidelines for the formation of a budget, and the principal will be expected to follow these guidelines.

Collective bargaining

Collective bargaining is an agreement between an employer and employee, usually involving the employee's labor union. The agreement typically states what terms have been agreed upon concerning wages, hours worked, and benefits, among other employment issues. A collective bargaining agreement cannot address every issue that might arise; however, there can be an unwritten agreement about how conflict will be resolved according to both the law and the customary practices of the school. Although a wide range of topics can be agreed upon, federal and state laws limit collective bargaining to some degree. The agreements made cannot violate any civil rights or reduce safety standards that are clearly stated under the Occupational Safety and Health Act. While there is not a requirement stating that the employer and union must reach an agreement, there should always be bargaining done in good faith between the parties involved.

Incremental and zero-based budgeting

Incremental budgeting uses the previous year's budget numbers to derive the current year's numbers. Once such details as student and staff numbers, course changes, inflation, and physical repairs have been determined for the current year, then last year's numbers are adjusted to reflect this year's needs. Incremental budgeting often uses formulas based on student demographics to arrive at staffing and equipment numbers. Incremental budgeting does not require administrators to revise all line items from year to year. When a school depends on a zero-based budgeting system, budgeting begins from scratch each year. Administrators must look at each line item and then estimate the money necessary for each in the upcoming year. Zero-based budgeting forces administrators to review each line item critically to determine if the item or category is still necessary; zero-based budgeting is a more objective method of budgeting, as it does not assume that all of last year's items will be continued during the upcoming year. Because zero-based budgeting is a more difficult and time-consuming method of budget preparation, most public schools use incremental budgeting.

Tax revenues

Because money derived from tax revenues rarely covers all of a school's budgetary needs, many schools depend on outside fundraising to supplement their budgets. Booster clubs, class-organized sales, and artistic performances and fairs are familiar to parents and vital to most schools. Vendors partner with schools to sell their products, which include everything from baked goods to stationery to toys and holiday crafts, and split the profits. Schools also seek grants from businesses and nonprofit organizations; such grants are normally targeted for specific subjects or programs in the school. Regardless of how the money is raised, most districts have guidelines for the collection and expenditure of fundraising revenue.

Marxist theory

Marxist theorists believe that organizations are created to benefit managerial control rather than to achieve efficiency. They also believe that workers must be stripped of their skills in order to become mindless repetitive workers who are a part of a machine. Since there is work division, a bureaucratization of organizations is created. Marxists also believe that hierarchy develops not as a way to coordinate work production, but as a way to control the means of accumulating capital. Marxists theorists see organizational structures as being similar to a nation; they are highly influenced by governmental and political structures. Marxists also believe that class stratification and conflict are caused by the social relations of workers in a society. Such conflict is not related to the individual characteristics of the workers, but is a result of their position in the labor system.

Complexity theory

The complexity theory is used in the domain of strategic management and organizational studies in order to understand how organizations can adapt to their environments. When an organization is able to share similar characteristics of its environment, then it is more likely to have sustainability. Recent studies of this theory have added to the understanding of how concepts from the complexity sciences can be used to understand organizational studies and strategic management. Theorist Karl Weick, for example, has applied the complexity theory to his loose coupling theory and interest in causal dependencies.

Garbage Can Model

Developed to explain certain behaviors that contradict the classical theory, the Garbage Can Model is based on the systemic-anarchic perspective that explains the decision-making process of an organization. According to the Garbage Can Model, problems within an organization trigger decision-making responses. As a result, the organization will go through the "garbage" in order to find a solution. This theory uses the term "garbage can" because the theory states that organizations brainstorm to find solutions that are then discarded when a final solution is reached. When different problems arise at a later time, organizations have the option of searching through the "garbage" of previously considered solutions in order to find an appropriate solution.

Henri Fayol's principles

Henri Fayol's first principle of management involves the division of work. He states that repetition of the same activity will increase output because the person performing the activity will increase his or her speed. Taking that fact into account, the work should be divided according to skill and given to the person who can perform that skill the fastest. The next principle describes the authority and responsibility of a person in a management position. Fayol states that an individual with authority has the right to give orders and expect obedience from those beneath him; however, with this authority comes with great responsibility. Discipline is outlined in another principle, as discipline is needed for an organization to run smoothly. Unity of command is also important, along with unity of direction. According to Fayol, individuals within an organization must have common goals and be able to follow orders. Fayol's next principle is the subordination of interests to the general interest, meaning that a person's interests should be focused on the success of the organization, not on his or her individual success. Fayol's other principles outline personnel, centralization, order, equity, stability, personnel tenure, and initiative.

Staffing numbers

Most districts require their schools to use standard formulas for determining the number of teachers and administrative staff hired. Most of these formulas are based on such student data as age, grade, and total number of students. School districts generally have set ranges of teacher-student ratios for their campuses. In districts that use campus-based decision making, an individual school might have more leeway in determining how many teachers and administrative personnel they can employ. Given the current scarcity of teachers applying for certification each year, many districts have had to raise teacher salaries to attract and retain skilled teachers, and it has become a struggle for schools to hire enough teachers while paying both new and veteran higher salaries. A complete picture of a district's teaching staff number is contained in Schedule II of the AEIS report.

Emergency plans

In the event of an emergency, a school must have a fully-developed plan for responding to the emergency so that staff members and students know what procedures they should follow in order to remain as safe as possible. Contagious disease outbreaks, fire, catastrophic weather, outbreaks of violence (whether by students, outsiders, or a terrorist attack), or environmental catastrophes are all situations for which a school can prepare ahead of time. A comprehensive and detailed plan outlining what students and staff members should do if any of these scenarios transpire must be not only established, but also practiced. Led by their principal, staff members should run emergency drills to rehearse where to go and what actions to take if an emergency strikes; students will go through similar drills. All staff members will have a copy of the disaster plan, the plan will be revised periodically, and the staff will meet periodically to discuss these revisions. Emergencies cannot be avoided and by their natures are unpredictable, but if a principal and his or her staff members have done their emergency preparation planning, then they can help minimize damage and loss.

Parents expect schools to make every possible effort to keep their children safe, and they also expect to be notified about things that happen to their children while they are in school. For this kind of communication to be successful, it is necessary that parents are familiar with the school's emergency plans. The school will have a procedure in place for notifying all parents in the event of an emergency. For parents, this plan clearly details who they should call in order to obtain information, and how and when parents can pick up their children from school. Today, thanks to cell phones and PDAs, parents learn of emergencies as soon they happen. Recently, for example, several schools have experienced lockdown situations due to violence or threatened violence, and students were calling and texting their parents as soon as the situations arose. However, student-to-parent contact does not absolve the school of its duty to make parents aware as soon as an emergency arises. When a situation is less dire than an immediate emergency but still of concern to parents and students—an unsuccessful kidnapping attempt near the campus or a student's contracting a serious illness for which other students need to receive treatment, for instance—the school is obligated to contact parents with all relevant information as soon as possible.

An administrator must work with local emergency personnel when making the disaster contingency plan. Local fire departments, police, hospitals and health care workers must be part of the planning; there should be a staff person or people to act as liaisons with these local emergency personnel in disaster preparation. In case of accidents, violence, bad weather or environmental events it will be necessary to call on fire, EMS or police (maybe all three), and the various departments and the school should have already worked together to plan for disaster. Most states and districts already require such planning and liaising for disaster prevention and limitation.

Staff development programs

The purpose of staff development programs is to improve schools in order to improve student performance. Administrators should select staff development programs that are related to both district and campus-level planning and decision making. If staff development is to be effective, it should focus on what the assessed needs are of the people who are participating in it. The content of staff development programs typically concentrates on how to improve specific skills. Because teachers often feel overwhelmed by the introduction of unfamiliar concepts every time they attend a staff development workshop, staff development is most effective when teachers can relate to the content being presented because of their prior experiences. Teachers should also be shown a demonstration of the strategic model that is to be implemented; if not, they might not understand how the program can be applied to their classrooms. As a result, they will not even attempt to put to use what they have been presented in staff development. Because modeling it may not be satisfactory enough for all teachers, there should be a follow-up to help with the implementation of a new skill.

Assessing performance

The evaluation methods an educator uses to measure student performance depend primarily on the curriculum being covered and the abilities of the students who are taking the class. In recent years, teachers have increasingly complained about assessing students through traditional written tests. Many teachers strive to implement alternative ways of assessing students' performance and levels of comprehension through active participation, a method that calls for students to perform tasks related to what they have learned in order to demonstrate his or her understanding. For instance, a student in a family and consumer sciences education class might be required to prepare a nutritionally balanced meal or to visit a local daycare center. Administrators can help teachers achieve success in using alternative means of assessment by encouraging them and supporting their innovative ideas. Administrators must first help teachers determine the major educational goals they want students to accomplish in a designated period of time. Next, administrators and teachers should agree upon the behaviors or skills students should be able to demonstrate regarding these goals before making a decision concerning how to assess the students' performance.

Developing tests

When administrators help teachers develop and evaluate valid tests, they have more confidence that the data gathered from these tests will be accurate and reliable. By providing staff development opportunities that focus on methods of developing classroom assessments, an administrator can sharpen a teacher's skills in creating tests that are suitable for students in his or her class. Before generating tests, a teacher will first analyze what information was taught to the students and then decide what objectives will be tested. Because testing every single objective is almost impossible, it is important for a teacher to choose the objectives that are most significant. Next, the teacher must decide what the weight will be for each objective, which sets the criteria by which the test will be scored. Once those decisions are made, then it is time for the teacher to select the format of each question. There are a variety of ways to ask a question: multiple choice, essay form, true/false, or fill in the blank. The next step is organizing how the questions will be arranged, followed by writing clear directions so that students understand what is expected of them when they are taking the test.

Equal opportunity for females

The goal of any school district is to provide an equal-opportunity environment for both genders. By keeping informed about current trends in both technology and gender issues in the field of education, campus administrators can be instrumental in ensuring that females have the same opportunities as males in areas of technology and are encouraged to pursue interests in computers and engineering. By developing appropriate educational programs, an administrator can effectively address the gap between genders in regard to technology. As a result, even if a female student does not demonstrate an interest in technology, she can be exposed to a curriculum that allows her to use technology in subjects that do interest her. Technology can be integrated in history, language arts, music, and many other subjects to enhance the learning of both male and female students.

Holding teachers accountable

To ensure that students are receiving the best education possible, effective administrators acknowledge the importance of holding teachers accountable for their teaching. Teachers can be held accountable by being required to provide administrators with copies of their lesson plans, by exhibiting examples of student work, and by clearly defining the goals of both the school and their classrooms. Unfortunately, some teachers feel as if their abilities are being called into question and become defensive when they are reminded that administrators will hold them accountable for what happens in their classrooms by monitoring their teaching methods and measuring their students' achievement. Despite opposition from teachers, administrators must clearly express to teachers what is expected of them in terms of accountability. Administrators can help teachers be accountable by providing them with necessary materials and always being willing to provide them support and encouragement. Teachers need to be reassured that they are important and that their voices and concerns are heard.

Teacher workshops

Workshops are one kind of instructional tool used to improve the skills of teachers. However, these workshops and other professional development programs should be evaluated in order to ensure their effectiveness. Evaluating a workshop can provide useful information to the agencies that fund these workshops, the institutions that sponsor them, and the workshop instructors themselves as they seek input about how to improve their presentations. Evaluations reflect whether participants have found a workshop to be applicable to teaching or otherwise valuable to their professional growth. From evaluations completed by participants, the instructor of a workshop can learn a variety of information that will help him or her plan future classes, determine the most successful procedures for conducting the workshop, decide what activities are most effective, and make changes if necessary. For extensive, detailed input, two different kinds of evaluations should be given: formative and summative. A formative evaluation completed during a workshop's program can be used to make immediate changes in the presentation or to review information that might have been unclear, while a summative evaluation at the end of a workshop can be used to assess how well participants have met the goals.

School-based management

In a school-based management situation, the training teachers receive can be delivered in a number of different ways. Funding for these training sessions comes from a variety of sources; it can come from statewide professional organizations or grants or by diverting funds from other budget areas. For instance, schools will often use a surplus of funds to send teachers to training, or they will make cuts in some areas of the school budget and then use that money for teacher training. Many statewide professional organizations or foundations are generous in helping sponsor teacher training or providing other support for professional development programs. In most cases, a school district will hold district-wide workshops for teachers and other staff members. The instructors for these workshops can be hired consultants or fellow staff members who have been trained to lead a workshop.

Site-based management

Site-based management is an organizational strategy that permits each campus within a district to plan and make its own decisions in directing and supporting the improvement of student performance. Campus-based planning and decision-making committees assume responsibility for such management decisions as hiring staff, scheduling, and budgeting for that particular campus. A site-based committee also develops, reviews, and revises the school's campus improvement plan, as well as its goals. Because teachers participate in curriculum development, a site-based management approach allows for more flexibility in deciding what instructional programs best meet the individual needs of students. Since planning and decision-making processes lie in the hands of administrators and teachers, teachers feel more empowered and in control of their teaching methods. This approach also provides a great deal of opportunity for group discussion about decisions regarding the school. A disadvantage of site-based management is that committee members can be confused about what their specific roles and responsibilities include. Also, power struggles can develop between administrators, teachers, and parents. A majority vote is usually the basis for resolving conflicts and finalizing decisions.

Staff development training

In most all school districts, staff development is a requirement for teachers and other staff members. Administrators and teachers should work together to avoid having training sessions selected by central-office staff who might never have even visited any of the schools and therefore know little about the needs of a school or its teachers. Schools that encourage teachers and administrators to work together to develop staff development training sessions have better results because the parties involved in selecting topics for training can decide what best supports the needs and goals of the school. If teachers and other staff members have input in choosing training sessions, then they will have a greater sense of responsibility and feel as if they are directly contributing to the improvement of the school. Teachers may also take a greater interest in the sessions and not feel they are obligated to go in order to fulfill a requirement.

Effective teacher evaluation

The purpose of the teacher evaluation system is for administrators to measure teacher competency and help teachers develop professionally. Evaluations also serve as means of providing teachers with feedback about their teaching methods and classroom needs, both strengths and deficiencies. Administrators ensure not only that state standards for teacher evaluations are implemented, but also that teachers have these standards clearly expressed to them before and after an evaluation. When an administrator is evaluating a teacher, he or she should consider elements that may not be addressed in state-established evaluation criteria, such as the variety of teaching methods a teacher can use. Effective evaluations include other sources of information about the teacher's performance besides an administrator's 45-minute visit to the classroom.

Management decisions

An administrator frequently acts as the manager of a school. When an administrator is required to make management decisions, his or her goal is to enhance both teaching and learning while supporting the mission of the school. Administrators in a managerial role coordinate activities that support the school's goals and make decisions that assist their staff members. Additionally, an administrator who acts as a manager has the responsibility of hiring personnel and maintaining or discontinuing educational programs.

Personnel decisions

An administrator's organizational and operational role in dealing with personnel is an important one. An administrator must always keep in mind that he or she is a powerful leader in the development of a school's community. As such, an administrator has the ability to change the dynamics of the school's community with every person he or she hires, which makes hiring individuals who share the common goals and interests of the campus a top priority. Another personnel decision involving an administrator concerns the appropriate placement of a new hire. After an employee is hired, an administrator must decide, usually with input from staff members and the district's superintendent, in what area or on what grade level the new staff member will be most beneficial to the students and school. Afterwards, administrators are responsible for monitoring the progress of the new staff member and ensuring that the he or she is equipped with the necessary resources to help the school achieve its goals.

Personnel role changes

When a school system decides to implement school-based management on its campuses, there is a major impact on all the roles of the stakeholders. A superintendent's input, direction, and support are needed to ensure proper implementation of the approach. A superintendent also has the responsibility of explaining to the community what school-based management is and why it is effective. A principal's role changes the most because he or she is looked upon as the school's leader and chief executive. A principal assumes the responsibility of creating programs for his or her campus instead of enforcing policies that have already been made by someone else. With this increased authority comes more accountability. Teachers are affected by school-based management as well. The most important change for teachers is that they have an equal voice in the decision-making process instead of simply following policies that have already been created for them.

Overlap of information

The Supervisor is expected to know how to use all the sources of information that can be gathered from the campus community: student information (ages, test scores, ethnicity, at-risk factors, etc.), teacher information, information about parents and caregivers (involvement, or lack thereof), community issues (safety, economics) and current trends in public education. With a thorough understanding of these data the Supervisor can then develop (propose) a definable and realistic vision for the campus. Part of realizing the vision is recognizing what is needed to implement (prepare) it – how much money it will cost, how many professional staff and in what capacities they will serve, what will be the physical demands for buildings, equipment, supplies, what specific kind of support is needed from the larger community. This preparation requires a broad, eagle's eye view of the campus' current state, which can only be arrived at through collection and evaluation of all the sources of data mentioned above. Armed with this data the Principal can assemble a coherent picture of what he or she will need.

Expectations for students

Administrators should set high expectations for students; however, they should take into account the fact that every student is unique and set expectations accordingly. One of the first considerations when an administrator is establishing expectations is the student's developmental level. An administrator needs to be aware of any learning disabilities or developmental deficiencies a student might have because expectations should not be set too high if they are not developmentally appropriate for students. Another factor an administrator should consider is the instructional level for the students. Expectations should not be set so high that they surpass a student's appropriate instructional level. A kindergartener, for instance, cannot be expected to perform on the same level as a sixth grader. The opposite is also true; expectations should not be set so low that students will be performing below grade level and not encouraged to achieve anything beyond that level.

Gaining support for change

Certain groups that will be affected the most when changes are implemented in a school include faculty, students, parents, the school board, the administration, and the state's department of public education. These groups are important in the change-making process because of their influence; each separate entity can provide either the most support or the most resistance to the changes proposed by administrators. Administrators must remember that every group will have its opinions, and the most professional approach is to respect, listen to, and accept those opinions even if the administrator knows that they will have no effect on the changes that will be implemented. One of the most important groups an administrator needs to consider during the change–making process is the faculty. It is crucial to get the faculty involved because if faculty members do not understand why change is needed, they will be less supportive and, as a result, the implementation of a new program might not be successful.

Innovation adoption

The first stage an administrator goes through during the adoption of an innovation is the awareness stage, which involves becoming aware of a new innovation without having sufficient information about it. Oftentimes during the awareness stage, an administrator does not have a strong enough interest in finding out more information about the subject. Next, during the interest stage, an administrator begins to show interest in an innovation, gathers more information about it, and begins to develop negative or positive feelings about the innovation. During the mental stage, an administrator will decide that the innovation is something worth trying, proceed to evaluate the innovation formally, and determine how it will be implemented. He or she may also ask respected members of the school community to assess the innovation. During the trial stage, the innovation is implemented on a trial basis. Following that is the adoption stage, when the innovation is fully implemented. The last stage is the integration stage, during which the new innovation becomes a routine.

Many times, innovations are unsuccessful because teachers do not understand what their responsibilities are in their new roles, even if they have had orientation before the process is implemented. Administrators should never assume that teachers will fully understand their roles after one or two orientation sessions because teachers may not initially be confident that they have the knowledge and skills necessary to implement an innovation in their classrooms. In addition to ensuring that teachers receive the proper training and assistance needed to fulfill their duties, an administrator should solicit feedback from staff and faculty in the beginning stages of implementation. Another reason innovations fail is due to a lack of materials teachers might need to carry through with the new program. If an administrator wants an innovation to succeed, it is his or her responsibility to make sure that a sufficient quantity of appropriate materials is available. Finally, innovations are often unsuccessful because certain aspects of the school's existing program have not been changed to assist with the teacher's new role.

Conflict initiation

Although all administrators want to avoid conflict, it is almost impossible to prevent conflict entirely when an individual or group is not performing at the level they should be and is resistant to change. In fact, situations may arise that call for administrators to initiate conflict themselves. Because an administrator is responsible for ensuring that all staff members are performing to the best of their abilities, conflict may be a necessary means by which to bring about improvement. If, for example, an administrator becomes involved in a situation where he or she observes a problem with a teacher but the teacher disagrees with that assessment, then avoiding conflict will most likely not be probable. It is important that all possible outcomes of conflict initiation are considered beforehand and that conflict is absolutely necessary for improvement to take place.

Dealing with conflict

In dealing with conflict, administrators have four primary options. One option is to use the cooperative approach, which involves an administrator's being willing to listen to other people's points of view and showing empathy toward those individuals. After these things have been accomplished, then an administrator can attempt to find a compromise that will lead to a mutually-satisfactory solution. Another approach to dealing with conflict is confirming, which means that an administrator communicates to the people involved in a situation that he or she feels they have a great deal of competency and that their capabilities are highly respected. Another option is to use the competitive approach, which views conflict as a win-lose battle; the only way for the conflict to end is for one of the groups involved in the conflict to back down from the conflict. The last option an administrator has is to use the avoidance approach. This approach is passive in that the groups stop discussing the situation, which brings an end to the conflict, but no issues are resolved.

Resolving conflict

Research has shown that administrators who use both the cooperative and confirming approaches for conflict resolution have much more success in resolving conflict than those administrators who choose use the competitive or avoidance techniques. The cooperative and confirming approaches are considered to be more successful because individuals feel that they are recognized for their competence. As a result, they feel a sense of security and value and are more likely to be motivated to resolve the conflict. The competitive approach is typically less effective. Oftentimes, administrators will use the competitive approach when they think they can win the conflict, while they use the avoidance approach when they are uncertain of how to handle the situation. The cooperative and confirming approaches require administrators to have strong interpersonal skills; if they lack these special skills, then it is best for the administrator to designate someone who does posses these skills to act as a facilitator in resolving conflict.

Power struggle bargaining

Administrators might find themselves in a situation in which all parties involved feel strongly about their objectives. As a result, conflict cannot be avoided, and the chance of an agreement is impossible without some kind of intervention. This situation is called power struggle bargaining. Administrators will do everything within their power to resolve this conflict; however, they remain convinced that the solution to a problem lies only within the option they support. Such steadfastness can hurt people's feelings and destroy many personal and professional relationships between individuals who are involved in the situation. Many times, a conflict may seem to be resolved, only to reappear in future situations, resulting in still more power struggle bargaining. At some times, it may be necessary for administrators to get involved in power struggle bargaining; however, if they want the conflict to end in their favor, they must assess their power and authority accurately to avoid what could be disastrous results for the school as a whole.

Conflict avoidance methods

Techniques that can be used for conflict resolution include conflict avoidance methods. One of these techniques is called the withdrawal method, where an administrator chooses not to argue in a certain situation and accepts whatever the outcome might be. When administrators act as if an issue does not matter to them personally, they are employing the strategy of indifference. An administrator can also avoid any circumstances that would cause conflict; this method is called isolation. Using the smooth over method involves an administrator's completely accepting a situation and minimizing any arguments that may arise from it. The consensus method allows people to discuss their views and try to persuade others to agree with them. Although these methods avoid conflict, they do not resolve it. Nevertheless, these methods may be necessary for administrators to use, especially in situations when one group feels powerless in changing the views of another group.

Problem-solving approach to conflict resolution

The problem-solving approach is another method of conflict resolution and can be the most effective. However, this method is usually successful only if the parties involved are willing to compromise and if agreement is actually possible. It is also important that all parties can contribute something valuable and are confident that the solution made will not exclude their interests. Groups should be allowed the opportunity to state their opinions, along with their conflicting positions. Groups should also restate the opinions and positions of their opponents as way of assuring them that their points of view have been heard and understood. Doing so also allows an administrator to be certain that groupa are clearly listening to each other. An administrator should then consult with the groups to clarify whether a conflict still exists. If so, group members should further discuss why their opinions and arguments are valid to them. When all members are finished stating their viewpoints, the administrator should ask the groups if they have anything further that they need to add to the discussion that will help in making a decision. Even when the problem-solving approach is used, there remains the possibility that conflict may still be unavoidable.

Fact finding

Once an administrator has heard each party's point of view in a dispute, it is important for the administrator to then examine the facts of the situation and determine which arguments are valid. Many times, people consider their opinions to be unquestionable facts; however, those facts need to be verified. It is very common for a person's emotions to distort his or her memory and the true facts of the situation. Administrators must also recognize that while individuals involved in the conflict can agree on the facts, their interpretations can be completely different. An administrator's goal in the process of fact-finding is to clarify the issues that the parties do agree upon and then identify and address the areas that are the source of disagreement. The administrator is put in a position to act as mediator, a role that is much easier to play if he or she is not one of the parties at conflict. If he or she is involved in the conflict, then it is best if a neutral person acts as mediator.

Adjusting staffing patterns

The formative assessment will take a snapshot of classes, staffing, student demographics, student to teacher ratios, curriculum and instruction. With that snapshot, campus and district administration will develop a program for adjusting staff patterns and classroom management in ways that they think - based on research, professional literature and examination of other schools – will improve student performance, facilitate classroom control, decrease disciplinary incidents, etc. Once the program has been implemented, the Principal, staff and teachers will monitor it, reporting regularly on various observations and management and, at the conclusion of an agreed time frame, another snapshot will be taken. This snapshot will measure the same factors that were measured prior to implementation of the adjusted staffing patterns and classroom management tools. And the summative assessment will show whether the program achieved what it was intended to achieve.

Staff assessment process

Teacher assessment tells you how the teacher is doing – how well or how poorly he's doing his job, how well or how poorly she is using her skills, whether she has the skills and the knowledge she should have, etc. But that is only the beginning. The second part – which many schools and school districts neglect – is professional development based on the results of the assessment. What weaknesses and areas needing improvement did the assessment reveal? What can the teacher learn, or do, to do her job better? Remember the design-implement-assess-modify paradigm that runs throughout the competencies – assessment should always be followed by, if not a modification, an enhancement or improvement.

Professional staff development

No matter how well you or your teachers are doing your jobs, you can do better. No matter how much you're doing, you can do more – or do it smarter. There is always room for improvement and that improvement comes as the result of education, skills enhancements, advanced training, professional growth – all of which comes through professional development. Teachers need to be challenged and grow and learn just like their students or they will stagnate, just like their students. Stagnating teachers cannot teach or inspire. Through professional development, which includes but need not be limited to conferences, workshops, advanced education, professional literature and independent research, teachers can increase their knowledge and sharpen their skills.

Conferences and teacher workshops are what most educators think of when they discuss professional development, but they need not limit themselves to that. Professional development may also be gained through professional literature – books and reports detailing current educational research and theory, or books by acknowledged expert educators covering their experiences and preferred methods. Teachers may also want to pursue further formal education, masters-level classes or similar programs at the university level. Peer to peer mentoring or consultation is also a valid method of professional development; districts may organize local seminars or programs for teachers to visit other schools and observe their programs or classes. Teachers may also apply for grants from government or private agency sources to conduct their own research into their areas of interest.

You have to take a studied, deliberate and pragmatic approach to teacher hiring. There is a shortage of qualified teachers nationwide; you must make efforts to recruit and hire the best, and the best for the areas in which you need them. You recruit and hire teachers according to your school's needs (because you will have done a needs assessment for this purpose already, naturally). Once teachers are hired, there must be in place an orientation and training program for them – you can't throw a teacher into the student shark pool and say "swim faster!" You must train them and help them adjust to your school. And you need to have in place, before the teachers are hired, an idea of how you plan to retain the good teachers, because competition between school districts is fierce in some places. Part of your teacher retention plan needs to be a comprehensive professional development program, one in which passionate and devoted teachers know they will have an opportunity to grow and expand their skills.

Assessment model

There are a number of assessment models in use among school districts; most districts in Texas use the Professional Development Assessment System for teacher assessments. Regardless of which assessment system a district chooses to use, the system should be consistent in the way it assesses teachers and staff; it should adhere to all state and legal guidelines; and all administrators should be trained and certified in its use. Just as in student testing, teacher testing should be carefully designed so that the test measures what it is meant to measure – a teacher's knowledge and skills set, and her expertise at using that knowledge and skill in the classroom. The assessment system should measure if, and how well, the teacher knows what she should know and if, and how well, she can impart that knowledge to her students. If the assessment model does not measure this, or if it is inconsistently applied from teacher to teacher or from school to school, it is not reliable and it will not be trusted by teachers. That is why it is necessary for all administrators with assessment responsibility to be trained and certified in the assessment model that the district uses.

Designing a professional development program

Two very important aspects of a professional development program should be legal issues and communication. The program must be in compliance with all state and local laws and regulations; school law and employment law is pretty voluminous concerning what teachers can and cannot be required to attend, learn, do, etc. Many school districts have binding agreements with unions concerning out of school hours and how much time can be required of teachers for extracurricular activities. Communication might be just as important. It is vital that the teachers understand, before they even show up, what the purpose of the particular program is – what will be required of them, what they will be expected to do, how the program is intended to benefit them. If they end up feeling that the program was irrelevant, poorly designed, not what it was advertised to be, they will be reluctant to participate in future development activities. Principals need to communicate clearly to teachers the importance of professional enrichment and to let teachers know that they, the Principals, are eager to help them, the teachers, take advantage of opportunities to enrich their skills and add to their expertise.

The needs assessment will determine what kind of professional development program is needed – who will be expected to use it, what it is supposed to accomplish for everyone who uses it, how much time and money will be involved. The Principal should ask for input from everyone who will be involved in the program, either in running it or, especially, in using it. In order for teachers and other staff members to actually use the program, they must buy into it – they need to have a voice in its design and selection. So the needs assessment must involve administrators and everyone who will use the program. It must be as comprehensive in scope as possible – taking a look at as many different professional enrichment opportunities as can be found and which can reasonably be expected to be useful (i.e., don't consider opportunities in areas 400 miles away when the school district is unlikely to approve airline fares). The needs assessment should be as objective as possible – look at the professional development needs of ALL staff members in ALL areas, not just the areas most popular (or problematic) at the moment. And include the school district in the needs assessment because the school district's money will likely be part of the budget.

Allocation of resources

Allocation is another name for a very familiar term in the competencies – alignment. Allocating time and money for professional development is simply a matter of correctly aligning your resources. You have teachers in various subjects at various grade levels; they all have a fixed amount of non-classroom time available in which to pursue professional enrichment opportunities; you have a fixed amount of money which you can devote to professional development; you have a fixed amount of time you can afford to let (and require) the teachers be out of the classrooms; you have (or should have) put together a program of various professional development opportunities your staff members can choose from. Now you need to match up staff members to program opportunities within time and budget constraints.

Development courses for adult learners

You need to keep in mind the needs and interests of adult learners, just as you try to pitch student education at the level of the kids you're targeting. Adults will be impatient with a poorly organized or overly long presentation – a tight format, maximizing the amount of information presented in the shorts time frame, will work best. However long or short the program, it should stick to the schedule advertised – if you say the class or the seminar is going to last 2 hours or 8 hours, it should not last 3 hours or 8.5 hours. This means you have to match the contents to the time frame available, and not try to cram too much or too complicated material into a short time frame. Make sure the program is relevant to your attendees – to *their* school and *their* needs. Adult learners are busy and often tired and stressed out by the time they show up for class; they've already worked a full day. Conduct the program or class at a time convenient to your attendees, and for teachers this will usually mean in the late afternoon or early evening. And maybe most importantly, provide food and drink – anyone who's ever done continuing education, no matter the field, will tell you that food and drink guarantees a higher attendance.

Professional development in technology matters

Technology now plays a leading role in instructional programs; children get their instruction in AV and multimedia formats, they use Web-based applications in the classroom, they use increasingly sophisticated equipment in laboratory settings, the school communicates with them and their parents via Web and email. Technology also forms a large part of the curriculum; we are living in a technology driven economy and students must be trained in its many uses and applications. So it's vital that teachers be trained in the uses and potential uses of technology for their teaching practices. Because technology, and particularly Internet and computer technology, advances so rapidly it is necessary for teachers to be trained on an ongoing basis; a minimum of yearly or semiannual workshops and refresher courses in computer and web use should be required of teachers in all school districts that have the financial and information infrastructure resources to provide it.

Administrators view of assessment

Administrators like that assessment can help improve a teacher's teaching. They also like that it serves as an accountability tool. It backs up their (the administrators') decisions for approving or denying tenure, promotions and demotions, and particularly because it can justify terminations. And of course because assessment is required by school boards and state bodies governing public schools. Administrators are less likely to look for, or hope for, a lot of variability in the design of the assessment system, as they will use it to assess many different people and so will take a more one-size-fits-all approach to testing.

Teacher's view of assessment

Teachers rate assessment programs based on how they are administered and how the people administering them are going to view the results (for lack of a better word, the "bias" or "agenda" that the assessors will be assumed to have). Teachers want assessment systems that help them become better teachers and help them see where their skills need improvement. They want an assessment system that realizes and allows for how complex a process teaching is, and that allows for all the different things that can affect student learning, all the many different conditions under which teachers work. And they want their assessments to take into account personal differences in teaching styles and beliefs about the nature and purposes of education in general.

Assessment of teacher's knowledge and skills

Two basic areas to be assessed are: the teacher's knowledge, and how the teacher uses that knowledge. All assessment systems attempt to answer those two questions; there are many different ways to do it, and many people disagree about which ways are most effective. Assessment comes down to measurement and interpretation, and the interpretation is a matter of professional judgment. The assessment model is supposed to identify and measure specific, discrete, clearly defined areas of knowledge and skill, and the assessor is trusted to be able to interpret the measurements. There is a lot of debate regarding what those specific, discrete and clearly defined areas should include, and there will be much that is inherently hard to measure – a teacher's teaching style, how he relates to his students, what types of material he uses in the classroom. There are factors affecting student learning outside a teacher's control – class size, school budget constraints, and local political pressures – how to account for that in grading a teacher's performance? And what kind of test should the teacher take himself? Several years ago almost 50% of the people taking the Massachusetts teacher assessment failed – it was considered to be poorly designed and unreasonably timed. Can such a test give an accurate picture of a teacher's knowledge and skill?

Teacher training

Every school has its own culture, processes and personality, even within the same district, so every time a teacher begins a new school, she will benefit from orientation and training specific to that school. Knowing the student body's demographics and cultural background; how the other teachers approach teaching; the school's recognized strengths and weaknesses; what you the Principally personally expect from teachers; what resources, including professional development, the school offers teachers; what out of classroom duties the teacher will be expected to carry – all of these are issues specific to each school, and the teacher needs to be familiar with them. Through orientation and training at the beginning of a teacher's tenure with a school will increase the likelihood that the teacher will remain at the school, and low teacher turnover is every Principal's desire.

Teacher recruiting, retention and dismissal

School districts poach each other's teachers on a regular basis. So, in addition to the difficulty caused by the fact that there are fewer people getting certified as teachers, once you've managed to hire enough qualified teachers you have to worry about keeping them. Some statistics claim that up to 50% of new teachers nationwide will not stay with teaching for a second year. School districts have begun different programs as an attempt to retain teachers, including merit pay programs, hiring and retention bonuses, letting teachers pick the schools they want to teach in, etc. All of these programs can present legal, financial or administrative problems. And it seems that dismissing teachers can be as difficult as hiring good ones in the first place. Thanks to several landmark Supreme Court decisions over the past two decades, it is now a very lengthy and legally complex process to fire a public school teacher; it involves a lot of documentation, counseling, notification and dealing with teachers' unions. Ideally, of course, one tries to hire only the best or the potential best in order to avoid the headaches of termination down the road, but it's not possible to avoid termination all the time.

Teacher supervision

The three models currently popular are clinical supervision, artistic supervision and peer assistance. Clinical supervision is the most widely used model and the most time consuming. It involves numerous conferences with the teacher under evaluation, observation of the teacher teaching, and analysis and interpretation of the lesson and data derived from observing the teacher. Artistic supervision tries to allow for the individuality, personality, and creativity of individual teachers – less of the scientific method, more intuition, more of an approach based on right-brain, artistic modes of thinking. The person who came up with this theory advocated watching a teacher's lesson the same way one might watch an artistic performance. Lastly, peer assistance involves experienced teachers observing and assisting teachers in their lesson plans and classroom management.

Peer assistance

Teachers do not often get the opportunity to watch other teachers teach – in most schools at least, teachers work by themselves in their classrooms. But some districts have begun evaluation programs in which teachers evaluate their peers; the National Education was opposed to the idea for a long time but has now come around to approving of it. It's not a widespread practice yet, but it has been implemented in some districts, with school board and union approval. In these districts, the teachers who do the evaluations do not have teaching duties themselves, so they have enough time to do fair and thorough assessments. Because of their experience, they are competent to assess all areas of teaching and to provide assistance to those teachers they are evaluating. In some districts, these teachers begin assisting teachers before they've assessed them, helping them plan lessons and develop teaching ideas. Some professionals have worried that teachers might tend to be lenient in their assessment of colleagues so that has not been the case in districts observed thus far.

Professional conflict

The school does not need a staff of professionals who agree with one another on everything, even if such a thing were possible. From disagreement comes (hopefully) dialog, and from dialog comes (eventually) consensus. Disagreements cause arguments, and arguments cause us to think about and reexamine our own ideas. If everyone reexamines his own ideas, and listens respectfully to others' ideas, consensus and accord comes about. And among professionals it usually leads to improvement or resolution of whatever was the topic of disagreement. The principal is not a shepherd leading a flock of docile sheep; he is a leader among leaders, a professional leading other professionals, and professionals have strong ideas, opinions, values and beliefs. That's what allows them to do such an emotionally and intellectually challenging job as teaching, and that's what makes a strong school and a campus culture of achievement.

Empowering staff

If the staff members have never been given or taught to exercise authority, they won't know what to do with it. You cannot tell an administrator that he's now in charge of planning science curriculum if he's never done it before, nor can a staff member who has never handled a budget suddenly be given budget oversight duties. Empowerment is a flashy word for responsibility – if you're empowered to do something, you are also responsible for how well or how poorly you do it. So before staff can be trusted to run things and make decisions they must be trained in what they're expected to do. And this training must be well planned, structured and monitored.

Analyzing staffing patterns, class schedules, and discipline

"Analyze the implications of various factors" just means to be aware of and consider everything that is involved in the education of the school's students. Notice change – recognize it, respond to it and, optimally, try to anticipate it. Take note of everything that affects how your teachers teach, and everything that affects how your students learn. Poorly designed class schedules make it difficult for students to get to their classes on time or have enough time to get the work done. Too few or (much rarer) too many teachers hinders effective instruction. Lax or inadequate discipline leads to badly managed classrooms, which disrupts learning and makes teaching impossible; overly strict or onerous discipline antagonizes students and parents and is not even effective in the long term. Staffing patterns, class scheduling formats, discipline practices and school organization structures affect students' daily lives, and that has a profound impact on their ability to learn.

Face time

The Superintendent is a manager of the whole school district, but most importantly he is a manager of people. He needs to stay in personal touch with all his staff and especially with his teachers and staff. If he wants to encourage them to grow and develop professionally, and to pursue professional development opportunities, he needs to do it in person. A show of personal concern, an effort at personal communication, is far more effective than sending emails and interoffice memos about upcoming conferences or new books. Teachers are busy, usually overworked, and professional development is one of those things that is easy to push down the "to do" list so that it never actually gets done. If the Superintendent has a personal relationship with his teachers he will be more attuned to their schedules, their time constraints, their particular professional concerns and he will be able to help them find the time and the appropriate venue for their professional development opportunities.

Health inventory

The "organizational health inventory" is a very popular management and human resource tool. The OHI attempts to take a comprehensive, 360 degree picture of the campus' staff. Ideally, input is sought from all campus stakeholders – administrative, teachers, admin staff, and other employees (custodial and kitchen staff, facilities staff, etc.) The OHI may contain questions which staff members are asked to answer, or it might contain a list of factors, assertions, assumptions (i.e., "the Superintendent discusses classroom management with teachers") with which respondents are asked to agree or disagree. How an OHI is designed, what it covers, how it weights questions and answers – all of these may vary. What's important is that an OHI be designed with input from all who will participate, so that it addresses issues relevant to the specific campus or district; that it be tested widely; that its use and interpretation be agreed upon by everyone involved. The OHI may be used as a formal or informal tool for assessing a school's health or dysfunction. It is a good tool for impartially (or as impartially as possible) describing staff members' perceptions of their relationship to the school and the school's administrative staff; it is probably more accurate than relying on anecdotal evidence. And it attempts to quantify what are for the most part intangible issues – collegiality, cooperation, job satisfaction, etc.

Superintendent professional development

Just as teachers will stagnate without ongoing education and professional enrichment, so will Superintendents. Leading and inspiring and mentoring a large group of professionals like teachers can be an emotionally and intellectually draining job, even if a very rewarding one. The Superintendent needs to recharge the mental batteries and stay current in the professional literature and theory just like his teachers do. If there are new and better methods for helping teachers handle classroom management, or for hiring and retaining the most talented teachers, or for developing effective school-family relationships, the Superintendent needs to know about them.

Conflict manager

Since conflict (or disagreement, to use a less loaded word) among professionals is not always avoidable, and many times actually a sign of a healthy and high-performing campus culture, it is the Superintendent's job to manage that conflict, not just make it go away. But the Superintendent cannot simply order everyone to come to an agreement. He must lead the way, by getting everyone talking, making everyone aware that their opinions are valued and will be respected, encouraging everyone to listen to what everyone else is saying, and making it clear to everyone that they themselves are responsible for forming a consensus, finding a solution. He treats them all like the dedicated professionals they are, thereby setting an example for the way they should treat each other. It is a hard thing to accomplish, but a person who cannot do it is not cut out for the Superintendentship.

Helping others lead

Because schools today must largely run themselves, and make decisions for themselves, school staff and teachers have a lot more responsibility than they used to. They now participate in the decisions that Superintendents once made alone. Collaborative decision making has meant empowerment of non- Superintendent administrative staff and teachers, and empowerment has meant responsibility. Responsibility means that the admin staff and teachers now making decisions have become leaders themselves, even if they don't technically oversee other people (and many times, they do). The Superintendent leads the professional staff, and the professional staff leads other staff members, and all together lead the school. It is one of the Superintendent's jobs to teach those professional staff how to lead others – how to seek input, manage conflict, build teams and consensus, how to make decisions with other people.

Authority and influence

Authority is decision making responsibility; if you have authority for something, you have the ability to make decisions about it and you have responsibility for those decisions. The Superintendent has authority over a great many things in the school district– personnel hiring and termination, budget, student discipline, building matters, overall curriculum design – he makes decisions about these areas, those decisions are valid and are implemented, and he is ultimately responsible for everything that happens in these areas, even things that are done by other people. Influence does not entail decision making responsibility or accountability. It is the Superintendent's ability to be involved in something, to have a say in matters, to be heard by those who do have decision making responsibilities and accountability. Influence is the ability to heard and heeded by those in authority. The Superintendent does not have authority over how the district will allocate funds, but he should have some influence in it.

Decision making

Everything that gets done in a school district gets done because decisions were made, and the Superintendent has a hand in almost every decision. What courses are taught, what teachers are hired or terminated, how and how much money is spent, dress codes and behavior codes and whether the school needs a new wing – all depend on decisions, decisions made at least in part by a Superintendent who has gathered and analyzed all the relevant data and applied his knowledge and expertise to the problem or situation. Superintendents must communicate with parents and students, and encourage and lead teachers, and they must write the checks and sign the work orders, yes – but most of all they make the decisions that keep the school district running. How to be decisive, how to use professional judgment, how and when to seek input when making decisions, how to know when a collaborative decision is necessary – all are necessary skills for a Superintendent.

Attributes of leadership

To be a truly effective leader the Superintendent must have the trust of the people he's leading. So he must have a coherent set of principles, a set of values that he adheres to in practice. He must be seen to be honest, impartial, and transparent in his dealings. He must have the necessary knowledge, expertise and experience to be a Superintendent. He needs to have a visible passion and devotion for his job, in order to inspire passion in those he leads. He must have fundamental business management skills so that he can competently handle budget and other administrative duties – school staff will not trust him to run the school effectively otherwise. He needs to have a clear vision of what the school and its culture needs to be, and he needs to know how to explain that vision to others. He should also have a stable personality – able to deal with conflicts and crises calmly and in a businesslike manner. And he must take responsibility for everything that happens on his watch, including mistakes and crises – he is the ultimate leader of the school and he takes ultimate responsibility for everything, and his people know that he will support them and not duck the hard calls or the negative feedback.

Practice Test

Practice Questions

1. A female member of a school's staff sends a letter to the superintendent of the school district. Her complaint is that her school's principal, who is male, calls her and other female employees by names such as "dear", "honey," and so on. The writer of the letter perceives this as disrespectful. In following up, the superintendent discovers the content of the complaint is confirmed as fact but also that the majority of the rest of the female staff do not perceive the principal as disrespectful in his forms of address. Which action by the superintendent regarding the complaint would be most suitable?

    a. Telling the letter writer that other females on the school staff do not agree with her about the names

    b. Telling the principal some staff are offended and the names do not set good examples for students

    c. Calling a meeting of female school staff and principal to review laws on workplace sexual harassment

    d. Calling a meeting with the principal about disrespect and asking him to make a public apology to staff

Questions 2–6 refer to the following information:

    Karen Arnold is a high school department chairperson and teacher with many years of experience. Her school has formed committees to plan and implement Professional Learning Communities (PLCs) in an effort to meet the adequate yearly progress (AYP) standard required of the school under the provisions of its Title I funding and in accordance with Superintendent Dr. Dillon's directive for all district schools to use PLCs to conform with the district's vision and mission statements. Ms. Arnold has filed a Level 1 complaint with her school's principal, Dr. Cleveland, alleging that he has hired only less-experienced and inexperienced teachers for the PLC planning committee, which will begin planning and writing curriculum in the summer and continue during the school year. She states this decision is motivated to save money and is discriminatory and ageist because these teachers are younger and paid less than she is; that the committee should include input from both new and experienced teachers; and that as a chairperson, she deserves the commensurate pay that she has been denied. She has talked with Dr. Cleveland and the curriculum director about this but did not receive acceptable responses. Dr. Cleveland's Level 1 response is that he accepted e-mail requests for committee membership over two weeks in August and sent an e-mail reminder two days prior to the request deadline. He states he did not receive an e-mail request from Ms. Arnold and did not know she wanted to serve on the PLC committee until receiving the formal complaint. He further alleges that salary and experience were not considered in hiring committee members. He denies her request to be on the committee. Ms. Arnold's Level 2 appeal states that Dr. Cleveland was well aware of her interest in committee membership through direct conversations, so his allegation of not knowing about it is not true. The school district's policy for complaints does encourage employees to pursue informal discussions with their principal or supervisor first and indicates a formal complaint may be filed if an informal conference does not resolve the issue. In the formal process, if the employee finds a Level 1 formal complaint is not satisfied by the principal or administrator's required written response, at Level 2, the employee may ask for a meeting with the assistant superintendent or designee to appeal the decision. If the Level 2 decision does not provide relief, the employee may request a meeting with the superintendent or designee at Level 3 to appeal it. The Level 3 administrator must respond in writing. If this does not provide relief, at Level 4, the employee can appeal it to the School Board. At each level, the employee can request copies of records, which must include documents from all previous levels.

2. Of the following choices, which action by Dr. Dillon, the superintendent, would be most likely to address the concerns raised by Ms. Arnold?
   a. Having the principal recommend employees to participate in the committee member hiring process
   b. Implementing a district policy of only hiring teachers without tenure to participate in hiring processes
   c. Adopting a district policy of giving every teacher the same pay for participating in the hiring processes
   d. Implementing a district policy to include representation of teachers in deciding on the hiring process

3. According to the policy of the school board, which of the following should Dr. Dillon do to respond to Ms. Arnold's Level 2 complaint?
   a. Dr. Dillon himself should meet with Ms. Arnold to discuss her grievance, following up with a summary of the meeting in a memo.
   b. Dr. Dillon should direct Dr. Cleveland, the high school principal, to meet with Ms. Arnold to talk about her concerns in this case.
   c. Dr. Dillon should assign his assistant superintendent to have a conference with Ms. Arnold, following up with a summary memo.
   d. Dr. Dillon should wait for the school district's decision about the PLC implementation before giving Ms. Arnold his response.

4. If Ms. Arnold decides to appeal the decision regarding her Level 2 grievance, what should Dr. Dillon's next action be in response to her appeal?
   a. Dr. Dillon should personally review Ms. Arnold's appeal and provide his response in writing.
   b. Dr. Dillon should automatically deny Ms. Arnold's appeal to advance it to the school board.
   c. Dr. Dillon should return the appeal to Dr. Cleveland, the principal, directing him to resolve it.
   d. Dr. Dillon should forward Ms. Arnold's Level 2 appeal to the district's legal team for review.

5. According to the summary of the school district's policy, at which level can Ms. Arnold request a meeting with the school board to address her grievance?
    a. Level 4
    b. Level 3
    c. Level 2
    d. Level 1

6. If Ms. Arnold carries her grievance to Level 4, which of the following is true of the district policy about her right to request copies of documents related to her complaint?
    a. Ms. Arnold may request copies of all Level 3 records for her case.
    b. Ms. Arnold may request copies of records from all previous levels.
    c. Ms. Arnold may request copies of documents from Levels 3 and 2.
    d. Ms. Arnold may not request copies of documents by district policy.

Questions 7–10 refer to the following information:

> In compliance with the No Child Left Behind (NCLB) Act, the state has identified Brookview Elementary as one school in the district not making adequate yearly progress (AYP) in one indicator, reading, for two or more years in a row, subjecting it to the law's school improvement requirements. District Superintendent Dr. Dillon sends a memo to parents of students at this school informing them of this status and of their right to request their children be transferred to another district public school. The memo also informs parents that the school can appeal the identification, that improvement requirements must be in force regardless for the whole school year, and that the entire school district will implement professional learning communities (PLCs) to address improvement requirements and to conduct data analysis of standardized test results made by school campus staff with assistance from their regional education service center to inform strategies for meeting requirements. Ms. Corcoran, the curriculum director, recommends that budget allocations within the district budget be transferred from District PLC Planning to Professional Development for the Brookview campus and from District Reading to Brookview ES Reading.

7. Dr. Dillon realizes that the new PLCs will necessitate added funding to plan and implement them. To accomplish this while ensuring all district schools have sufficient budget allocations, which of the following would be best for him to do?
    a. To forward Ms. Corcoran's memo to all principals and ask them to transfer Campus Professional Development funds to District Planning for the PLC initiative
    b. To forward Ms. Corcoran's memo to each school's Campus Advisory Committee and ask them to vote on transferring campus fund allocations to school district level
    c. To share Ms. Corcoran's budgetary allocation projections with all principals and request their ideas for securing more funding for PLC planning and implementation
    d. To expect that, because the federal government has mandated the PLC initiative, it will allocate the funds Ms. Corcoran has projected will be necessary to support it

8. Who will analyze standardized test result data to inform Brookview's failure to meet AYP in reading and design solutions to meet school improvement requirements?
    a. The employees of the school campus
    b. The regional education service center
    c. The PLC
    d. All of the groups listed above

9. The superintendent has informed parents that they have which of the following rights?
    a. The right to appeal the district's implementation of requirements for a whole school year
    b. The right to appeal the state identification of the school as requiring school improvements
    c. The right to request the transfers of their children to a school in a different school district
    d. The right to request transfers of their children to another campus within the same district

10. Brookview ES was identified as not making AYP:
    a. by a local agency to comply with a state law.
    b. by a state agency to comply with a state law.
    c. by a state agency to comply with federal law.
    d. by a federal agency to comply with a federal law.

11. In one school district, the ethnicity of the student body is 75% White, 12% Hispanic, 8% African-American, 3% Native American, and 2% Asian or Pacific Islander. The same school's teaching staff as ethnically 92% White, 4% Hispanic, 1.5% Native American, 1.5% Asian or Pacific Islander, and 1% African-American. In considering this report, which of these should the superintendent realize?
    a. The proportion of Asian and Pacific Islander students is not represented in the teaching staff.
    b. The ethnic diversity of the district student population is not matched in the teaching staff.
    c. The teaching staff in the district reflects an ethnic diversity similar to that of the students.
    d. The proportion of African-American students is overrepresented in the district teaching staff.

12. A superintendent of a school district is formulating the district's vision for the coming years and realizes that curriculum improvements in reading are necessary throughout the district. To convey the necessity for these improvements to the principals and teachers in her district, which of these should the superintendent do first?

 a. She should ask the district reading coordinator to collaborate with all schools to evaluate their needs and strengths in reading instruction and find strategies for enhancing student reading performance.

 b. She should ask the district reading coordinator to sum up current district teaching practices and explore new, evidence-based reading instruction practices that are suitable for every age and grade level.

 c. She should have leaders at each school immediately implement a new reading program so students will demonstrate progress by the next time they must take state-required standardized assessments.

 d. She should have the reading coordinator collaborate with the financial officers to estimate current reading expenditures and estimate the projected costs for a variety of available curriculum packages.

13. Superintendent Dr. Harris has reviewed the state's statistics for her district. She wants to support district teachers and other staff in feeling valued by "celebrating small successes." She can recognize many achievements; however, which area of district achievement requires additional progress before celebrating it?

 a. The district has a low rate for identification of students requiring special education services.

 b. Of the district's students who failed subject assessments the year before, a significant number passed.

 c. Of the indicators shown for college readiness in high school students, most have increased.

 d. The indicators reflect high student achievement for ninth-grade mathematics and sciences.

Questions 14–17 are based on the following information:

 Dr. Dennis has just become superintendent of Flowery Branch Independent School District (FBISD). After meeting with school principals, he observes that the district has no technology plan. Technological resources are in short supply and not distributed evenly across the district. Technology in the district's school libraries is partial and needs to be updated. Several school Campus Improvement Plans refer to using technology but only on a limited basis. In addition, the capacity of the district for networking is insufficient, and comparatively few of its teachers have had staff development training in utilizing state-of-the-art educational technology. Dr. Dennis sets goals for his first year to see that a comprehensive technology plan is developed for the district and to have that plan's implementation begin. His first step is to form a Technology Planning Committee (TPC). This committee produces the district technology vision, which the school board of trustees approves. The mission statement they write for the district's new technology plan begins: "FBISD has a commitment to ensuring all of its students are prepared to engage in lifelong learning and successful work in this Age of Information."

14. Which specific student goals would most meet the mission indicated?
   a. "All students will be proficient in using software resources and online databases for research by graduation."
   b. "All students will be fluent in one or more programming languages often used in workplaces by graduation."
   c. "All students will actively use diverse technologies for solving problems and communicating by graduation."
   d. "All students will know how to save, access, and manipulate quantitative data via using technology by graduation."

15. After developing a district-wide technology plan, which of the following necessary changes should take priority?
   a. Have all district schools integrate full technology use in their Campus Improvement Plans.
   b. Obtain sufficient technology resources for all district schools and distribute these evenly.
   c. Provide staff development for all district teachers to use current educational technology.
   d. Upgrade the district infrastructure to enable full networking and automation of libraries.

16. Which of the following should Dr. Dennis do to assure credibility, community support, and grant approval for his district's new technology plan?
   a. Make sure the TPC's implementation includes a publicly issued technical report specifying which hardware is installed in each of the district's facilities
   b. Make sure the TPC's implementation includes a cost-benefit analysis of the district's expenditures for initiatives to improve school campus infrastructures
   c. Make sure the TPC's implementation plan evaluates the effects of different technologies and directs program changes and decisions using objective data
   d. Make sure the TPC's implementation includes seeking and obtaining district experts' and community leaders' endorsements of the new technology plan

17. In order to ensure that the district's new technology plan has the best potential to succeed and is a realistic one, which of these should Dr. Dennis do regarding the TPC?
   a. He should encourage the TPC to develop the technology plan so it necessitates minimal monetary support coming from the school district.
   b. He should have the TPC represent all stakeholder groups, including members with different attitudes about, and backgrounds in, technology.
   c. He should direct the TPC to develop the new technology plan modeled very closely on plans other school districts in the state have produced.
   d. He should engage an instructional technology expert from outside of the school district as a consultant who will be more objective.

18. On TV, a local channel airs a news item wherein a teachers' group repeats rumors that their district superintendent is approving the hiring of younger and newer teachers for the committee planning their professional learning community (PLC) to reduce salary expenses. This group is threatening to file a federal lawsuit on the grounds of age discrimination. Which choice would be the superintendent's most suitable course of action?

   a. Tell the president of the school board of the news item, describe the hiring plan to all board members and employees, and then contact the news media.

   b. Disregard the news item, continue the process planned for hiring the committee, and call the local newspaper later on to provide correct information.

   c. Inform local media of the intended committee-hiring process, tell the school board of the news item, then answer teachers' questions during a meeting.

   d. Ask the school board president to be the official media liaison, explain the committee-hiring process, and then report about the event to the superintendent.

19. In the wake of recent publicized school shootings and discovering students bringing guns to schools, the officials of a school district plan to conduct a survey of parents, students, and other community members regarding the relative safety of our schools. Which of the following is a significant advantage of making a survey like this?

   a. It can show community members that their attitudes and behaviors have a direct impact on school safety.

   b. It can give the district officials a better idea of how realistic their community's perceptions are of this issue.

   c. It can tell district officials what behaviors community members think should be disciplined most strongly.

   d. It can provide additional motivation for employees of the district and schools to make school safety a priority.

20. In response to the incidence of student fights in his district's high schools, the superintendent firmly believes a district policy should be adopted to report all such fights to the police. Of the following, which most represents a drawback of adopting such a policy?

   a. Implementing this policy could prevent student conflict resolution and thus lead to more off-campus violence.

   b. Implementing this policy could decrease the cooperation of students with the police officers on their campuses.

   c. Implementing this policy could support public perceptions that this district has worse safety issues than others.

   d. Implementing this policy could make teachers perceive they are receiving unfair blame for disciplinary issues.

21. A superintendent is contemplating a recommendation to the school board to establish a district-wide police force for middle and high school campuses. Which choice best represents the MOST suitable superintendent action to resolve the MOST likely possible drawback to this plan?

    a. For the perceptions social service workers and school counselors will have of role conflicts with police, to educate all district employees in the necessity of campus police presence.

    b. For the perceptions of principals that police reflect negatively on principals' management of discipline, encourage principal–police collaboration and publicly support principals.

    c. For the perceptions that police are less experienced than educators in dealing with young individuals, invite district employees to report specific concerns about police to their principals.

    d. For the perceptions many parents and students will likely have of campus police as being threatening, educate community stakeholders about police's roles as role models and protectors.

22. Superintendent Jackson attends a baseball game at one of his district high schools. A member of the school board who is also in attendance yells insults at the umpire every time he objects to his calls. Of the following, which would be the best action by the superintendent the first time he observes this?

    a. He should do nothing initially but make a note to himself to watch for this behavior at future games.

    b. He should formally reprimand the behavior in writing as violating the school sportsmanship tradition.

    c. He should privately talk with this school board member about positive role modeling for the students.

    d. He should recommend an anger management course before he evaluates the school board member.

23. The school board and superintendent are collaborating in developing a new district vision statement. Some board members recommend that this statement incorporate wording expressing their commitment to providing all students with preparation for their lives in our "Information Age." However, some other board members challenge this recommendation because they are not sure a vision statement should refer to this topic. Which of the following would be the best response by the superintendent?

    a. Telling the board vision statements should identify both specific goals and strategies to implement the goals

    b. Telling the board that reflection of emerging trends and issues in education is appropriate in a vision statement

    c. Telling the board any language that will incite controversy in the school district should not be in vision statements

    d. Telling the board it is proper to identify any significant deficiencies the district must address in vision statements

24. In a city whose population is rapidly expanding, community stakeholders in the school district feel that its career preparation curriculum should be modified to account for demographic changes. To develop this curriculum to be more current and effective, which choice best reflects the role of the superintendent's office?

a. To function as liaison with business groups that can help identify specific skills associated with succeeding occupationally

b. To conduct research investigating the teaching approaches and best-practice principles to prepare students for their careers

c. To design and distribute a survey to students and their parents that will help identify particular student career objectives

d. To draft a list of potential career training courses to offer students and get principals' and teachers' review and feedback on it

25. A school district is engaged in the implementation of a new vision and a new strategic plan. In this endeavor, which choice best characterizes the main role of the board of trustees?

a. To convey the beliefs and values that underlie the district's vision and goals to stakeholders

b. To develop district policies that help to guide the attainment of the district vision and goals

c. To look for and locate funding sources that will help the district to attain its vision and goals

d. To identify procedures and practices of operation that can meet the district vision and goals

26. A school district is implementing professional learning communities (PLCs) to improve district teaching. The superintendent wants to make sure school principals and teachers know how to utilize data about student performance to this end. Of the following, which would allow the superintendent to combine showing principals and teachers how to use PLCs with informing them of trends found in aggregated data about the district?

a. Provide the data at a general principals' meeting, giving them time to problem solve collaboratively.

b. Directly forward the data to all principals with a directive to improve student test scores by next year.

c. Collaborate using vertically established teams reviewing the data with campus leaders and teachers.

d. Send a memo to the leadership teams giving principals' opinions about the data and what they imply.

27. The chairpersons of academic departments in a high school express to their principal during a meeting that they view professional learning communities (PLCs) as unnecessary because the reason for recent declines in their school's student performance indicators is the change in the student body's socioeconomic status rather than the teachers' instruction. Which strategy would help the superintendent motivate this group's participation in the district PLC initiative?

    a. Collaborate with these department chairpersons to track their current students' progress over an extended time period.

    b. Issue all principals a memo that participating is mandatory and they should reprimand in writing any employees who object.

    c. Discuss the school data with the principal to gain a wider comprehension of every area showing deficient performance.

    d. Tell the principal to work with the team on how to use the PLC for implementing strategies to meet diverse learner needs.

28. A new superintendent found that her district had no comprehensive technology plan and formed a technology planning committee (TPC) to develop one. Rather than have the technology program perceived as a separate one, she wants it to be integrated into the district's curriculum. She decides to solicit the curriculum development committees for each subject department to support the TPC's efforts. Which of the following would best accomplish this?

    a. Have them review and approve every component of the TPC's plan that is relevant to their respective subject areas of the curriculum.

    b. Have them furnish the members of the TPC with a copy of their respective curricula and any other information they might request.

    c. Have them review specific instructional software packages for their respective curriculum areas and recommend which to purchase.

    d. Have them revisit their respective curriculum areas in light of which kinds of technologies could promote learning and how so.

29. An effective plan for professional development relative to instructional technology should incorporate which of the following guidelines or principles?

    a. National educational foundations and organizations should provide grant funding to support professional development.

    b. The district should support teachers to visit and observe other schools and workplaces where people utilize current technologies.

    c. The various learning styles and needs of professionals should be addressed by offering different kinds of opportunities for training.

    d. Professional development trainers should be chosen from the district's most proficient teachers of math, science, and business.

30. A superintendent develops and implements a set of processes whereby school administrators, members of the curriculum planning committees, and all other teachers collaborate in systematically reviewing district curriculum. The review reveals that some transfer students in high school placed in grade-level subject classes did not complete the prerequisite classes in their previous schools. This relates most to assuring appropriate _____.

    a. sequence.
    b. alignment.
    c. content.
    d. scope.

31. A new superintendent evaluates the district's curricula and finds need for improvement. Which is the best foundation for the superintendent to give district staff direction for curricular improvements?
    a. Best practices identified informally by experienced teachers
    b. Best practices identified by a large body of research evidence
    c. Best practices identified in another district in a different state
    d. Best practices identified by a new pilot program in one school

32. A superintendent has initiated district professional learning communities (PLCs) to promote improvements in teaching practices and student performance. This superintendent distributes an article by an education scholar about PLCs to all district principals and staff. This article describes the constructivist theory of learning, noting that each student brings unique experiences, knowledge, and beliefs to school; that individual students, and teachers as well, actively construct their own knowledge in a variety of ways; and that PLCs model constructivism in learning. It advocates learner-centered rather than teacher-centered instruction and collective learning addressing student needs and professional effectiveness. Based on these points, how should district principals and staff modify their practices?
    a. They should score their assessment tests using the normal (bell) curve.
    b. They should group their students according to their achievement levels.
    c. They should modify their instruction according to their students' needs.
    d. They should modify the grade levels or the courses that they teach.

33. The superintendent and other officials of a school district concur that, to support school safety, their developmental guidance program should emphasize teaching the students social skills, problem-solving skills, and conflict resolution skills and techniques. What is the main strength of this strategy?
    a. It will establish a school environment where student behavior is disciplined through peer pressure, not adult coercion.
    b. It will enable members of the community to see that not all student safety issues can be eliminated by school officials.
    c. It will distribute discipline issues to be a burden shared equally among the administrators, teachers, and students.
    d. It will enable students to see that they are empowered to change their and others' behaviors to make their schools safer.

34. Regarding motivation, from Albert Bandura's Social Learning Theory, which term refers to a person's perception of his or her ability to perform a task successfully?
    a. Self-efficacy
    b. Self-image
    c. Self-concept
    d. Self-esteem

35. The teachers in a school district commonly use classroom strategies including active student participation; activating students' familiarity, experience, and prior knowledge; modeling; communicating learning requirements to students; giving students feedback; arranging positive consequences; and making use of natural consequences. These strategies are most associated with which theory of motivation?
    a. The ARCS Motivational Theory
    b. Maslow's Theory of Motivation
    c. The Equity Theory of Motivation
    d. Expectancy Theory of Motivation

36. According to the Expectancy Theory of Motivation, a student's belief that she or he will get a reward for meeting performance expectation(s) reflects which component of behavior in motivation?
    a. Motivational force
    b. Instrumentality
    c. Expectancy
    d. Valence

37. In one school district, most administrators and teachers believe that socioeconomically disadvantaged students cannot focus on learning if their needs for shelter, safety, and food are not met first. This attitude best reflects which type of theory of motivation?
    a. Social
    b. Biological
    c. Humanistic
    d. Psychoanalytic

38. A superintendent who has spearheaded an initiative for her district to establish professional learning communities (PLCs) shares an article about these with district personnel. In it, the author expounds research on evidence-based principles of PLCs, including common values, beliefs, and vision for a school; supportive leadership, with the community sharing decision-making authority; structural support like the resources, time, and space to learn; trust, caring, and respect in community relations; intentional, collective, reciprocal learning that meets students' needs and increases professionals' effectiveness; and shared practices among peers leading to improvements on individual and organizational levels. Based on this information, which of these areas of professional development are most supportive of implementing PLCs in the district?
    a. The district's historical perspective, pedagogy, and practice
    b. The district's curriculum, design, articulation, and alignment
    c. The district's curriculum, its pedagogy, and its assessments
    d. The district's stated vision, mission, values, and goals

39. In order not only to implement PLCs in the school district but also maintain them in the future, the district superintendent feels that the changes this initiative will bring must be integrated into the school district's culture. Which of the following must the school leadership team consider to effect such changes in the district and school culture?

    a. How the members can plan professional development programs and effective strategies for follow-up

    b. How the members can assign school campus staff, manage disciplining students, and schedule classes

    c. How the members can develop district benchmarks, standard assessments, and desegregation of data

    d. How the members can express values they share, reflect in dialogues, and make time for celebrations

40. A school district has planned new professional learning communities (PLCs) to improve instruction and student performance. Initially, some teachers objected to the process of selecting members for the PLC planning committees, claiming discrimination by hiring less-experienced teachers with lower salaries to save costs. The district has now been implementing the PLCs for the past several months. As part of this initiative, district personnel have created standard assessments for all students. As a result, clear evidence of improved student achievement is emerging in the state education agency's performance data, generating much enthusiasm in participating teachers. To communicate this success and also promote continuing improvements, which choice is the superintendent's best first step?

    a. Give the school board president the performance data to put on the next regular board meeting's agenda to inform budgetary decisions.

    b. Give local media a press release on the PLC initiative's success, emphasizing it is despite a publicized controversy over committee selection.

    c. Ask the curriculum director to compile and share performance data at the next principals' meeting to report on the PLC initiative's progress.

    d. Send school principals performance data and ask them to share it with the teachers who disagreed over the committee selection process.

41. In one school district, the teachers at all its elementary schools have completed participating in a course of professional development training sessions in making observational assessments in the classroom. To make sure that district elementary school students gain the most benefit from this training their teachers have had, which of the following should district administrators do?

    a. Follow up on the training by sending the teachers bimonthly surveys to report their using observational assessments.

    b. Establish a program of consultations and activities to follow up on all teachers participating in the training applying new skills.

    c. Establish a requirement that all teachers who participated in the training must pass a test on observational assessments.

    d. Request that the teachers who participated in the training give presentations on observational assessment at their schools.

42. Good staff development trainers know the principles of adult learning. For example, adult learners appreciate being treated with respect. Which of the following correctly identifies other adult learning principles applicable to staff development training?
    a. Adults care more than children that learning is relevant to their goals.
    b. Adult learners bring the same experience and knowledge as children.
    c. Adults have less concern than kids about how practical the learning is.
    d. Adults are more externally motivated and other-directed than youth.

43. Effective staff development training utilizes teaching approaches consistent with adult learning principles. Which of these is an approach LEAST congruent with the principles of adult learning?
    a. Problem-oriented
    b. Didactic in nature
    c. Collaborative
    d. Egalitarian

44. A teacher in a public school district has filed a grievance that she perceived discrimination in the process for selecting PLC committees. The superintendent receives a letter from a group of other teachers from the same school, stating they plan to join in with the first teacher's pending complaint. What part of the school board's policy applies to the superintendent's response if they do file an official grievance?
    a. Notice to employees
    b. Guiding principles
    c. Consolidating complaints
    d. Jurisdictional referral

45. Teachers in a school district ask for a raise in their salaries the next school year. To support this request, they cite the average pay rate in their state, pointing out that their salaries are lower than this. They also note that the district has difficulty keeping teachers because of the low pay. The superintendent is relaying the teachers' request to the school board. In the district's report, which data would the superintendent find to verify these statements by the teachers?
    a. District teachers' average years' experience
    b. District teachers' distribution by experience
    c. The turnover rate for the district's teachers
    d. The average salary for the district's teachers

46. Data in state reporting show that a certain school district spends much less on security and monitoring services per student than the state's per-student rate. This district's tax rate exceeds the average tax rate for the state. In this district's elementary schools, class sizes range from 17 to 20.3, while state figures for this indicator range from 19 to 22.1. In the Actual Revenue Information indicators, the district's operating expenditures for instruction are lower per student than the state's, while the district spends more per student on co-curricular activities than the state's per-student figure. Based on this information, which of the following reflects the influence of community values on this district's budgetary and programmatic decision making?
    a. Spending for security and monitoring services exceeds the state average.
    b. The taxes in the district's community exceed average taxes in the state.
    c. District elementary school class sizes are limited to 21 or fewer students.
    d. Instruction is underfunded while co-curricular activities are overfunded.

Questions 47–50 refer to the following information:

Over the past twelve years, the student population in one school district has experienced significant growth. As a result, the district's elementary school, which was already an old, deteriorating building, is now also crowded beyond capacity. The school board has accordingly proposed replacing it with a new elementary school, hiring a firm of architects to draft the plans and estimate the total construction costs. The state government agrees to fund part of these expenses, but the district must raise the remaining funds via a bond issue, which must receive a majority district vote for approval. A faction of district members voices serious objections to the bond issue.

47. Of the following, which trends should carry the most weight while planning the new school building's design?

    a. Demographic projections of cultural and ethnic changes in district community populations

    b. Potential long-term changes to state regulations of facilities dedicated to special education

    c. The state's total budget for building new public schools undergoing changes in its amounts

    d. Population growth projections for the district's communities within the next twelve years

48. When the district superintendent reviews the architectural plans for the new school, she or he needs to be cognizant of which federal and state regulations?

    a. Regulations specifying minimum acceptable amounts of insulation in the ceilings and walls

    b. Regulations specifying how much floor space has to be allotted for each of the classrooms

    c. Regulations dictating building designs that provide accessibility to students with disabilities

    d. Regulations dictating building materials made in the USA be used everywhere they can be

49. When a school district's new superintendent begins the position, someone offers information that, when its schools were constructed, the building materials could have included asbestos. Which of the following would be the best way for the new superintendent to respond?

    a. Hiring a contractor right away to initiate the procedures for eliminating all materials containing asbestos from schools

    b. Hiring a licensed professional inspector to determine if asbestos exists in district schools and, if so, to plan for managing this

    c. Putting together a committee from stakeholders in the district to study the topic and draft an asbestos removal plan

    d. Requesting that the local board of health inspect all district schools and report findings to the superintendent's office

50. A district's school board is reviewing bids for food services for its schools from different vendors. Of these, one offers a significantly lower bid than the others. However, one board member raises the consideration that she has heard some negative feedback from others about that vendor's services. Which of the following should the superintendent do pursuant to this discussion?

    a. Ask other customers who have hired the vendor in question about the services' quality.

    b. Advise the school board to decline the low bid and hire a vendor who is more reputable.

    c. Advise the school board to contract with the low bidder to comply with state regulations.

    d. Disclose the low bid amount to all vendors involved and then reopen bidding procedures.

51. A school district's superintendent, school board, and other officials have agreed to the need for a new school building on one campus. To begin the process of planning for construction, which of the following should be the superintendent's first action?

    a. Collaborating with representatives of the campus and district in developing the proposed new school's instructional requirements

    b. Scheduling a consultation with the contracted architectural firm to talk about various options for the designing of the new school building

    c. Arranging a series of public forms for holding discussions about requirements in space and instruction of the proposed new school building

    d. Requesting that the principal designated for the proposed new school produce a short report of needs expected for the amount of space

Questions 52 and 53 are based on the following information:

> Superintendent Hay's district plans to build a new library for one school campus. Superintendent Hay is contemplating working with city administrators to construct it as a public library to be shared among school and community users. Some other community groups have also asked Dr. Hay about using school facilities when school is not in session and the buildings are empty. Dr. Hay's administrative staff is small, and its members have no experience with planning facilities; therefore, he plans to contract with an independent professional consultant to help in planning for the new library.

52. Arranging for joint use of a facility among the school and other organizations confers which of the following as a main benefit?

    a. It coordinates and brings into alignment the sources of funding and structures of authority of multiple agencies.

    b. It addresses insufficient space in growing communities and uses limited public resources more efficiently.

    c. It relieves time limitations of the custodial staff by reducing the requirements in maintenance for the building.

    d. It is supported by solid research evidence that joint facility use is effective and complies with building codes.

53. Which of the following best characterizes the kind of working relationship Dr. Hay should have with the independent contractor he plans to hire as a planning consultant?

    a. He should ask the consultant to be the administrator of the planning process to sustain its efficacy and efficiency.

    b. He should ask an architect to produce long-term plans for the district, so the library is aligned with the district's needs.

    c. He should ask the consultant to apply the long-term plans for the district and library to meet district student needs.

    d. He should ask the consultant to make decisions about educational aspects of the new library as an expert in these.

54. One school in a district has been notified by the state that it did not show adequate yearly progress (AYP) for student performance in Language Arts. The superintendent and principal confer to address this. The superintendent then communicates in writing to parents of students at this school that the school must comply with Stage 1, Year 1 school improvement requirements for the coming school year. If the school does not make progress to meet the Stage 1 requirements, which will the ensuing Stage 2 requirements involve?

    a. To restructure the campuses rated academically unacceptable and replace the principals at each one of these campuses

    b. To make on-site audits of the student assessment procedures on each campus with an academically unacceptable rating

    c. To satisfy Year 1 requirements and pay for tutoring low-income students and other supplemental educational services

    d. To remove the school principal's authority, replace school staff, make the school days longer, or revise the curriculum

55. Population growth in a school district has necessitated building a new school. Construction will be partially funded by state government, with the remaining funds to be raised through a bond issue. This bond issue requires a district majority vote for approval, and one community group is against it. For the bond election, which of these is most important as the superintendent's responsibility?

    a. The superintendent is an advocate for the students to promote meeting their educational needs.

    b. The superintendent serves as an intermediary between the community and the board of trustees.

    c. The superintendent serves as a mediator for community members on opposing sides of the issue.

    d. The superintendent is an organizer of those supporting the bond issue to lobby for helping it pass.

- 129 -

56. Residents in a community have expressed to their new superintendent of schools their desire for involvement in activities to improve their district schools. To that end, the superintendent is exploring strategies for fostering such community school engagement. Of the following, which would best enable the superintendent to include members of the community in the district's educational decisions?
    a. Ask members of the community to provide input into how to assign district personnel.
    b. Ask members of the community to take part in developing and revising school curricula.
    c. Ask members of the community to give expertise and time for physical plant upgrades.
    d. Ask members of the community to evaluate performance of faculty and administrators.

57. According to the Governmental Accounting Standards Board (GASB), Service Efforts and Accomplishments (SEA) Reporting includes these among its categories: Input indicators report resources used for specific services/programs. Output indicators report services provided and units produced by a given service provider or program. Outcome indicators report results of a service or program. Efficiency indicators report the inputs or expenses per unit of output or outcome. Based on these definitions, which of the following is an example of an efficiency indicator?
    a. The number of teachers employed in an elementary school
    b. The number of students who graduated from a high school
    c. The cost for each student who is graduated by a high school
    d. The change in student test scores via instructional programs

58. Among the following, which is valid regarding the significance of good school budget planning?
    a. School goods and services are subject to supply and demand as in all markets.
    b. Education is unlike other goods and service that take priority in public interest.
    c. Decisions about school district operations involve lesser complexity in planning.
    d. The planning process is crucial for achieving consensus among all stakeholders.

Answers and Explanations

1. B: The majority of female staff's perception of the principal's nicknames as inoffensive could indicate he does not consciously intend disrespect by using them and also suggests a positive relationship between staff and principal. Therefore, reprimanding the principal and asking for a public apology (D) is not most appropriate, especially as only one staff member complained. However, her complaint must be acknowledged and not discredited simply for lack of agreement (A). As the principal's address may not constitute sexual harassment and most staff members do not perceive it as such, a meeting to review laws (C) is also not the best action. The superintendent should make the principal aware of how his habit is perceived by some and that it is therefore also better for students not to learn it from him.

2. D: Ms. Arnold indicated that she told the principal she wanted to serve on the PLC committee, which he denied. She also pointed out the need to include teachers of various experience levels on the committee. Dr. Dillon's ensuring that teachers' interests and input are represented in the committee-hiring process(es) would address her complaint regarding representation. Because her concerns include that the principal has not done this and continues to refuse to do so, having him recommend employees to participate in the process (A) will not address these concerns. Teachers without tenure (B) are the same younger, less-experienced or new teachers already hired for the committee; focusing on them to participate in committee-hiring processes would ignore or exacerbate her concerns. Paying all teachers the same for participating in the committee selection process (C) is irrelevant: Ms. Arnold's complaint was that she was not allowed to collect her designated pay grade in the summer for committee membership.

3. C: The superintendent should not meet with the teacher himself (A) to address a Level 2 complaint because the district policy states that, at Level 2, the employee may request a meeting with the assistant superintendent or designee. Dr. Dillon should not direct the principal to meet with the teacher (B) both because this does not conform with the policy and moreover because the principal's hiring decision was the subject of the teacher's complaint; she addressed her Level 1 complaint to him as policy requires; and he denied it. The policy provides for the teacher to meet with the assistant superintendent at Level 2, not for the superintendent simply to wait for a district-level decision on the entire PLC initiative (D).

4. A: According to the summary given of the school district's policy, if Ms. Arnold appeals the response to her Level 2 complaint, at Level 3, the superintendent must himself respond in writing to her appeal. When escalated, all grievances should proceed through the successive levels defined in the policy; the superintendent should NOT automatically deny the teacher's appeal to escalate it to the school board (B), which hears Level 4 complaints. The teacher can appeal to the school board at Level 4 if the superintendent's written response to her Level 3 appeal does not provide her with relief. Returning the appeal to the principal (C) who already denied the Level 1 complaint would also clearly violate this district policy and would be counterproductive. Forwarding the appeal to the district's legal team (D) also does not adhere to the stated district policy.

5. A: According to the summary of the district policy, Level 1 grievances (D) must be addressed to the teacher's principal. If the principal's written response does not afford

relief, Level 2 complaints (C) are assigned to the assistant superintendent or designee. If the written response at this level does not bring relief, the teacher can appeal at Level 3 (B) to the superintendent. If the superintendent's written response does not give the complainant relief, she can appeal at Level 4 to the school board.

6. B: The summary states that, according to the school district's policy, Ms. Arnold is entitled to request copies of all records from the previous levels of her complaint. This includes Levels 1, 2, and 3—not only Level 3 (A) or only Levels 3 and 2 (C). According to the summary of the district policy, it is not true that Ms. Arnold may not request copies of these records (D).

7. C: Since the PLC initiative is to be district wide, all school principals in the district should contribute their ideas and resources for securing the extra funding needed. Asking principals to transfer funds from campus to district level (A), or asking them to vote on doing so (B), are the reverse of what is needed and what Ms. Corcoran has recommended and will not support the PLC initiative. Expecting the federal government to allocate funds (D) is not realistic: The federal law mandates school improvement requirements, but securing adequate funding is left to the individual states or local school districts as part of their responsibility to comply with federal law and their decisions on how to accomplish this.

8. D: As well as planning and writing curriculum, the PLC (C) will initiate and facilitate analysis of the data on standardized test results to inform its strategies for meeting Brookview's school improvement requirements under NCLB as identified by the state. The PLC will include school campus employees (A), who will receive assistance from the regional education service center (B). Thus, these are all involved.

9. D: The description of the superintendent's memo includes informing parents they have the right to request their children be transferred from Brookview to another school within the same school district. It does NOT say the superintendent informed them of a right to request transfers of their children to a school in a different school district (C). It describes appealing the state's identification of the school's status as the school's right, NOT the parents' right (B). The superintendent has informed parents that, regardless of appealing the identification, the district must implement improvement requirements for the whole school year; he has NOT informed parents they have a right to appeal this implementation by the school (A).

10. C: The state identified Brookview ES as not making AYP to comply with the No Child Left Behind (NCLB) Act, which is a federal law making state and local schools accountable for student progress. NCLB is not a state law (A). The identification was to comply with a federal, not a state law (B). The identification was to comply with a federal law but was made not by a federal agency (D).

11. B: The district's student body is 75% White, while the district's teaching staff is 92% White. Therefore the White ethnicity is overrepresented among teaching staff relative to its proportion among students. This also means that the teaching staff does NOT reflect a similar ethnic diversity as that of the students (C). As 1.5% of the teaching staff is Asian or Pacific Islander, therefore it cannot be said that this ethnic group is not represented at all in the teaching staff (A). The proportion of African-American students is 8%, while that of

teaching staff is 1%. Therefore, the percentage of African-American students is underrepresented in the teaching staff, NOT overrepresented (D).

12. A: The first action for the superintendent to take of those listed would be to have the teachers and coordinator of reading instruction determine which of their teaching practices are effective and where they need improvement and to identify which teaching techniques can increase their students' achievement in reading. She should not ask the coordinator to change all current teaching practices in favor of new ones (B); this would be "throwing out the baby with the bathwater." Current teaching practices found effective should be maintained and only ineffective ones modified or replaced. Immediately instituting a whole new reading program in an accountability-pressured race to increase test results (C) misses the point of better teaching and learning in reading, and uninformed assessing of what does or does not work in the current program will likely backfire. While costs might need to be estimated if a new curriculum is adopted (D), this would not be the first thing to do: Evaluating the strengths and needs of the current curriculum could indicate modifying it rather than replacing it, which would incur no additional costs or different costs than a new curriculum package.

13. A: A low identification rate does not indicate that few students in Superintendent Harris's district need special education services but rather that district personnel are not recognizing, evaluating, and determining eligibility for enough students with special needs to receive them. Hence, this rate needs improvement. If statistics show a high proportion of students previously failing the subject assessments who passed it the following year (B), this shows the district has improved these students' achievement on this standardized assessment—a success to be celebrated. If the majority of indicators for high school students' college readiness have increased (C), this is another example of educational success. And if the statistics indicate high levels of achievement in two subject areas for most students at a specific grade level (D), these are also indices of success and reasons to celebrate.

14. C: All students actively using various technologies to facilitate problem-solving and communication activities best meets the overall mission of preparing them to pursue lifelong learning and successful workplace performance. Proficiency in using technology for research (A) is a narrower goal less likely to promote lifestyles of continuing learning and success in a variety of workplaces. Fluency in programming languages (B) is only one aspect of technology; it could promote success in programming jobs only but is less likely to promote success in varied jobs and an interest in continuing to learn throughout life. Knowing how to use technology to store, access, and manipulate numbers (D) would support success only in jobs primarily requiring those specific skills and not the many other jobs students will end up doing; and knowing how to use technology only to save, find, and work with numbers would not prepare students for interest and success in lifelong learning.

15. D: Before current instructional technology can be obtained and installed, the district will need to upgrade the existing infrastructure to support the installation and operation of new devices (B). Staff development for teachers to learn how to use the newest educational technology (C) is necessary but not until they have it to use (or at least soon enough before the schools acquire it so they do not forget what they have learned or the information taught becomes outdated). For them to have the equipment, the infrastructure must first be developed to support its use. Schools can be directed to incorporate full technology use in their Campus Improvement Plans (A) once the TPC has informed district management as to

the specific nature of the technology they will have, which again depends on infrastructure improvements.

16. C: Dr. Dennis can obtain credibility in the community and approval for funding grants for the new district technology plan by making sure that objective data are provided to support evaluations of the impacts different technologies will have and to inform the changes and decisions he and the TPC will make regarding their program. A public technical report specifying facility hardware (A) will not gain the interest or comprehension of most community leaders and funding grantors. A cost-benefit analysis (B) is inappropriate here: While various technology costs can be calculated or estimated, the benefits of lifelong learning and future workplace success can be appreciated qualitatively but not measured quantitatively. Choice (D) is backwards: Specific plans, such as proving the effects of technologies and the reasons for program decisions, will gain community and grantor credibility, which in turn will be more likely to win their endorsements than trying to obtain these first, which would be difficult without first establishing credibility and support.

17. B: The superintendent should form the TPC such that it represents all those invested in the school district, including stakeholders whose attitudes and backgrounds regarding technology differ. This is more likely to attain committee input representative of the same variety of perspectives and knowledge present in the school district's community. Representing these viewpoints is more likely to attain success for the technology plan, and the varied knowledge brought to the committee is more likely to make it more realistic. Focusing plan design on the least district monetary support (A) is unrealistic in itself and would likely compromise plan success. Making this district's plan very close to those of other districts in the state (C) is unrealistic as each district has different characteristics, strengths, and needs; such a cookie-cutter approach could seriously interfere with a specific district plan's success. While an outside consultant might or might not be objective (D), she or he lacks knowledge and experience of the specific district, community, and students that its members have, which will better inform committee decisions.

18. A: Whether the rumors are true or untrue, the superintendent should not ignore the broadcast (B). Calling the newspaper is less appropriate than contacting the TV station as the report was a TV, not newspaper, story (B). The superintendent should not give informing the media precedence over the school board (C). As teachers first heard the rumors, repeated them on the news, and would be most directly affected by them if true, the superintendent should not leave them for last and then only answer their questions (C). She or he should detail the hiring process to them and other staff sooner, right after informing the school board's president of the news coverage. The superintendent is responsible to address this situation rather than delegate the president of the school board (D) because superintendents are supposed to communicate effectively with and influence the media positively regarding district vision, mission, and activities and also because she or he likely knows more details of the committee-hiring process than the school board president.

19. B: Of the choices given, the best advantage of making a public opinion survey is that it can provide district officials with a way to compare community perceptions of an issue like school safety with the local reality of the issue. Asking people their opinions is not the most directly effective way to convey to them that what they think and do affect the issue (A). Asking people how safe they feel their schools are is not a direct way to find out which behaviors they feel should be disciplined most (C). The officials could better motivate

district and school staff to prioritize school safety with incentives affecting those employees more directly than citing public opinions (D) would do.

20. C: If all high school fights in the district become a matter of police record, the public in this district's community could easily perceive that school safety is more problematic there than in other school districts. Reporting fights to the police would not preclude also providing conflict resolution procedures at the schools (A). Reporting fights to community police would not necessarily make students less cooperative with campus police (B); it might even reinforce their cooperation by association. Making high school fights a matter of police record would not automatically make teachers feel implicated for inadequate student discipline (D), especially if there is a campus police presence.

21. D: Students and parents previously unaccustomed to a campus police presence are initially likely to perceive officers at middle and high schools as threatening. The superintendent can ameliorate this perception by influencing community members to view police officers as positive role models for students and protectors of their safety and welfare to prepare them for establishing a district police force. Social service workers and school counselors are not likely to view police as creating role conflicts (A) as these employees do not typically view their own roles as enforcing laws or maintaining the peace like the roles of police officers. While some principals who are insecure about their public images may view police presence as reflecting negatively on their own discipline (B), others may welcome police support. Public support and encouraging collaboration may not resolve the insecurities of the former. The perception of police as less experienced with young individuals (C) is invalid as police departments have juvenile offender divisions whose officers have such experience.

22. C: This avoids humiliating the board member by speaking privately and accentuates positive, not negative, behaviors in emphasizing role modeling for students (rather than telling the member she or he is a negative role model). Doing nothing and waiting to see the behavior repeated (A) would not communicate Superintendent Jackson's position on this behavior at the present time. The board member will then likely repeat it, so saying nothing this time only delays the necessity of the conversation. While the behavior is indeed unsportsmanlike, a formal written reprimand (B) upon first observation is excessive, not giving the board member any opportunity to rectify it. Recommending anger management before the next evaluation (D) presumes the board member has a problem, which Superintendent. Jackson cannot identify based only on this event, and he is not qualified to diagnose such a problem without a psychologist's evaluation. Also, making behavior change a contingency for a favorable evaluation unethically pressures the board member rather than encouraging setting a more positive example.

23. B: A district vision statement is an appropriate place for language reflecting trends and issues that are currently emerging in education. Vision statements are broader and more general than strategic plans that detail specific goals and strategies (A). A school district's vision statement is meant to communicate what the district wants to accomplish, which inspires its planning and strategies. (Its mission statement is more related to how it will accomplish its vision.) Composing the vision statement should be guided by the members' ideas of the district's potential, where they want it to go and what they want it to be, rather than being restricted by avoiding any possible controversy (C). The vision statement should show what the district hopes to do overall, not specific deficiencies it hopes to remediate (D).

24. A: Of the choices given, the most applicable role for the superintendent's office is as a link with business groups that have the workplace knowledge and experience to help the school district target the most necessary skills for workplace success in its updated or new career preparation curriculum. Conducting research into best teaching approaches and practices (B) is the role of researchers rather than administrators. While surveying students and parents about students' career goals (C) will reveal student interests and preferences, this information alone is not useful in redesigning the curriculum without knowing what skills the schools need to teach the students for them to succeed in the workplace. The same is true of listing possible courses and getting principals' and teachers' feedback on them (D): This will not tell whether the proposed courses will teach students the skills they will need to be able to succeed in the city's businesses.

25. B: The main role of the board of trustees is to develop policies for the school district that promote attainment of the district's stated vision and goals. Communicating beliefs and values that underlie the district vision and goals to stakeholders (A) is more a role of the superintendent's office. Seeking and locating funding to support district visions and goals (C) is a more a role of school principals and others designated by the superintendent. Facilitating the identification and application of best practices and procedures of operation to meet the district vision and goals (D) is a superintendent's function.

26. C: The superintendent should work together with leadership and instructional levels to review the district data, both informing principals and teachers of district trends reflected by analysis of the data and showing how PLCs can address these trends to improve district instruction and hence student performance. Simply providing data to principals and expecting them to problem solve (A) does not involve the superintendent or teachers in the processes of analysis and problem solving. Sending the principals data with a directive to improve test scores (B) not only leaves the superintendent, campus leaders, and teachers out of the process but also gives principals no help in understanding the data or trends implied by the data and formulating strategies to improve teaching and student performance. Sending a memo to leadership teams with principals' opinions (D) does not afford collaboration by anybody: The superintendent, principals, other campus leaders, and teachers get no chance to work together to analyze trends and use this information to form strategies to improve teaching and learning.

27. D: The socioeconomic changes in the school's community means its students now fall into the category of diverse learners. The superintendent can help shift the chairpersons' view of the PLC as unnecessary because their own teaching performance has not changed to the view that the PLC will help them find better instructional strategies for their more diverse student body. Seeing the PLC as a positive teaching aid to address student needs that have changed, instead of a needless attempt to improve general teaching quality that has not changed, will help motivate the chairs, who in turn can help motivate their teachers. Tracking student progress longitudinally (A) will not motivate the chairs but simply confirm performance declines. Using coercive orders (B) is not a way to generate positive motivation to try something new. Going over the data with the principal to analyze areas of deficient performance (C) may add to the superintendent's understanding of these, but this will not motivate the chairs to use the PLC to improve them.

28. D: To enlist the support of the curriculum development committees to integrate new technology into an existing curriculum, the superintendent should ask the committee for

each subject area to review their portions of the curriculum to see how they can use technology to enhance their instruction and what kinds of technologies would be appropriate to apply. Simply having them review the parts of the TPC's plan that apply to the curriculum in their subjects (A) is getting their approval but not their support through participation and meaningful input. Similarly, having them give the TPC copies of their parts of the curriculum (B) is not support; the TPC could get this information in other ways, and providing copies does not entail contributing ideas about how to integrate technology into instruction in each subject area. Reviewing and recommending instructional software (C) is premature: First, the curriculum planners must consider how technology can be an integral part of the curriculum.

29. C: Just as teachers are directed to accommodate the diverse learning styles and needs of students, professional development training should accommodate these in its students who are teachers. Teachers will be more motivated to learn how to use and integrate new technology in instruction when offered choices among training opportunities fitting how they learn best. Stipulating funding sources (A) is not a guideline or principle and may be unrealistic. As a district may or may not be able to support teacher visits and observations (B), this should also not be a guideline or principle; qualified experts in current technology and training can instruct teachers systematically, giving them far more than they can get from observational visits. (When or if feasible, such visits could serve to inspire enthusiasm and motivation but are no substitute for training.) Trainers should not be just proficient math, science, and business teachers (D) but qualified to use and teach technology and instruct teachers in the applications of instructional technology.

30. A: Placement in grade-level subjects without prior completion of prerequisite subjects relates to the sequence of instruction. Out-of-sequence instruction will cause the majority of students' performance to suffer. Alignment (B) relates to things such as assuring that curricula are consistent with accountability standards; that instruction conforms with the curriculum; that different schools across the same district design and teach compatible curricula; that school campus plans, budgets, and staff development are congruent with school campus needs, and so on. Content (C) relates to what material is taught in the overall curriculum, in individual subject areas, and so on. Scope (D) relates to the extent and comprehensiveness of the curriculum overall, of the individual courses, and so on, to encompass everything the students will need to learn to succeed in higher education, employment, and life.

31. B: Effective superintendents should be able to give their staff direction to improve curricula based on solid research evidence from multiple well-designed studies that all support the same best practices. While the experience of effective teachers (A) has great value and should never be ignored, in some cases, what works for certain teachers does not for others due to a myriad of factors (e.g., demographics of the student body and community, developmental levels, learning styles, teaching styles, teacher–student relationships, etc.) Informal contributions may help other teachers but do not constitute systematic evidence of more universal best practices obtained through controlled investigations. Best practices for a different district and state (C) may not apply to the needs and characteristics of the superintendent's district or the laws, regulations, and policies of that district's state. Best practices identified in one school's new pilot program (D) also lack the credibility and universality of best practices consistently supported by findings from many different research studies.

32. C: Based on the summary of points made about PLCs as operating from a perspective of constructivism, the district principals and staff can best modify their teaching practices by orienting their instruction to the needs of their particular students. Scoring assessment tests on a normal curve (A) is a device to even out the highest and lowest outlying scores, which minimizes individual differences rather than responding to them. Grouping students by achievement levels (B) is counter to the constructivist and PLC principle of collective and reciprocal learning. Changes in teaching practices to incorporate these principles will not necessarily require changing the courses taught or the students' grade levels (D).

33. D: The skills named all enable ways to promote positive behaviors and social interactions and constructively resolve disagreements. Teaching students to solve problems, interact appropriately with others, and settle differences among themselves empowers them. From this empowerment proceeds the realization of their own autonomy and control and how exercising these can ultimately place much of their schools' safety in their hands. This constitutes discipline through proactive and cooperative behaviors, not peer pressure (A). The purpose of this strategy is to equip students with the skills they need to take responsibility for their behavior, not to prove to community members that school officials are not omnipotent in safety issues (B). The idea is not for all school members to share discipline equally as a "burden" (C) but to preclude many occasions for disciplinary action by officials by teaching students how to initiate and maintain constructive social behaviors that will naturally prevent and replace destructive ones.

34. A: Bandura coined the term *self-efficacy* to refer specifically to an individual's feeling that she or he is competent to accomplish a certain task successfully, for example, a school or work task. Efficacy is a synonym with effectiveness. Self-image (B) is a broader term referring to the way one sees oneself overall. Self-concept (C) is similar to self-image; it refers to the way one conceives or thinks of oneself. Some people use (B) and (C) interchangeably; some do not. Self-esteem (D) refers to how well one thinks of oneself. Some people also interchange high or low self-esteem with positive or negative or good or poor self-image. Bandura coined *self-efficacy* more to mean an individual's attitude about his or her confidence in his or her own ability to accomplish a specific thing, which is more related to motivation to learn and perform rather than to mean a person's overall sense of self-worth, as the other choices do.

35. A: The ARCS Motivational Theory, proposed by John Keller, posits four factors for stimulating and sustaining motivation in learning: attention, relevance, confidence, and satisfaction. Applying this theory in classrooms, teachers use active student participation to arouse students' attention; activate students' prior knowledge, experience, or familiarity and model behaviors for them to provide relevance; inform students of learning requirements and give them feedback to inspire confidence; and use positive and natural consequences to evoke student satisfaction (i.e., students feel more satisfied with the outcomes of their efforts are congruent with their expectations) to maintain motivation. Abraham Maslow's Theory of Human Motivation (B) posits a hierarchy of needs, from the most basic survival needs to the highest need for self-actualization (realizing one's fullest potential). Equity Theory (C) (John Stacy Adams) posits motivation as a function of inputs and outputs, that is, our perceptions of whether resources are distributed equitably (= fairly) or not in interactions. Expectancy Theory (D) (Victor Vroom) posits motivational components: Motivational Force = Expectancy x Instrumentality x Valence.

36. B: Expectancy Theory proposes three components: expectancy, instrumentality, and valence. The theory's formula is that Motivational Force (A) = Expectancy x Instrumentality x Valence. Expectancy (C) means Effort → Performance; that is, one believes that one's effort will result in achieving the desired goals for performance. Instrumentality (B) means Performance → Outcome; that is, a student believes she or he will get some reward for meeting the performance expectation(s). Valence (D) means the value a person gives to such a reward according to his or her sources of motivation, personal values, goals, and needs.

37. C: Humanistic theories propose natural motivation to attain our fullest potential and barriers to this. Maslow's theory and Hierarchy of Needs is most famous, that we must satisfy basic needs like safety, shelter, sleep, and nourishment before higher-level needs for belonging, love, esteem, and self-actualization. (Carl Rogers proposed another well-known humanistic theory.) Social (A) theories emphasize the role of social interactions in learning and motivation, including Bandura's Social Learning Theory, showing children learn vicariously from observing others' behaviors and consequences, and by imitating models; and Vygotsky's sociocultural theory, often applied in classrooms, shows students can perform at higher levels with assistance than autonomously (the Zone of Proximal Development). Biological (B) theories include Instinct theory: As spiders spin webs and birds build nests, human babies cry to survive; Arousal Theory, that managing arousal levels maintains comfort; and Hull's Drive Reduction Theory, that internal biological drives motivate performance. Psychoanalytic (D) theories derive from Freud's original theory that all behavior, including learning, is to ensure our survival or prevent our destruction.

38. D: The summary of the part of the article described in the question refers most to qualities related to the vision, mission, values, and goals of the district. The summary does not refer specifically to the historical perspective, pedagogy, instructional practices {(A), (C)}; curriculum {(B), (C)}; design, articulation, or alignment of the curriculum (B), or the assessments (C) used by the district.

39. D: Addressing topics like expressing the values they share in common, engaging in dialogues for the purpose of reflection on their practices and experiences, and finding time to celebrate successes is most related to effecting changes in the district and school campus culture. Planning professional development (A) is more specifically related to improving teachers' instructional performance. Assigning staff, managing student discipline, and scheduling classes (B) are activities more related to the regular administration of the district's campuses than to changing the culture. Developing benchmarks and assessments for all students and desegregating data (C) are more related to setting academic standards and using data to evaluate district progress toward meeting those standards.

40. C: When the principals of all the district's schools meet, this is a good opportunity to present them with the positive feedback of improved student performance data. It communicates success and gives the principals themselves positive reinforcement, which they can also communicate to their teachers, and it also shows them evidence that the PLC initiative is effective to support its continuation and promote further improvements. These data can also be used later at board meetings to justify budget allocations for the PLCs (A), but this is not the most logical first step for the superintendent's specifically communicating success and promoting further improvements. Using the improved performance data to refute some teachers' initial objections to inequities they perceived in the committee selection process and the controversy these objections created is too combative and

adversarial—whether communicated within the district to principals and teachers (D) or publicly in the media (B)—to be a good first step for sharing success and furthering improvements.

41. A: The best way for district administrators to see that the elementary school students will benefit from the training their teachers had is to obtain documentation that the teachers are applying what they learned in the training by actually conducting the classroom observational assessments taught in the training. Surveying the teachers regularly to report when they are doing this is a way to obtain such documentation. Providing follow-up consultations and activities (B) gives the teachers additional input beyond the training, but it does not determine whether the teachers are actually applying what they learned. Requiring all participating teachers to pass a test (C) assesses what they learned from the training but again does not assess whether they are applying what they learned. Similarly, asking the participating teachers to make presentations at their schools (D) would enable the teachers to share what they learned with other teachers and staff but would not determine whether they are actually making the observational assessments they learned about in the training.

42. A: Principles of adult learning include that adult learners are more oriented to relevant information and more goal-oriented in their learning than younger students are. While we recognize that children do bring prior experience and knowledge to new learning, adults bring much greater foundations of existing knowledge and life experiences to their new learning than children do (B). Adult learners are also more practical regarding learning than children (C): They want to learn information that they can apply directly to their work activities. This is generally true of all adult learners, and teachers in particular may be even more interested in how they can apply new learning to their instructional practices. Children, especially younger ones, can often be motivated by external rewards; and younger children often need direction from adults to motivate them to accomplish some tasks. In contrast, adults generally have attained greater internal motivation and self-direction (D).

43. B: Traditional lecturing, instructor-centered approaches—although most teachers and other educated adults are quite experienced with these from their own educations—are not consistent with adult learning principles. Most teachers encountering this type of approach in staff development trainings will be bored and less engaged. (In fact, current teaching theories and practices discourage this kind of approach with children as well in favor of experiential, inquiry-based, active-constructivist learning.) Applying the principles of adult learning to staff development training results in instructional approaches that are oriented to problem solving (A), involves collaboration between instructors and adult learners and among learners (C), and features more equality between learner and instructor (D) than is typical when teaching children.

44. C: Because the group's filing a grievance about the same issue that the first teacher filed about, the superintendent's response falls under the part of the school board policy addressing the consolidation of multiple complaints over the same issue. The part about notice to employees (A) would apply to the superintendent's initiating contact to inform staff of something rather than responding to complaints. The part of the policy on guiding principles (B) covers the values and concepts that underlie the school district's vision, mission, and so on. The policy portion on jurisdictional referral (D) covers the procedures to follow when an issue has been directed to the superintendent that is not within his or her

jurisdiction, and he or she needs to refer it to the employee, office, or department under whose jurisdiction the issue falls.

45. D: The data for the district teachers' average salary will prove their claim that this figure is lower than the average teacher salary for their state. The average years of experience of the district teachers (A), if it is lower than the state average, could support a rebuttal that teacher salaries are determined by years of experience rather than supporting the teachers' asking for a raise. Teacher distribution by experience (B) is irrelevant to the issue. District teachers' turnover rate (C) would support their claim that the district has difficulty keeping teachers but would not support their contention that average salaries lower than the state average are the cause.

46. D: The district described spends more on co-curricular activities than on instruction compared to the state figures. This reflects the influence of community values in that the co-curricular activities are more popular in this community and district than the instructional activities. According to the summary of data, this district does not exceed the state average expenditures for security and monitoring services (A) but spends much less. Taxes in this district do exceed the average state tax rates (B), but this does not reflect school district decisions about budget allocations for various programs; it reflects decisions by the local government regarding taxation. District elementary class sizes are slightly smaller than the state average (C), but this does not reflect decisions regarding programs or budget allocations for them; it reflects the ratio of existing students to available teachers.

47. D: Because a primary reason for building a new elementary school, in addition to its age and poor condition, is the growth of the student population, planning to design the new school building should allow for projections of additional population growth. This affords a better chance of constructing a new facility that will accommodate ongoing expansion of the elementary student body rather than constructing a facility whose capacity will become outdated in the same length of time as the existing building. Projected cultural and ethnic changes in the community (A) will not affect new building design the way population growth will. According to the information given, the school to be replaced is the district's elementary school, not a dedicated special education school (B). Planning the new construction will involve current budget amounts, not future budget projections (C). Moreover, the state budget's future size—especially if it decreases—is yet another reason to plan construction with future population size in mind.

48. C: Federal laws like the IDEA, the ADA, Section 504 of the Rehabilitation Act, and corresponding state laws mandate that students with disabilities have the right to a free, appropriate public education in the least restrictive environment possible; prohibit discrimination against persons with disabilities in accessing public facilities; and forbid organizations' denying or excluding persons with disabilities from federally funded programs, services, or other benefits. The superintendent should make sure the architects' plans for the new school building provide this access. Laws on minimum insulation (A) are typically included in state and local building codes. Minimum requirements, rules, guidelines, and laws for classroom floor space (B) are found in state government codes and state Education Departments' publications. There are no laws requiring use of building materials made in the USA (D).

49. B: The superintendent should employ a professional inspector who is licensed, and hence trained, to find hazardous substances like asbestos in building materials. Because the

- 141 -

information the superintendent received was not proof of asbestos, but only that the building materials could have included it, the first step is for a qualified professional to determine or rule out its presence. Thus, hiring a contractor to remove something that may not be there (A) is premature. Members of a committee formed from district stakeholders (C) are concerned but not qualified even to identify asbestos in buildings, let alone to draft a plan for removal. Also, regarding (A) and (C), even if asbestos is present, it could be impossible to remove. The board of health (D) can provide accurate information on the health hazards of asbestos in buildings, but does not likely have the expertise for finding and managing it.

50. A: Because one board member has heard negative reports about the service quality of the lowest bidding vendor, the superintendent should solicit feedback from other customers who have contracted with this vendor to see whether any corroborate such reports and, if so, how many do. The experiences and perceptions of actual customers of this vendor can inform the superintendent's and board's contracting decisions. Deciding simply to refuse the lowest bid based only on hearsay (B) without seeking additional evidence from the bidder's real customers is not as informed a decision. While state regulations may require accepting the lowest bid (C), such rules are unlikely to mean acceptance regardless of service quality. They are more likely to indicate acceptance of the lowest bid from among those providing services of similar, acceptable quality.

51. A: Of the choices listed, the first action the superintendent should take is to consider the student body's instructional needs, which are most important in determining all design and construction decisions. This consideration precedes discussing design options with the architects (B). Moreover, the state mandates that school districts must prepare specifications for new schools proposed, including the number of students, grade level distribution of the student body, instructional programs needed for the students, and support areas and specialized classrooms that the school will require. Providing these specifications will meet the state requirements, whereas public forums discussing space and instructional requirements (C) will not. Similarly, determining space requirements should not be assigned to the designated principal alone (D) and should also not precede obtaining campus and district-wide consensus regarding the educational needs of the intended student body.

52. B: Because today's economy has federal and state budgets squeezed harder than ever, one way for superintendents to exercise fiscal responsibility is to partner with other organizations in jointly using facilities to save money while also improving community services. Community nonschool groups' utilizing facilities that are otherwise left empty outside school hours can support these aims. However, local policies and practices mainly determine such cooperative initiatives today as there is not yet much research to support their effectiveness (D). While joint use has obvious advantages of making better use of limited public space and resources, it also incurs additional maintenance requirements and demands on custodial staff (C) through more hours of building use and more users. It also does not coordinate and align multiple agencies' funding and authority (A) because the school and nonschool groups each have different policies, systems, procedures, and structures of decision making, which complicate their interaction.

53. C: The superintendent is responsible for being the administrator of planning and implementing new facilities, so Dr. Hay should not assign this duty to an outside consultant (A). As an educator, the superintendent has the best knowledge of the school system's

current and future educational programs, so Dr. Hay should also be the one to develop long-term plan for the school district (B) and to make educationally related decisions about the new library (D). Although administrators with limited staff lacking expertise in facility planning often feel the need to resort to other professionals' judgments, the superintendent will do better to take the responsibility for developing plans for the library and long-term plans for the school district in collaboration with district stakeholders and then ask the independent consultant to apply these plans throughout the planning and construction of the library.

54. C: According to the federal regulations for meeting AYP, if Stage 1 school improvement requirements for Year 1 are not met, Stage 2 requirements include that the school meets the requirements for Year 1 and also pays for supplemental educational services, for example, tutoring low-income students. The regulations do not mandate replacing principals and restructuring campuses (A); additionally, the question indicates only one school failed to meet AYP. The same both apply to auditing assessment procedures on multiple campuses (B). Neither do the regulations related to AYP dictate downgrading principal authority, replacing school staff, extension of school hours, or curriculum revision (D).

55. A: The most important responsibility of the superintendent is to be an advocate for his or her district's students and make sure that the school system meets their educational needs. This takes precedence over interceding between community stakeholders and the school board (B); interceding between those community stakeholders in favor of the bond issue and those opposed to it (C); or organizing those in favor of it to lobby to get it passed (D). The superintendent's first responsibility is always to the students and their education.

56. B: Of the choices given, the best way for the superintendent to respond to community members' desire for involvement in efforts to improve schools in their district is to invite their participation in curricular planning and revision. Meaningful curriculum design can closely influence school improvements, and community stakeholders' ideas can be valuable contributions. They are in general more likely to identify instructional needs in their schools than for most to have administrative knowledge about personnel assignments (A). Similarly, the majority of community members are unlikely to have expertise or time to contribute to physically improving school facilities (C). They are also not qualified to evaluate the performance of teaching and administrative staff (D); moreover, residents with children attending the schools may not be objective about these.

57. C: The cost, that is, expense, per student graduating, that is, per unit of output or outcome, is an efficiency indicator (and a cost-effectiveness indicator), according to the GASB's definitions. The number of teachers employed in an elementary school (A), that is, the resources used for a specific service or program, is an input indicator. The number of students graduating from a high school (B), that is, the units produced or services provided by a given provider or program, is an output indicator. The change in student test scores via instructional programs (D), that is, the result of a service or program, is an outcome indicator.

58. D: The process of planning a school district's budget is imperative to allowing district citizens to express their desires and to arriving at consensus agreements among the community members, the members of the school board, and the faculty and staff of the campuses or district about district operations and the direction they will take in the future. Good planning of school budgets is also important because the characteristics of goods and

services provided by school districts are frequently NOT subject to the same rules of supply and demand that apply in most business markets (A); hence, the school budget, rather than supply and demand, is then the limiting force. Goods and services, such as instruction, that schools provide ARE crucial priorities in the public interest (B). Another reason for the importance of planning budgets judiciously is that school district operations are so diverse and broad in scope that making good decisions DOES require more comprehensive planning (C).

Secret Key #1 - Time is Your Greatest Enemy

Pace Yourself

Wear a watch. At the beginning of the test, check the time (or start a chronometer on your watch to count the minutes), and check the time after every few questions to make sure you are "on schedule."

If you are forced to speed up, do it efficiently. Usually one or more answer choices can be eliminated without too much difficulty. Above all, don't panic. Don't speed up and just begin guessing at random choices. By pacing yourself, and continually monitoring your progress against your watch, you will always know exactly how far ahead or behind you are with your available time. If you find that you are one minute behind on the test, don't skip one question without spending any time on it, just to catch back up. Take 15 fewer seconds on the next four questions, and after four questions you'll have caught back up. Once you catch back up, you can continue working each problem at your normal pace.

Furthermore, don't dwell on the problems that you were rushed on. If a problem was taking up too much time and you made a hurried guess, it must be difficult. The difficult questions are the ones you are most likely to miss anyway, so it isn't a big loss. It is better to end with more time than you need than to run out of time.

Lastly, sometimes it is beneficial to slow down if you are constantly getting ahead of time. You are always more likely to catch a careless mistake by working more slowly than quickly, and among very high-scoring test takers (those who are likely to have lots of time left over), careless errors affect the score more than mastery of material.

Secret Key #2 - Guessing is not Guesswork

You probably know that guessing is a good idea. Unlike other standardized tests, there is no penalty for getting a wrong answer. Even if you have no idea about a question, you still have a 20-25% chance of getting it right.

Most test takers do not understand the impact that proper guessing can have on their score. Unless you score extremely high, guessing will significantly contribute to your final score.

Monkeys Take the Test

What most test takers don't realize is that to insure that 20-25% chance, you have to guess randomly. If you put 20 monkeys in a room to take this test, assuming they answered once per question and behaved themselves, on average they would get 20-25% of the questions correct. Put 20 test takers in the room, and the average will be much lower among guessed questions. Why?
    1. The test writers intentionally write deceptive answer choices that "look" right. A test

taker has no idea about a question, so he picks the "best looking" answer, which is often wrong. The monkey has no idea what looks good and what doesn't, so it will consistently be right about 20-25% of the time.

2. Test takers will eliminate answer choices from the guessing pool based on a hunch or intuition. Simple but correct answers often get excluded, leaving a 0% chance of being correct. The monkey has no clue, and often gets lucky with the best choice.

This is why the process of elimination endorsed by most test courses is flawed and detrimental to your performance. Test takers don't guess; they make an ignorant stab in the dark that is usually worse than random.

$5 Challenge

Let me introduce one of the most valuable ideas of this course—the $5 challenge:

You only mark your "best guess" if you are willing to bet $5 on it.
You only eliminate choices from guessing if you are willing to bet $5 on it.

Why $5? Five dollars is an amount of money that is small yet not insignificant, and can really add up fast (20 questions could cost you $100). Likewise, each answer choice on one question of the test will have a small impact on your overall score, but it can really add up to a lot of points in the end.

The process of elimination IS valuable. The following shows your chance of guessing it right:

If you eliminate wrong answer choices until only this many remain:	Chance of getting it correct:
1	100%
2	50%
3	33%

However, if you accidentally eliminate the right answer or go on a hunch for an incorrect answer, your chances drop dramatically—to 0%. By guessing among all the answer choices, you are GUARANTEED to have a shot at the right answer.

That's why the $5 test is so valuable. If you give up the advantage and safety of a pure guess, it had better be worth the risk.

What we still haven't covered is how to be sure that whatever guess you make is truly random. Here's the easiest way:

Always pick the first answer choice among those remaining.

Such a technique means that you have decided, **before you see a single test question**, exactly how you are going to guess, and since the order of choices tells you nothing about which one is correct, this guessing technique is perfectly random.

This section is not meant to scare you away from making educated guesses or eliminating choices; you just need to define when a choice is worth eliminating. The $5 test, along with a pre-defined random guessing strategy, is the best way to make sure you reap all of the benefits of guessing.

Secret Key #3 - Practice Smarter, Not Harder

Many test takers delay the test preparation process because they dread the awful amounts of practice time they think necessary to succeed on the test. We have refined an effective method that will take you only a fraction of the time.

There are a number of "obstacles" in the path to success. Among these are answering questions, finishing in time, and mastering test-taking strategies. All must be executed on the day of the test at peak performance, or your score will suffer. The test is a mental marathon that has a large impact on your future.

Just like a marathon runner, it is important to work your way up to the full challenge. So first you just worry about questions, and then time, and finally strategy:

Success Strategy

1. Find a good source for practice tests.
2. If you are willing to make a larger time investment, consider using more than one study guide. Often the different approaches of multiple authors will help you "get" difficult concepts.
3. Take a practice test with no time constraints, with all study helps, "open book." Take your time with questions and focus on applying strategies.
4. Take a practice test with time constraints, with all guides, "open book."
5. Take a final practice test without open material and with time limits.

If you have time to take more practice tests, just repeat step 5. By gradually exposing yourself to the full rigors of the test environment, you will condition your mind to the stress of test day and maximize your success.

Secret Key #4 - Prepare, Don't Procrastinate

Let me state an obvious fact: if you take the test three times, you will probably get three different scores. This is due to the way you feel on test day, the level of preparedness you have, and the version of the test you see. Despite the test writers' claims to the contrary, some versions of the test WILL be easier for you than others.

Since your future depends so much on your score, you should maximize your chances of success. In order to maximize the likelihood of success, you've got to prepare in advance.

This means taking practice tests and spending time learning the information and test taking strategies you will need to succeed.

Never go take the actual test as a "practice" test, expecting that you can just take it again if you need to. Take all the practice tests you can on your own, but when you go to take the official test, be prepared, be focused, and do your best the first time!

Secret Key #5 - Test Yourself

Everyone knows that time is money. There is no need to spend too much of your time or too little of your time preparing for the test. You should only spend as much of your precious time preparing as is necessary for you to get the score you need.

Once you have taken a practice test under real conditions of time constraints, then you will know if you are ready for the test or not.

If you have scored extremely high the first time that you take the practice test, then there is not much point in spending countless hours studying. You are already there.

Benchmark your abilities by retaking practice tests and seeing how much you have improved. Once you consistently score high enough to guarantee success, then you are ready.

If you have scored well below where you need, then knuckle down and begin studying in earnest. Check your improvement regularly through the use of practice tests under real conditions. Above all, don't worry, panic, or give up. The key is perseverance!

Then, when you go to take the test, remain confident and remember how well you did on the practice tests. If you can score high enough on a practice test, then you can do the same on the real thing.

General Strategies

The most important thing you can do is to ignore your fears and jump into the test immediately. Do not be overwhelmed by any strange-sounding terms. You have to jump into the test like jumping into a pool—all at once is the easiest way.

Make Predictions

As you read and understand the question, try to guess what the answer will be. Remember that several of the answer choices are wrong, and once you begin reading them, your mind will immediately become cluttered with answer choices designed to throw you off. Your mind is typically the most focused immediately after you have read the question and digested its contents. If you can, try to predict what the correct answer will be. You may be surprised at what you can predict.

Quickly scan the choices and see if your prediction is in the listed answer choices. If it is, then you can be quite confident that you have the right answer. It still won't hurt to check the other answer choices, but most of the time, you've got it!

Answer the Question

It may seem obvious to only pick answer choices that answer the question, but the test writers can create some excellent answer choices that are wrong. Don't pick an answer just because it sounds right, or you believe it to be true. It MUST answer the question. Once you've made your selection, always go back and check it against the question and make sure that you didn't misread the question and that the answer choice does answer the question posed.

Benchmark

After you read the first answer choice, decide if you think it sounds correct or not. If it doesn't, move on to the next answer choice. If it does, mentally mark that answer choice. This doesn't mean that you've definitely selected it as your answer choice, it just means that it's the best you've seen thus far. Go ahead and read the next choice. If the next choice is worse than the one you've already selected, keep going to the next answer choice. If the next choice is better than the choice you've already selected, mentally mark the new answer choice as your best guess.

The first answer choice that you select becomes your standard. Every other answer choice must be benchmarked against that standard. That choice is correct until proven otherwise by another answer choice beating it out. Once you've decided that no other answer choice seems as good, do one final check to ensure that your answer choice answers the question posed.

Valid Information

Don't discount any of the information provided in the question. Every piece of information may be necessary to determine the correct answer. None of the information in the question is there to throw you off (while the answer choices will certainly have information to throw you off). If two seemingly unrelated topics are discussed, don't ignore either. You can be confident there is a relationship, or it wouldn't be included in the question, and you are probably going to have to determine what is that relationship to find the answer.

Avoid "Fact Traps"

Don't get distracted by a choice that is factually true. Your search is for the answer that answers the question. Stay focused and don't fall for an answer that is true but irrelevant. Always go back to the question and make sure you're choosing an answer that actually answers the question and is not just a true statement. An answer can be factually correct, but it MUST answer the question asked. Additionally, two answers can both be seemingly correct, so be sure to read all of the answer choices, and make sure that you get the one that BEST answers the question.

Milk the Question

Some of the questions may throw you completely off. They might deal with a subject you have not been exposed to, or one that you haven't reviewed in years. While your lack of knowledge about the subject will be a hindrance, the question itself can give you many clues that will help you find the correct answer. Read the question carefully and look for clues. Watch particularly for adjectives and nouns describing difficult terms or words that you don't recognize. Regardless of whether you completely understand a word or not, replacing it with a synonym, either provided or one you more familiar with, may help you to understand what the questions are asking. Rather than wracking your mind about specific detailed information concerning a difficult term or word, try to use mental substitutes that are easier to understand.

The Trap of Familiarity

Don't just choose a word because you recognize it. On difficult questions, you may not recognize a number of words in the answer choices. The test writers don't put "make-believe" words on the test, so don't think that just because you only recognize all the words in one answer choice that that answer choice must be correct. If you only recognize words in one answer choice, then focus on that one. Is it correct? Try your best to determine if it is correct. If it is, that's great. If not, eliminate it. Each word and answer choice you eliminate increases your chances of getting the question correct, even if you then have to guess among the unfamiliar choices.

Eliminate Answers

Eliminate choices as soon as you realize they are wrong. But be careful! Make sure you consider all of the possible answer choices. Just because one appears right, doesn't mean that the next one won't be even better! The test writers will usually put more than one good answer choice for every question, so read all of them. Don't worry if you are stuck between two that seem right. By getting down to just two remaining possible choices, your odds are now 50/50. Rather than wasting too much time, play the odds. You are guessing, but guessing wisely because you've been able to knock out some of the answer choices that you know are wrong. If you are eliminating choices and realize that the last answer choice you are left with is also obviously wrong, don't panic. Start over and consider each choice again. There may easily be something that you missed the first time and will realize on the second pass.

Tough Questions

If you are stumped on a problem or it appears too hard or too difficult, don't waste time. Move on! Remember though, if you can quickly check for obviously incorrect answer choices, your chances of guessing correctly are greatly improved. Before you completely give up, at least try to knock out a couple of possible answers. Eliminate what you can and then guess at the remaining answer choices before moving on.

Brainstorm

If you get stuck on a difficult question, spend a few seconds quickly brainstorming. Run through the complete list of possible answer choices. Look at each choice and ask yourself, "Could this answer the question satisfactorily?" Go through each answer choice and consider it independently of the others. By systematically going through all possibilities, you may find something that you would otherwise overlook. Remember though that when you get stuck, it's important to try to keep moving.

Read Carefully

Understand the problem. Read the question and answer choices carefully. Don't miss the question because you misread the terms. You have plenty of time to read each question thoroughly and make sure you understand what is being asked. Yet a happy medium must be attained, so don't waste too much time. You must read carefully, but efficiently.

Face Value

When in doubt, use common sense. Always accept the situation in the problem at face value. Don't read too much into it. These problems will not require you to make huge leaps of logic. The test writers aren't trying to throw you off with a cheap trick. If you have to go beyond creativity and make a leap of logic in order to have an answer choice answer the question, then you should look at the other answer choices. Don't overcomplicate the problem by creating theoretical relationships or explanations that will warp time or space. These are normal problems rooted in reality. It's just that the applicable relationship or explanation may not be readily apparent and you have to figure things out. Use your common sense to interpret anything that isn't clear.

Prefixes

If you're having trouble with a word in the question or answer choices, try dissecting it. Take advantage of every clue that the word might include. Prefixes and suffixes can be a huge help. Usually they allow you to determine a basic meaning. Pre- means before, post- means after, pro - is positive, de- is negative. From these prefixes and suffixes, you can get an idea of the general meaning of the word and try to put it into context. Beware though of any traps. Just because con- is the opposite of pro-, doesn't necessarily mean congress is the opposite of progress!

Hedge Phrases

Watch out for critical hedge phrases, led off with words such as "likely," "may," "can," "sometimes," "often," "almost," "mostly," "usually," "generally," "rarely," and "sometimes." Question writers insert these hedge phrases to cover every possibility. Often an answer choice will be wrong simply because it leaves no room for exception. Unless the situation calls for them, avoid answer choices that have definitive words like "exactly," and "always."

Switchback Words

Stay alert for "switchbacks." These are the words and phrases frequently used to alert you to shifts in thought. The most common switchback word is "but." Others include "although," "however," "nevertheless," "on the other hand," "even though," "while," "in spite of," "despite," and "regardless of."

New Information

Correct answer choices will rarely have completely new information included. Answer choices typically are straightforward reflections of the material asked about and will directly relate to the question. If a new piece of information is included in an answer choice that doesn't even seem to relate to the topic being asked about, then that answer choice is likely incorrect. All of the information needed to answer the question is usually provided for you in the question. You should not have to make guesses that are unsupported or choose answer choices that require unknown information that cannot be reasoned from what is given.

Time Management

On technical questions, don't get lost on the technical terms. Don't spend too much time on any one question. If you don't know what a term means, then odds are you aren't going to get much further since you don't have a dictionary. You should be able to immediately recognize whether or not you know a term. If you don't, work with the other clues that you have—the other answer choices and terms provided—but don't waste too much time trying to figure out a difficult term that you don't know.

Contextual Clues

Look for contextual clues. An answer can be right but not the correct answer. The contextual clues will help you find the answer that is most right and is correct. Understand the context in which a phrase or statement is made. This will help you make important distinctions.

Don't Panic

Panicking will not answer any questions for you; therefore, it isn't helpful. When you first see the question, if your mind goes blank, take a deep breath. Force yourself to mechanically go through the steps of solving the problem using the strategies you've learned.

Pace Yourself

Don't get clock fever. It's easy to be overwhelmed when you're looking at a page full of questions, your mind is full of random thoughts and feeling confused, and the clock is ticking down faster than you would like. Calm down and maintain the pace that you have set for yourself. As long as you are on track by monitoring your pace, you are guaranteed to have enough time for yourself. When you get to the last few minutes of the test, it may seem like you won't have enough time left, but if you only have as many questions as you should have left at that point, then you're right on track!

Answer Selection

The best way to pick an answer choice is to eliminate all of those that are wrong, until only one is left and confirm that is the correct answer. Sometimes though, an answer choice may immediately look right. Be careful! Take a second to make sure that the other choices are not equally obvious. Don't make a hasty mistake. There are only two times that you should stop before checking other answers. First is when you are positive that the answer choice you have selected is correct. Second is when time is almost out and you have to make a quick guess!

Check Your Work

Since you will probably not know every term listed and the answer to every question, it is important that you get credit for the ones that you do know. Don't miss any questions through careless mistakes. If at all possible, try to take a second to look back over your answer selection and make sure you've selected the correct answer choice and haven't made a costly careless mistake (such as marking an answer choice that you didn't mean to mark). The time it takes for this quick double check should more than pay for itself in caught mistakes.

Beware of Directly Quoted Answers

Sometimes an answer choice will repeat word for word a portion of the question or reference section. However, beware of such exact duplication. It may be a trap! More than likely, the correct choice will paraphrase or summarize a point, rather than being exactly the same wording.

Slang

Scientific sounding answers are better than slang ones. An answer choice that begins "To compare the outcomes…" is much more likely to be correct than one that begins "Because some people insisted…"

Extreme Statements

Avoid wild answers that throw out highly controversial ideas that are proclaimed as established fact. An answer choice that states the "process should used in certain situations, if…" is much more likely to be correct than one that states the "process should be discontinued completely." The first is a calm rational statement and doesn't even make a definitive, uncompromising stance, using a hedge word "if" to provide wiggle room, whereas the second choice is a radical idea and far more extreme.

Answer Choice Families

When you have two or more answer choices that are direct opposites or parallels, one of them is usually the correct answer. For instance, if one answer choice states "x increases" and another answer choice states "x decreases" or "y increases," then those two or three answer choices are very similar in construction and fall into the same family of answer choices. A family of answer choices consists of two or three answer choices, very similar in construction, but often with directly opposite meanings. Usually the correct answer choice will be in that family of answer choices. The "odd man out" or answer choice that doesn't seem to fit the parallel construction of the other answer choices is more likely to be incorrect.

Special Report: How to Overcome Test Anxiety

The very nature of tests caters to some level of anxiety, nervousness, or tension, just as we feel for any important event that occurs in our lives. A little bit of anxiety or nervousness can be a good thing. It helps us with motivation, and makes achievement just that much sweeter. However, too much anxiety can be a problem, especially if it hinders our ability to function and perform.

"Test anxiety," is the term that refers to the emotional reactions that some test-takers experience when faced with a test or exam. Having a fear of testing and exams is based upon a rational fear, since the test-taker's performance can shape the course of an academic career. Nevertheless, experiencing excessive fear of examinations will only interfere with the test-taker's ability to perform and chance to be successful.

There are a large variety of causes that can contribute to the development and sensation of test anxiety. These include, but are not limited to, lack of preparation and worrying about issues surrounding the test.

Lack of Preparation

Lack of preparation can be identified by the following behaviors or situations:

Not scheduling enough time to study, and therefore cramming the night before the test or exam
Managing time poorly, to create the sensation that there is not enough time to do everything
Failing to organize the text information in advance, so that the study material consists of the entire text and not simply the pertinent information
Poor overall studying habits

Worrying, on the other hand, can be related to both the test taker, or many other factors around him/her that will be affected by the results of the test. These include worrying about:

Previous performances on similar exams, or exams in general
How friends and other students are achieving
The negative consequences that will result from a poor grade or failure

There are three primary elements to test anxiety. Physical components, which involve the same typical bodily reactions as those to acute anxiety (to be discussed below). Emotional factors have to do with fear or panic. Mental or cognitive issues concerning attention spans and memory abilities.

Physical Signals

There are many different symptoms of test anxiety, and these are not limited to mental and emotional strain. Frequently there are a range of physical signals that will let a test taker know that he/she is suffering from test anxiety. These bodily changes can include the following:

Perspiring
Sweaty palms
Wet, trembling hands
Nausea
Dry mouth
A knot in the stomach
Headache
Faintness
Muscle tension
Aching shoulders, back and neck
Rapid heart beat
Feeling too hot/cold

To recognize the sensation of test anxiety, a test-taker should monitor him/herself for the following sensations:

The physical distress symptoms as listed above
Emotional sensitivity, expressing emotional feelings such as the need to cry or laugh too much, or a sensation of anger or helplessness
A decreased ability to think, causing the test-taker to blank out or have racing thoughts that are hard to organize or control.

Though most students will feel some level of anxiety when faced with a test or exam, the majority can cope with that anxiety and maintain it at a manageable level. However, those who cannot are faced with a very real and very serious condition, which can and should be controlled for the immeasurable benefit of this sufferer.

Naturally, these sensations lead to negative results for the testing experience. The most common effects of test anxiety have to do with nervousness and mental blocking.

Nervousness

Nervousness can appear in several different levels:

The test-taker's difficulty, or even inability to read and understand the questions on the test
The difficulty or inability to organize thoughts to a coherent form
The difficulty or inability to recall key words and concepts relating to the testing questions (especially essays)
The receipt of poor grades on a test, though the test material was well known by the test taker

Conversely, a person may also experience mental blocking, which involves:

Blanking out on test questions
Only remembering the correct answers to the questions when the test has already finished.

Fortunately for test anxiety sufferers, beating these feelings, to a large degree, has to do with proper preparation. When a test taker has a feeling of preparedness, then anxiety will be dramatically lessened.

The first step to resolving anxiety issues is to distinguish which of the two types of anxiety are being suffered. If the anxiety is a direct result of a lack of preparation, this should be considered a normal reaction, and the anxiety level (as opposed to the test results) shouldn't be anything to worry about. However, if, when adequately prepared, the test-taker still panics, blanks out, or seems to overreact, this is not a fully rational reaction. While this can be considered normal too, there are many ways to combat and overcome these effects.

Remember that anxiety cannot be entirely eliminated, however, there are ways to minimize it, to make the anxiety easier to manage. Preparation is one of the best ways to minimize test anxiety. Therefore the following techniques are wise in order to best fight off any anxiety that may want to build.

To begin with, try to avoid cramming before a test, whenever it is possible. By trying to memorize an entire term's worth of information in one day, you'll be shocking your system, and not giving yourself a very good chance to absorb the information. This is an easy path to anxiety, so for those who suffer from test anxiety, cramming should not even be considered an option.

Instead of cramming, work throughout the semester to combine all of the material which is presented throughout the semester, and work on it gradually as the course goes by, making sure to master the main concepts first, leaving minor details for a week or so before the test.

To study for the upcoming exam, be sure to pose questions that may be on the examination, to gauge the ability to answer them by integrating the ideas from your texts, notes and lectures, as well as any supplementary readings.

If it is truly impossible to cover all of the information that was covered in that particular term, concentrate on the most important portions, that can be covered very well. Learn these concepts as best as possible, so that when the test comes, a goal can be made to use these concepts as presentations of your knowledge.

In addition to study habits, changes in attitude are critical to beating a struggle with test anxiety. In fact, an improvement of the perspective over the entire test-taking experience can actually help a test taker to enjoy studying and therefore improve the overall experience. Be certain not to overemphasize the significance of the grade - know that the result of the test is neither a reflection of self worth, nor is it a measure of intelligence; one grade will not predict a person's future success.

To improve an overall testing outlook, the following steps should be tried:

Keeping in mind that the most reasonable expectation for taking a test is to expect to try to demonstrate as much of what you know as you possibly can.
Reminding ourselves that a test is only one test; this is not the only one, and there will be others.
The thought of thinking of oneself in an irrational, all-or-nothing term should be avoided at all costs.
A reward should be designated for after the test, so there's something to look forward to. Whether it be going to a movie, going out to eat, or simply visiting friends, schedule it in advance, and do it no matter what result is expected on the exam.

Test-takers should also keep in mind that the basics are some of the most important things, even beyond anti-anxiety techniques and studying. Never neglect the basic social, emotional and biological needs, in order to try to absorb information. In order to best achieve, these three factors must be held as just as important as the studying itself.

Study Steps

Remember the following important steps for studying:

Maintain healthy nutrition and exercise habits. Continue both your recreational activities and social pass times. These both contribute to your physical and emotional well being.
Be certain to get a good amount of sleep, especially the night before the test, because when you're overtired you are not able to perform to the best of your best ability.
Keep the studying pace to a moderate level by taking breaks when they are needed, and varying the work whenever possible, to keep the mind fresh instead of getting bored. When enough studying has been done that all the material that can be learned has been learned, and the test taker is prepared for the test, stop studying and do something relaxing such as listening to music, watching a movie, or taking a warm bubble bath.

There are also many other techniques to minimize the uneasiness or apprehension that is experienced along with test anxiety before, during, or even after the examination. In fact, there are a great deal of things that can be done to stop anxiety from interfering with lifestyle and performance. Again, remember that anxiety will not be eliminated entirely, and it shouldn't be. Otherwise that "up" feeling for exams would not exist, and most of us depend on that sensation to perform better than usual. However, this anxiety has to be at a level that is manageable.

Of course, as we have just discussed, being prepared for the exam is half the battle right away. Attending all classes, finding out what knowledge will be expected on the exam, and knowing the exam schedules are easy steps to lowering anxiety. Keeping up with work will remove the need to cram, and efficient study habits will eliminate wasted time. Studying should be done in an ideal location for concentration, so that it is simple to become interested in the material and give it complete attention. A method such as SQ3R (Survey, Question, Read, Recite, Review) is a wonderful key to follow to make sure that the study habits are as effective as possible, especially in the case of learning from a

Copyright © Mometrix Media. You have been licensed one copy of this document for personal use only. Any other reproduction or redistribution is strictly prohibited. All rights reserved.

textbook. Flashcards are great techniques for memorization. Learning to take good notes will mean that notes will be full of useful information, so that less sifting will need to be done to seek out what is pertinent for studying. Reviewing notes after class and then again on occasion will keep the information fresh in the mind. From notes that have been taken summary sheets and outlines can be made for simpler reviewing.

A study group can also be a very motivational and helpful place to study, as there will be a sharing of ideas, all of the minds can work together, to make sure that everyone understands, and the studying will be made more interesting because it will be a social occasion.

Basically, though, as long as the test-taker remains organized and self confident, with efficient study habits, less time will need to be spent studying, and higher grades will be achieved.

To become self confident, there are many useful steps. The first of these is "self talk." It has been shown through extensive research, that self-talk for students who suffer from test anxiety, should be well monitored, in order to make sure that it contributes to self confidence as opposed to sinking the student. Frequently the self talk of test-anxious students is negative or self-defeating, thinking that everyone else is smarter and faster, that they always mess up, and that if they don't do well, they'll fail the entire course. It is important to decreasing anxiety that awareness is made of self talk. Try writing any negative self thoughts and then disputing them with a positive statement instead. Begin self-encouragement as though it was a friend speaking. Repeat positive statements to help reprogram the mind to believing in successes instead of failures.

Helpful Techniques

Other extremely helpful techniques include:

Self-visualization of doing well and reaching goals
While aiming for an "A" level of understanding, don't try to "overprotect" by setting your expectations lower. This will only convince the mind to stop studying in order to meet the lower expectations.
Don't make comparisons with the results or habits of other students. These are individual factors, and different things work for different people, causing different results.
Strive to become an expert in learning what works well, and what can be done in order to improve. Consider collecting this data in a journal.
Create rewards for after studying instead of doing things before studying that will only turn into avoidance behaviors.
Make a practice of relaxing - by using methods such as progressive relaxation, self-hypnosis, guided imagery, etc - in order to make relaxation an automatic sensation.
Work on creating a state of relaxed concentration so that concentrating will take on the focus of the mind, so that none will be wasted on worrying.
Take good care of the physical self by eating well and getting enough sleep.
Plan in time for exercise and stick to this plan.

Beyond these techniques, there are other methods to be used before, during and after the test that will help the test-taker perform well in addition to overcoming anxiety.

Before the exam comes the academic preparation. This involves establishing a study schedule and beginning at least one week before the actual date of the test. By doing this, the anxiety of not having enough time to study for the test will be automatically eliminated. Moreover, this will make the studying a much more effective experience, ensuring that the learning will be an easier process. This relieves much undue pressure on the test-taker.

Summary sheets, note cards, and flash cards with the main concepts and examples of these main concepts should be prepared in advance of the actual studying time. A topic should never be eliminated from this process. By omitting a topic because it isn't expected to be on the test is only setting up the test-taker for anxiety should it actually appear on the exam. Utilize the course syllabus for laying out the topics that should be studied. Carefully go over the notes that were made in class, paying special attention to any of the issues that the professor took special care to emphasize while lecturing in class. In the textbooks, use the chapter review, or if possible, the chapter tests, to begin your review.

It may even be possible to ask the instructor what information will be covered on the exam, or what the format of the exam will be (for example, multiple choice, essay, free form, true-false). Additionally, see if it is possible to find out how many questions will be on the test. If a review sheet or sample test has been offered by the professor, make good use of it, above anything else, for the preparation for the test. Another great resource for getting to know the examination is reviewing tests from previous semesters. Use these tests to review, and aim to achieve a 100% score on each of the possible topics. With a few exceptions, the goal that you set for yourself is the highest one that you will reach.

Take all of the questions that were assigned as homework, and rework them to any other possible course material. The more problems reworked, the more skill and confidence will form as a result. When forming the solution to a problem, write out each of the steps. Don't simply do head work. By doing as many steps on paper as possible, much clarification and therefore confidence will be formed. Do this with as many homework problems as possible, before checking the answers. By checking the answer after each problem, a reinforcement will exist, that will not be on the exam. Study situations should be as exam-like as possible, to prime the test-taker's system for the experience. By waiting to check the answers at the end, a psychological advantage will be formed, to decrease the stress factor.

Another fantastic reason for not cramming is the avoidance of confusion in concepts, especially when it comes to mathematics. 8-10 hours of study will become one hundred percent more effective if it is spread out over a week or at least several days, instead of doing it all in one sitting. Recognize that the human brain requires time in order to assimilate new material, so frequent breaks and a span of study time over several days will be much more beneficial.

Additionally, don't study right up until the point of the exam. Studying should stop a minimum of one hour before the exam begins. This allows the brain to rest and put things in their proper order. This will also provide the time to become as relaxed as possible when going into the examination room. The test-taker will also have time to eat well and eat sensibly. Know that the brain needs food as much as the rest of the body. With enough food and enough sleep, as well as a relaxed attitude, the body and the mind are primed for success.

Avoid any anxious classmates who are talking about the exam. These students only spread anxiety, and are not worth sharing the anxious sentimentalities.

Before the test also involves creating a positive attitude, so mental preparation should also be a point of concentration. There are many keys to creating a positive attitude. Should fears become rushing in, make a visualization of taking the exam, doing well, and seeing an A written on the paper. Write out a list of affirmations that will bring a feeling of confidence, such as "I am doing well in my English class," "I studied well and know my material," "I enjoy this class." Even if the affirmations aren't believed at first, it sends a positive message to the subconscious which will result in an alteration of the overall belief system, which is the system that creates reality.

If a sensation of panic begins, work with the fear and imagine the very worst! Work through the entire scenario of not passing the test, failing the entire course, and dropping out of school, followed by not getting a job, and pushing a shopping cart through the dark alley where you'll live. This will place things into perspective! Then, practice deep breathing and create a visualization of the opposite situation - achieving an "A" on the exam, passing the entire course, receiving the degree at a graduation ceremony.

On the day of the test, there are many things to be done to ensure the best results, as well as the most calm outlook. The following stages are suggested in order to maximize test-taking potential:

Begin the examination day with a moderate breakfast, and avoid any coffee or beverages with caffeine if the test taker is prone to jitters. Even people who are used to managing caffeine can feel jittery or light-headed when it is taken on a test day. Attempt to do something that is relaxing before the examination begins. As last minute cramming clouds the mastering of overall concepts, it is better to use this time to create a calming outlook.
Be certain to arrive at the test location well in advance, in order to provide time to select a location that is away from doors, windows and other distractions, as well as giving enough time to relax before the test begins.
Keep away from anxiety generating classmates who will upset the sensation of stability and relaxation that is being attempted before the exam.
Should the waiting period before the exam begins cause anxiety, create a self-distraction by reading a light magazine or something else that is relaxing and simple.

During the exam itself, read the entire exam from beginning to end, and find out how much time should be allotted to each individual problem. Once writing the exam, should more time be taken for a problem, it should be abandoned, in order to begin another problem. If there is time at the end, the unfinished problem can always be returned to and completed.

Read the instructions very carefully - twice - so that unpleasant surprises won't follow during or after the exam has ended.

When writing the exam, pretend that the situation is actually simply the completion of homework within a library, or at home. This will assist in forming a relaxed atmosphere, and will allow the brain extra focus for the complex thinking function.

Begin the exam with all of the questions with which the most confidence is felt. This will build the confidence level regarding the entire exam and will begin a quality momentum. This will also create encouragement for trying the problems where uncertainty resides.

Going with the "gut instinct" is always the way to go when solving a problem. Second guessing should be avoided at all costs. Have confidence in the ability to do well.

For essay questions, create an outline in advance that will keep the mind organized and make certain that all of the points are remembered. For multiple choice, read every answer, even if the correct one has been spotted - a better one may exist.

Continue at a pace that is reasonable and not rushed, in order to be able to work carefully. Provide enough time to go over the answers at the end, to check for small errors that can be corrected.

Should a feeling of panic begin, breathe deeply, and think of the feeling of the body releasing sand through its pores. Visualize a calm, peaceful place, and include all of the sights, sounds and sensations of this image. Continue the deep breathing, and take a few minutes to continue this with closed eyes. When all is well again, return to the test.

If a "blanking" occurs for a certain question, skip it and move on to the next question. There will be time to return to the other question later. Get everything done that can be done, first, to guarantee all the grades that can be compiled, and to build all of the confidence possible. Then return to the weaker questions to build the marks from there.

Remember, one's own reality can be created, so as long as the belief is there, success will follow. And remember: anxiety can happen later, right now, there's an exam to be written!

After the examination is complete, whether there is a feeling for a good grade or a bad grade, don't dwell on the exam, and be certain to follow through on the reward that was promised...and enjoy it! Don't dwell on any mistakes that have been made, as there is nothing that can be done at this point anyway.

Additionally, don't begin to study for the next test right away. Do something relaxing for a while, and let the mind relax and prepare itself to begin absorbing information again.

From the results of the exam - both the grade and the entire experience, be certain to learn from what has gone on. Perfect studying habits and work some more on confidence in order to make the next examination experience even better than the last one.

Learn to avoid places where openings occurred for laziness, procrastination and day dreaming.

Use the time between this exam and the next one to better learn to relax, even learning to relax on cue, so that any anxiety can be controlled during the next exam. Learn how to relax the body. Slouch in your chair if that helps. Tighten and then relax all of the different muscle groups, one group at a time, beginning with the feet and then working all the way up to the neck and face. This will ultimately relax the muscles more than they were to begin with. Learn how to breathe deeply and comfortably, and focus on this breathing going in and out as a relaxing thought. With every exhale, repeat the word "relax."

As common as test anxiety is, it is very possible to overcome it. Make yourself one of the test-takers who overcome this frustrating hindrance.

Additional Bonus Material

Due to our efforts to try to keep this book to a manageable length, we've created a link that will give you access to all of your additional bonus material.

Please visit http://www.mometrix.com/bonus948/texessuper195 to access the information.